Praise for Jurgen Wolff

"He's full of encouraging examples and practical tips, many of them more far-reaching than they seem at first glance. Wolff suggests a number of ways to get the imagination going, such as his 'What if?' exercise."
Financial Times

"The real genius of *Your Writing Coach* is its accessibility to writers of all personalities and genres. Logic and good business practices meet creativity and self-exploration in these 248 pages, leading writers down a path of personalized success. The title is apt; Jurgen Wolff's engaging style ensures that his encouragement will be echoing in writers' ears for years to come."
Anastasia K Bond, Oregon Writers' Colony newsletter

"*Your Writing Coach* is the real deal—no fluff or padding, just concentrated insider knowledge. By far the best book on writing I have read."
Rupert Widdicombe, writer and journalist

"Absorbing and inspiring, *Your Writing Coach* is destined to become an instant classic. Wolff's treasure trove of advice and insider secrets will prove to be an indispensable friend to all those who aspire to the writing life."
***Amanda Barry Hirst, author of* PR Power**

"*Your Writing Coach* is an antidote to the bad advice aspiring writers are often given. There are only two books on writing I recommend—Stephen King's and this one."
***William F. Owen, author of* Blackfoot Is Missing**

"*Your Writing Coach* will help you find the insights of the writing craft. Pick it up and let it guide you to success."
***Xavier Koller, Academy Award-winning director,*
Journey of Hope**

"Jurgen Wolff demystifies the writing process in a ~~~
understand steps guaranteed to ~~
Phil Doran, author of the bests

Dedicated to the memory of John Hixon,
a fine young writer who had much more to give.

YOUR CREATIVE WRITING MASTERCLASS

Advice from the best on writing successful

novels, screenplays and short stories

JURGEN WOLFF

NICHOLAS BREALEY
PUBLISHING

London • Boston

First published by
Nicholas Brealey Publishing in 2012

3–5 Spafield Street	20 Park Plaza, Suite 1115A
Clerkenwell, London	Boston
EC1R 4QB, UK	MA 02116, USA
Tel: +44 (0)20 7239 0360	Tel: (888) BREALEY
Fax: +44 (0)20 7239 0370	Fax: (617) 523 3708

www.nicholasbrealey.com
www.YourCreativeWritingMasterclass.com

© Jurgen Wolff 2011
The right of Jurgen Wolff to be identified as the author of this work
has been asserted in accordance with the Copyright, Designs and
Patents Act 1988.

ISBN: 978-1-85788-578-1

British Library Cataloguing in Publication Data
A catalogue record for this book is available from the
British Library.

All rights reserved. No part of this publication may be reproduced, stored
in a retrieval system, or transmitted, in any form or by any means,
electronic, mechanical, photocopying, recording and/or otherwise without
the prior written permission of the publishers. This book may not be lent,
resold, hired out or otherwise disposed of by way of trade in any form,
binding or cover other than that in which it is published, without the
prior consent of the publishers.

Illustrations by the author.

FSC
Mixed Sources
Product group from well-managed
forests and other controlled sources
Cert no. SGS–COC–2061
www.fsc.org
© 1996 Forest Stewardship Council

Printed in the UK by Clays Ltd, St Ives plc.

Contents

Introduction

You want to write a novel, a screenplay, a play, or a short story. You probably have lots of ideas, but perhaps you're unsure of how to structure your plot or how to make your characters come alive on the page. Where can you look for guidance and models? One of the reasons I wanted to write this book is that in my classes at the University of Southern California and private workshops all over the world over the last 20 years, I've noticed writers looking in all the wrong places.

Aspiring screenwriters were looking to the top-grossing films of the moment, or the hottest TV shows of the day.

Aspiring novelists were taking their cue from the latest best-seller lists.

Sometimes there are excellent novels on the bestseller lists, and some superb movies make a lot of money at the box office. But often the result of emulating the hit of the moment is a watered-down version of the original.

There is a better place to look: the great classic novels of the past two centuries, as well as more recent books and films that have shown enduring qualities.

The core of this book is advice from past masters like Jane Austen, Robert Louis Stevenson, Vladimir Nabokov, Anton Chekhov, and Charles Dickens, as well as current writers like Martin Amis, JK Rowling, Ray Bradbury, Elmore Leonard, and Salman Rushdie.

Of course, hearing advice is not the same as applying it. That's why I've added a wealth of exercises to help you make the transition from one to the other. Whether you're starting with a glimmer of an idea or already have a first draft you'd like to polish so you can launch it confidently into the marketplace, a combination of advice and applications can guide you to success.

While you will find a lot of support and guidance here, this book isn't about a quick fix. Those looking for some kind of magic template or fill-in-the-blanks form won't find them here. The writers quoted in these pages invested not only their time but also their heart and soul in what they wrote. They accepted the fact that writing well requires courage, perseverance, and an independent spirit. That doesn't mean they always had confidence in what they were writing, though. As you'll read, many of them experienced anxiety every time they faced a blank page, and sometimes they felt like imposters for daring to assume, or even hope, that others would find their words of interest. They continued anyway, and their willingness to tread this difficult path has brought enjoyment and enlightenment to millions around the world. If you are ready to embark on your own version of that adventure, this book is for you.

A quick tour of what awaits

We start with a look at what inspires writers and how you can draw on your memories, your dreams, and even your fears to feed your imagination. This section also emphasizes the importance of letting ideas germinate, allowing your subconscious mind to do some of the work before you move to the keyboard.

Because great characters are the foundation of enduring works of fiction, the next section includes several chapters on creating characters that come alive on the page and live on in the memory of readers or movie-goers. You'll find an organic method for discovering characters rather then inventing them. We also discuss the huge importance of status, both actual and perceived, in the relationships between your characters. There's a chapter on how to let the dialogue reflect your characters, and also the link between character and setting. When all these are aligned, you may find that the characters seem to be taking over the story, and we look at the nature of that experience too.

The next section is about the integration of character and plot. Here you'll find out how to pick the most appropriate point of view, how to exploit the conflicts that drive your characters, and practical methods for planning your plot. Crafting a power-ful opening, using foreshadowing, dealing with the difficult mid-dle, and bringing your story to a rewarding end are all covered, as are the question of theme and the process of rewriting.

The fourth group of chapters is all about finding your style. I emphasize that style must serve the story, not call attention to the cleverness of the writer. To that end, I look at how to use clarity and simplicity, conciseness, appropriate detail, and elegant word choice to make your story compelling.

Next we turn to the process of writing itself. This includes the questions of what setting and props can support your writing, how to build your confidence, how to deal with critics (includ-ing a harsh inner critic), and how to overcome writer's block.

The final main section prepares you for the writer's life. Topics include what fame and success mean to a writer, what kind of daily routine to strive for, how to enjoy the writer's life despite its sometimes precarious nature, and what the outlook is now for the novelist and screenwriter. This part ends with a con-sideration of the responsibilities that come with being a writer.

Visit the website www.YourCreativeWritingMasterclass.com and you'll find even more advice from top authors, more ways to apply their suggestions, and the ability to share your experiences of incorporating these lessons in your own work. There are also video biographies, reviews, and resources.

The material on the website and the highly practical advice and exercises in this book combine to create a masterclass that one can only dream of: Charles Dickens drops in to demonstrate how to create exciting characters, Ernest Hemingway helps you figure out how to write concisely and powerfully, and Jane Austen shows you how to make the reader warm to an unsympa-thetic character—followed by another hundred or so expert authors from the past and present. They stand ready to be your mentors and coaches. My hope is that their examples and the exercises in this book will help you create what only you can write in the way that works best for you.

PART I
FINDING INSPIRATION

What inspired great works that are still read decades or even centuries after they were written? What did master writers do when they were stuck for an idea? What methods gave some of them a never-ending flow of stories?

In this section you'll discover the sometimes ordinary, sometimes strange ways in which authors such as Anton Chekhov, Robert Louis Stevenson, Mary Shelley, and Gabriel García Márquez found their inspiration and their starting points. I'll also look at how their methods can help you to move forward with your writing.

1

It starts with (someone else's) words

Do you remember the first book that had an impact on you? Perhaps it was one that was read to you or the first one you were able to read yourself. Or was there a book later in your childhood that had an influence you didn't discern at the time?

Many noted authors have said they were deeply moved by what they read as youngsters. In some cases it was one particular book that made them want to be writers and to which they still return for inspiration years later.

Even once a writer is established, a classic author may serve as their mentor. Martin Amis has said:

> When I am stuck with a sentence that isn't fully born, it isn't there yet, I sometimes think, How would Dickens go at this sentence, how would Bellow or Nabokov go at this sentence? What you hope to emerge with is how you would go at that sentence, but you get a little shove in the back by thinking about writers you admire.

If that sounds like a strategy you'd like to employ, it can be handy to have the masters nearby. Hanging near my desk is a collection of postcard portraits of nine of my writing heroes: Shakespeare, Samuel Johnson, Dickens, Stevenson, Conrad, Wilde, Bertrand Russell, Somerset Maugham, and Graham Greene. I got the postcards at the National Portrait Gallery and had them framed. Having them watch as I write makes it very easy to stay humble, but most of the time it's more inspirational than daunting to have them looking down on me with what I interpret as benevolent gazes.

You don't have to limit yourself to the greats. William Faulkner's advice was:

Read, read, read. Read everything—trash, classics, good and bad, and see how they do it. Just like a carpenter who works as an apprentice and studies the master. Read! You'll absorb it.

WILLIAM FAULKNER (1897–1962)
Faulkner's most famous novels are *The Sound and the Fury*, *As I Lay Dying*, and *Absalom, Absalom!*. In 1949 he won the Nobel Prize for Literature, and went on to win two Pulitzer Prizes. In 1987 the US Postal Service issued a 22-cent stamp bearing his image.

Vladimir Nabokov advocates reading poetry:

You have to saturate yourself with English poetry in order to compose English prose.

For Maya Angelou, the Bible is the greatest inspiration:

The language of all the interpretations, the translations, of the Judaic Bible and the Christian Bible, is musical, just wonderful. I read the Bible to myself. I'll take any translation, any edition, and read it aloud, just to hear the language, hear the rhythm, and remind myself how beautiful English is.

Being changed—and changing others

In a letter to Oprah Winfrey published in the magazine *O*, Harper Lee, author of *To Kill a Mockingbird*, referred to her love of books when she was young and said:

Now, 75 years later in an abundant society where people have laptops, cell phones, iPods and minds like empty rooms, I still plod along with books.

The young Lee couldn't have imagined that some day her own book would have a profound effect.

A survey of lawyers active in the civil rights movement in the 1960s and 1970s revealed that many of them were inspired by the novel *To Kill a Mockingbird* (published in 1960) or its film version (made in 1962). The novel won a Pulitzer Prize for Fiction in 1962 and in 1999 it was voted Best Novel of the Century by the *Library Journal*. It was the reclusive author's only published book, although it is rumored that she has continued to write, just not for publication.

Eudora Welty found that Virginia Woolf was

the one who opened the door. When I read To the Lighthouse, I felt, Heavens, what is this? I was so excited by the experience I couldn't eat or sleep. I've read it many times since, though more often these days I go back to her diary. Any day you open it to will be tragic, and yet all the marvellous things she says about her work, about working, leave you filled with joy that's stronger than your misery for her.

GABRIEL GARCIA MARQUEZ (b 1927)
Márquez's works include *One Hundred Years of Solitude, Love in the Time of Cholera,* and *Autumn of the Patriarch.* Due to his political views on imperialism and his personal friendship with Fidel Castro, he was denied a US visa until Bill Clinton's administration. Many of his works have been adapted into films, particularly in Mexico.

It was the works of Kafka that literally shocked Gabriel García Márquez into writing:

One night a friend lent me a book of short stories by Franz Kafka. I went back to the pension where I was staying and began to read The Metamorphosis. *The first line almost knocked me off the bed. I was so surprised. The first line reads, "When Gregor Samsa woke up one morning from unsettling dreams, he found himself changed in his bed into a monstrous vermin…" When I read the line I thought to myself that I didn't know anyone was allowed to write things like that. If I had known, I would have started writing a long time ago. So I immediately started writing short stories.*

The influence of that tale on Márquez's development as a leading writer of magical realism is clear.

Ralph Ellison told the *Paris Review*:

In 1935 I discovered Eliot's The Waste Land, *which moved and intrigued me but defied my powers of analysis... At night I practiced writing and studied Joyce, Dostoyevsky, Stein, and Hemingway. Especially Hemingway; I read him to learn his sentence structure and how to organize a story.*

Let the library inspire you

Ray Bradbury advises:

You must lurk in libraries and climb the stacks like ladders to sniff books like perfume and wear books like hats upon your crazy heads.

That's harder to do now that libraries are being turned into multimedia centres in which actual books sometimes are the quaintest and most neglected element, but it's good advice nonetheless. Until iPads and Kindles and other ereaders can give off the lovely musty smell of an old book (and probably it's only a matter of time), at least those of us brought up on traditional books will always have a place in our hearts for them and for libraries.

It was in the Redwood City Public Library that I found my most influential childhood books: Enid Blyton's series of Famous Five books, rather idealized stories of the sleuthing adventures of a group of four English children and their dog. That library had the whole series of 21 volumes and I whipped through them, enjoying the England of my (and Blyton's) imagination. Surely that had some influence on my decision, many years later, first to study in the UK and eventually to move to London. Perhaps in 20 years there will be a huge wave of British immigration prompted by the Harry Potter books.

Look beyond the word

Sometimes inspiration comes from another branch of the arts. Salman Rushdie says:

> Much of my thinking about writing was shaped by a youth spent watching the extraordinary outburst of world cinema in the sixties and seventies. I think I learned as much from Bunuel and Bergman and Godard and Fellini as I learned from books.

For Stephen Sondheim, seeing a rather obscure movie called *Hangover Square* was formative:

> It was a moody, romantic, gothic thriller starring Laird Cregar, about a composer in London in 1900 who was ahead of his time. And whenever he heard a high note he went crazy and ran around murdering people. It had an absolutely brilliant score by Bernard Herrmann, centred around a one-movement piano concerto.

Sondheim said his *Sweeney Todd* was an homage to Herrmann.

While you can be inspired by the words and experiences of others, you'll be drawing on your own as you write. In the next chapter I look at how to use your memories and fears as a source.

FROM ADVICE TO ACTION!

In today's busy world it can be a challenge to find the time to read, but it's still one of the best ways to feed your mind. How long has it been since you've read some of the classic authors like Joyce, Dostoyevsky, Hemingway, or Dickens?

I have a friend who plans reading sessions into a very busy schedule because it nourishes his brain and brings an hour of peace into an otherwise hectic day. If you looked at his calendar you'd find entries like "5pm–6pm: Melville" or "1pm–2pm: Joyce."

Is there a famous work you've always intended to read or a classic movie you've meant to watch but haven't gotten around to?

ACTION: Make an appointment with yourself to read a book or see a film that's noted as a classic. You may also want to revisit some of your favorites. There are a few books I go back to from time to time and find new virtues each visit: *The Seven Pillars of Wisdom* by TE Lawrence, *The Courage to Create* by Rollo May, and Joseph Conrad's *Lord Jim*. The equivalent films for me are *Citizen Kane*, *Treasure of the Sierra Madre*, *Lawrence of Arabia*, *High Noon*, *The Godfather* I and II, *Day for Night* (and the list goes on).

Consider the books and films you found most formative, choose one you think would warrant rereading or reviewing, and schedule the required time. This time read it not only for enjoyment but to analyze what made the book or film so powerful for you. What can you learn from that author's methods that might help you make your own writing more vivid and influential? For starters, consider:

- What is the story about, in a sentence or two?
- What is at stake for the protagonist?
- What does the story reveal about the characters, and how?
- How does the opening capture your interest?
- How do the action and the central conflict escalate?
- What are the story's surprises?
- What emotions does it evoke in you? How does it do that?

I invite you to share your most special books on the website www.YourCreativeWritingMasterclass.com, so that everyone can benefit from your experience.

2
Memories and fears

What were the most significant events of your child-hood? Do you find yourself drawing on them, directly or indirectly, in your writing? Many writers do. Willa Cather claimed:

Most of the basic material a writer works with is acquired before the age of fifteen.

F Scott Fitzgerald gave it a bit longer:

A writer can spin on about his adventures after thirty, after forty, after fifty, but the criteria by which these adventures are weighed and valued are irrevocably settled at the age of twenty-five.

The theme of much of Fitzgerald's work was rooted in his own youth:

That was always my experience—a poor boy in a rich town; a poor boy in a rich boy's school; a poor boy in a rich man's club at Princeton... However, I have never been able to forgive the rich for being rich, and it has coloured my entire life and works.

This ambivalence is reflected in how the narrator of *The Great Gatsby* first describes Jay Gatsby:

Gatsby, who represented everything for which I have an unaffected scorn. If personality is an unbroken series of successful gestures, then there was something gorgeous about him, some heightened sensitivity to the promises of life, as if

he were related to one of those intricate machines that reg-
isters earthquakes ten thousand miles away... Gatsby
turned out all right at the end; it is what preyed on Gatsby,
what foul dust floated in the wake of his dreams that tem-
porarily closed out my interest in the abortive sorrows and
short-winded elations of men.

George Bernard Shaw supported the idea of writing about your own experience:

The man who writes about himself and his own time is the
only man who writes about all people and about all time.

Eudora Welty reassures us that we don't need to have had a particularly dramatic life in order to draw on it for inspiration:

I am a writer who came out of a sheltered life. For all seri-
ous daring starts from within.

The memory need not be clear—in some cases, according to Josip Novakovich, it may be a memory that is just out of reach or mysterious in some way that has the most powerful effect. He says:

So, from my experience (no doubt it works differently for dif-
ferent people)—I think that an incomplete memory, or the
memory of an experience not fathomed, provides the
strongest impetus to imagine, invent, mold, create. It's the
moments just missed that drive you crazy, crazy to live in an
imaginary past.

Haruki Murakami points out:

I think memory is the most important asset of human
beings. It's a kind of fuel; it burns and it warms you. My
memory is like a chest: There are so many drawers in that

chest, and when I want to be a fifteen-year-old boy, I open up a certain drawer and I find the scenery I saw when I was a boy in Kobe. I can smell the air, and I can touch the ground, and I can see the green of the trees. That's why I want to write a book.

It is well known that Charles Dickens's childhood informed many of his books. He had happy early years, but that period ended when his father was sent to debtor's prison. The rest of the family joined him there, except Charles, who boarded with a family friend and had to work 10-hour days pasting labels on shoe polish to pay for his board and help his family.

Although not all the specifics are the same, many elements of *David Copperfield* echo Dickens's experience. Even though David never knew his father, who died before he was born, his early life is happy enough. But his mother marries a man who is cruel to him and then his mother and her new baby die. His stepfather sends him to work at a grim factory in London. This is how David Copperfield describes his feelings at being put to work washing and labeling bottles for many hours a day—which we can be sure was informed by Dickens's memories of his own misery:

> *No words can express the secret agony of my soul as I sunk into this companionship… and felt my hopes of growing up to be a learned and distinguished man, crushed in my bosom. The deep remembrance of the sense I had, of being utterly without hope now; of the shame I felt in my position; of the misery it was to my young heart to believe that day for day what I had learned, and thought, and delighted in, and raised my fancy and emulation up by, would pass away from me, little by little, never to be brought back anymore; cannot be written… I mingled my tears with the water in which I was washing the bottles; and sobbed as if there were a flaw in my own breast, and it were in danger of bursting.*

Sometimes memories can be used for a particular image. On her website JK Rowling writes:

> *I was a rotund baby. The description in* Philosopher's Stone *of the photographs of "what appeared to be a beach ball wearing different coloured bobble hats" would also apply to the pictures of my early years.*

Your goal in referring to your memories is not writing your auto-biography, but rather mining your past for characters and events you can use as part of your fiction, especially those elements that carry an emotional weight and can inject your projects with their energy.

Ideas for novels and screenplays usually don't pop into your mind full-blown, although there are some notable exceptions. JK Rowling again:

> *It was after a weekend's flat-hunting, when I was travelling back to London on a crowded train, that the idea for Harry Potter simply fell into my head. I had been writing almost continuously since the age of six but I had never been so excited about an idea before. To my immense frustration, I didn't have a functioning pen with me, and I was too shy to ask anybody if I could borrow one. I think, now, that this was probably a good thing, because I simply sat and thought, for four (delayed train) hours, and all the details bubbled up in my brain, and this scrawny, black-haired, bespectacled boy who didn't know he was a wizard became more and more real to me.*

Thus it was that, thanks partly to the ramshackle state of British Rail, that a billion-dollar enterprise was born in a period of a mere four hours.

Generally, ideas take time to blossom, and the next chapter suggests ways to encourage that process.

FROM ADVICE TO ACTION!

Did you have the disadvantage of a happy childhood? Even so, there may be a rich source of material there for the taking.

ACTION: Some ways to get back in touch with those times are looking at family albums, watching old family movies, and reminiscing with relatives. Some questions that might stir up useful memories:

- What do you consider the most important event in your childhood? In your life since your childhood?
- Who influenced you the most when you were growing up?
- Who were your closest friends when you were growing up? What brought you together?
- As a child, did you have imaginary friends? What were they like?
- What was the happiest part of your life so far? The unhappiest?
- Which of these memories seem the most likely to be transformable into a story?
- What would you change to make it work better as fiction?

Writing as therapy

Some authors are inspired by their own anxieties. Jean Rhys is one of many accomplished authors for whom writing is a kind of therapy. She said:

> I've never written when I was happy. I didn't want to. But I've never had a long period of being happy... You see, there's very little invention in my books. What came first with most of them was the wish to get rid of the awful sadness that weighed me down. I found when I was a child that if I could put the hurt into words, it would go.

Edna Ferber had a rather dark view of the personality of writers, presumably including herself:

> *I think that to write well and convincingly, one must be somewhat poisoned by emotion. Dislike, displeasure, resentment, fault-finding, imagination, passionate remonstrance, a sense of injustice—they all make fine fuel.*

EDNA FERBER (1885–1968)

Ferber's best-known works are *Show Boat, So Big*, and *Giant*. She refused to allow *Show Boat* to be made into a musical until Jerome Kern explained that he wanted to use it to change the genre. Her first writing job was as a reporter for her town's newspaper at age 17.

William Styron agreed:

> *The good writing of any age has always been the product of someone's neurosis... Writing is fine therapy for people who are perpetually scared of nameless threats—for jittery people.*

Tennessee Williams said:

> *My work is emotionally autobiographical. It has no relation-ship to the actual events of my life, but it reflects the emo-tional currents of my life. I try to work every day, because you have no refuge but writing. When you're going through a period of unhappiness, a broken love affair, the death of someone you love, or some other disorder in your life, then you have no refuge but writing.*

That was the case in the creation of the film *Taxi Driver*. Its writer Paul Schrader says:

> *My marriage broke, I was in debt, I had an ulcer, I had no place to stay, I had quit the American Film Institute. I spent three weeks cruising in my car along the sewers of the city. I was living in a metal box, surrounded by people, but absolutely alone. I came to screenplay writing as self-therapy. I wrote about a taxi driver who was full of anger,*

suicidal. I needed the power of art: if I didn't separate from this person, he was becoming me or I was becoming him. That's how I created Travis Bickle.

Of course, solitude can be constructive as well as destructive, and in the next chapter we'll see how that works, and how dreams can also inspire fiction.

FROM ADVICE TO ACTION!

One of the great delights of being a writer is that we can create our own worlds, and they can be much more satisfactory than the one we live in. In our fictional world the bookworm can be popular, the skinny kid can get even with the bullies... wait, this is getting too autobiographical.

Seriously, you don't have to write a "misery memoir" to take advantage of the therapeutic effects of writing about the things that have troubled you or still do. I speak from experience, as the author of a play called *Killing Mother* (oops, too much information!).

ACTION: Take an inventory of the ways you have found life unsatisfactory. Which of them might make the basis of a story you'd like to write?

One way to be more aware of the elements of your life you could use for inspiration is to take a piece of paper, turn it sideways, and draw one column for each decade so far. Now jot down the most important events in each. The first decade would start with your birth and might include your first day at school, the birth of a brother or sister, and perhaps the death of a pet— whatever sticks in your memory and has some emotion attached.

Notice what patterns emerge and how you feel about them. Even if no ideas or themes become obvious immediately, this exercise may stir up your subconscious mind and plant the idea for a story that will emerge later.

3
Solitude and dreams

odern studies of creativity have confirmed that ideas often come when we are not chasing them, but that's not a new finding. Francis Bacon, Sr. advised:

Write down the thoughts of the moment. Those that come unsought for are commonly the most valuable.

Friedrich Nietzsche advocated solitary exercise as a stimulus:

We do not belong to those who have ideas only among books, when stimulated by books. It is our habit to think outdoors—walking, leaping, climbing, dancing, preferably on lonely mountains or near the sea where even the trails become thoughtful.

Henry Miller went a step further:

What the budding artist needs is the privilege of wrestling with his problems in solitude—and now and then a piece of red meat.

And we can follow Franz Kafka yet further:

You do not need to leave your room. Remain sitting at your table and listen. Do not even listen, simply wait, be quite still and solitary. The world will freely offer itself to you to be unmasked, it has no choice, it will roll in ecstasy at your feet.

Charles Dickens was a master of finding a healthy balance of solitude and conviviality. His biographer, Michael Slater, reveals that Dickens's normal daily routine was four hours at his desk in the morning, then a 12-mile walk in the afternoon, then dinner, frequently including house guests, and party games until bedtime. Slater suggests that many of the ideas Dickens translated into prose in those four hours occurred to him during the walks. He writes:

> On 21 June Dickens found he needed an exceptionally long country walk of fourteen miles to begin thinking through what he later called, with reference to the whole novel [David Copperfield] that "very complicated interweaving of truth and fiction".

FROM ADVICE TO ACTION!

It's ironic that the simplest activities—sitting quietly on a park bench for an hour or taking an aimless stroll through a new neighborhood—seem to have turned into luxuries. Walk down any city street and you'll see that half or more of your fellow pedestrians are talking or texting on their phones or listening to music. They're here but their minds are somewhere else.

The drive toward 24/7 connectivity means that the traditional oases of calm—15 minutes sipping a coffee at a sidewalk café or 10 minutes browsing in a bookshop—are no longer safe from interruption.

The benefits of technology are awesome, but as someone observed, every silver lining has a cloud, and for writers the elimination of solitude is one great big cumulus.

ACTION: You still have a choice. You can leave behind your mobile phone and go for a walk. You can turn on the answer machine and take a long bath. You can go to a park and meditate. And, in the stillness of those moments, you can begin to conceive a story that only you can tell. Try scheduling at least 15 minutes a day of such uninterrupted time.

Night-time and dreams

There are some authors who feel inspired in the morning, but generally they tend to be night people. HP Lovecraft put it this way:

> At night, when the objective world has slunk back into its cavern and left dreamers to their own, there come inspirations and capabilities impossible at any less magical and quiet hour. No one knows whether or not he is a writer unless he has tried writing at night.

Some authors don't just write at night, they write in their sleep, in the form of dreams. Possibly the most famous dreamer and a resulting book are Mary Shelley (at the time, Mary Wollstonecraft Godwin) and her novel *Frankenstein*. Here's how it happened, as she described in her introduction to the book:

> When I placed my head upon my pillow, I did not sleep, nor could I be said to think... I saw—with shut eyes, but acute mental vision—I saw the pale student of unhallowed arts kneeling beside the thing he had put together. I saw the hideous phantasm of a man stretched out, and then, on the working of some powerful engine, show signs of life, and stir with an uneasy, half-vital motion. Frightful must it be; for supremely frightful would be the effect of any human endeavor to mock the stupendous Creator of the world... I opened [my eyes] in terror. The idea so possessed my mind, that a thrill of fear ran through me, and I wished to exchange the ghastly image of my fancy for the realities around... I could not so easily get rid of my hideous phantom; still it haunted me. I must try to think of something else. I recurred to my ghost story—my tiresome, unlucky ghost story! O! if I could only contrive one which would frighten my reader as I myself had been frightened that night! Swift as light and as cheering was the idea that broke

*upon me. "I have found it! What terrified me will terrify oth-
ers; and I need only describe the spectre which had haunted
my midnight pillow." On the morrow I announced that I had
thought of a story. I began that day with the words, "It was
on a dreary night of November," making only a transcript of
the grim terrors of my waking dream.*

One of the two most successful book series of all time was
inspired by a dream. The website of *Entertainment Weekly*,
EW.com, reported:

*On June 2, 2003, [Stephenie] Meyer had a dream about a
human girl meeting a vampire in the woods. The next morning the English-major grad from Brigham Young University got
up, started writing for the first time in her life, and just three
months later finished a 500-page book about a regular girl
named Bella and her gorgeous vampire boyfriend, Edward.*

**ROBERT LOUIS
STEVENSON (1850–94)**
Stevenson's best-known
works are the novels
*Treasure Island,
Kidnapped*, and *Strange
Case of Dr Jekyll and Mr
Hyde*. He was also a
poet and essayist. He
ranks among the 30
most-translated authors
in the world, just below
Charles Dickens.

Another story that originated in a dream was
Robert Louis Stevenson's *Strange Case of Dr Jekyll
and Mr Hyde*. In his travel memoir *Across the
Plains*, one chapter is devoted to his account of his
nightmares as a child and how he eventually came
to harvest them for plots for his tales. Here is how
he describes the process that led to Dr Jekyll:

*For two days I went about racking my brains for
a plot of any sort; and on the second night I
dreamed the scene at the window, and a scene
afterward split in two, in which Hyde, pursued
for some crime, took the powder and underwent
the change in the presence of his pursuers.*

Of course, it's rare for a dream to provide an
entire plot, and Stevenson was clear that he
fleshed out the bones of the idea:

All the rest was made awake, and consciously, although I think I can trace in much of it the manner of my Brownies [his name for the powers at work during his dreams]. The meaning of the tale is therefore mine, and had long pre-existed in my garden of Adonis, and tried one body after another in vain; indeed, I do most of the morality, worse luck! and my Brownies have not a rudiment of what we call a conscience. Mine, too, is the setting, mine the characters. All that was given me was the matter of three scenes, and the central idea of a voluntary change becoming involuntary.

A more recent master of horror, Stephen King, also depends on his nightmares for material. In an interview with UK writer Stan Nicholls, King revealed the origin of the novel *Misery*:

Like the ideas for some of my other novels, that came to me in a dream. In fact, it happened when I was on Concorde, flying over here, to Brown's. I fell asleep on the plane, and dreamt about a woman who held a writer prisoner and killed him, skinned him, fed the remains to her pig and bound his novel in human skin. His skin, the writer's skin. I said to myself, "I have to write this story." Of course, the plot changed quite a bit in the telling. But I wrote the first forty or fifty pages right on the landing here, between the ground floor and the first floor of the hotel... Dreams are just another part of life. To me, it's like seeing something on the street you can use in your fiction. You take it and plug it right in.

Allan Gurganus agrees, and is fascinated by how one type of dreaming turns into another:

There's a strange combination in writing of using images and fragments from actual dreams, but also finding a way to have a governed conscious dream life, which is what writing is... The joy of being a storyteller is precisely that I have two dream lives, at least two: the one that happens the eight hours a night that I close my eyes, and also the one that happens the rest of the time when I open my eyes.

**RAY BRADBURY
(b 1920)**

Bradbury is best known for *Fahrenheit 451, The Martian Chronicles*, and *The Illustrated Man.* Widely considered to be a science fiction writer, Bradley considers himself to be a fantasy writer. He never attended college, choosing instead to pursue his education in public libraries.

Ray Bradbury is a proponent of using the semi-dream state that we experience just as we are waking up. In an interview with Gavin Grant at Booksense.com, he said:

I think that's why people like my work, because they know it's very honest work, very intuitive, and it's very dreamlike. These things come to me a lot of times while I'm waking up in the morning around 7 o'clock. I don't dream things, but there's a time between waking up and being fully awake when your mind is relaxed and things come to you and you are surprised by them and you jump out of bed and run and write them down.

That happens with, I would say, 60% of my work. I don't believe in dreams. People say, "Have you ever dreamt a story?" That's never happened to me. I do believe in that relaxed state that when you're waking up you're not thinking intellectually, but you're perceiving things in that state before you're fully awake.

It's not only nightmares that serve as raw material for your writing. Some years ago I had the experience of dreaming the beginning of a story that I thought could make a good comedy screenplay about a failed author who decides to write a children's book. I got up and wrote the first six pages. The next night, my dream picked up where the first one left off and I got up and wrote another six pages. I was overjoyed—at this rate, I would have a complete screenplay in three weeks!

Unfortunately, at that point the dreams stopped, but the first 12 pages pretty much remained as I dreamed them, in the film called *The Real Howard Spitz.*

One easy way to get in the habit of capturing your dreams is to use the practice Julia Cameron calls "morning pages." She recommends that you write three pages, longhand, in a stream-of-consciousness manner, to get and maintain a creative flow. They're for your eyes only with no idea of publication or being used, but it would be natural for some of your dream material to be included.

FROM ADVICE TO ACTION!

ACTION: The biggest challenge is remembering your dreams, but you can train yourself to do so. Keep a pen and paper or a tape recorder on your bedside table. Before you go to sleep, remind yourself that it's your intention to remember your dreams. When you wake up, immediately jot down or record anything you recall from your dreams. At first you may find you only come up with one image or a little bit of a conversation. The more you do this, though, the more you will remember. At that point you can become more selective and make a note only of the dreams that seemed to have some emotional impact, because those are the ones most likely to serve as the raw material or inspiration for a story that will be meaningful to you.

4

Germination

Successful authors recognize the need for an idea to flower. Inspiration doesn't just mean being hit with one idea suddenly; it can also mean cultivating it, allowing it to grow in our subconscious, and letting it emerge when it's ready.

Here is how the prolific detective novel author Georges Simenon described his process to the *Paris Review*:

> Unconsciously I probably always have two or three, not novels, not ideas about novels, but themes in my mind. I never even think that they might serve for a novel; more exactly, they are the things about which I worry. Two days before I start writing a novel I consciously take up one of these ideas. But even before I consciously take it up I first find some atmosphere... I might remember such-and-such a spring, maybe in some small Italian town, or some place in the French provinces or in Arizona... and little by little, a small world will come into my mind, with a few characters. These characters will be taken partly from people I have known and partly from pure imagination... And then the idea I had before will come around and stick around them. They will have the same problem I have in my mind myself. And the problem—with those people—will give me the novel.

Jack Kerouac's version of the process has some similarities:

> You think out what actually happened, you tell friends long stories about it, you mull it over in your mind, you connect it together at leisure, then when the time comes to pay the rent again you force yourself to sit at the typewriter, or at the writing notebook, and get it over with as fast as you can...

and there's no harm in that because you've got the whole story lined up."

He wrote *On the Road* in three weeks.

Martin Amis described his experience this way:

MARTIN AMIS (b 1949) Amis wrote *Money, The Information,* and *London Fields.* He refused to read novels as a child and young adult, reading only comic books; his high school headmaster described him as "unusually unpromising." Many of his novels are loosely autobiographical, including *Money,* in which there is a character with his name.

What happens is what Nabokov described as a throb. A throb or a glimmer, an act of recognition on the writer's part. At this stage the writer thinks, Here is something I can write a novel about... The idea can be incredibly thin—a situation, a character in a certain place at a certain time. With Money, for example, I had an idea of a big fat guy in New York, trying to make a film. That was all.

A specific image was William Faulkner's starting point for *The Sound and the Fury*:

It began with a mental picture. I didn't realize at the time it was symbolical. The picture was of the muddy seat of a little girl's drawers in a pear tree, where she could see through a window where her grandmother's funeral was taking place and report what was happening to her brothers on the ground below. By the time I explained who they were and what they were doing and how her pants got muddy, I realized it would be impossible to get all of it into a short story and that it would have to be a book.

Alice Walker describes her inspiration for her best-known novel and also the time it took to develop into a full story:

I don't always know where the germ of a story comes from, but with The Color Purple I knew right away. I was hiking through the woods with my sister, Ruth, talking about a lovers' triangle of which we both knew. She said, "And you know, one day The Wife asked The Other Woman for a pair of her drawers." Instantly the missing piece of the story I was mentally writing—about two women who felt married to the same man—fell into place. And for months—through illnesses, divorce, several moves, travel abroad, all kinds of heartaches and revelations—I carried my sister's comment delicately balanced in the centre of the novel's construction I was building in my head.

What most of these elements have in common is that they seem to just appear and start a train of thought. As Ernest Hemingway said:

I never had to choose a subject—my subject rather chose me.

FROM ADVICE TO ACTION!

ACTION: Whether your starting point is an image or a feeling or an overheard remark, capture it as quickly as possible. Your options include jotting it down in a notebook, texting it to yourself, dictating it to your phone (many phones have recording functions or you can just leave a voicemail for yourself), or taking a photo. For some writers it's the act of recording the idea that is more important than referring to it later. Just noting it is enough to implant it in their mind, where it can continue to grow.

As with a seed, it's not a good idea to pull up the idea too often to see whether it's ready yet. Leave it alone and it will surface when the time is right.

One way to give yourself some visual prompts is to engage in a practice I wrote about in my book *Creativity Now!* Suggested by innovation and strategy manager Richard Stomp, it's called streetcombing. It's like beachcombing, but instead of gathering shells you're looking for interesting visual images and collecting them with your camera.

It doesn't matter whether or not you actually use any of these images in your writing; the very act of consciously looking for interesting images changes the way you see everything. Suddenly your eyes and brain are much more sensitive to the strange and wonderful things happening all around you.

You can do the same thing with what you hear. Most writers are natural eavesdroppers anyway, but for a day make an effort (unobtrusively, of course) to jot down as many snatches of overheard conversation as you can. At the end of the day, they will coalesce into a conversation worthy of Beckett—and they may just prompt an idea for a character or a story.

You can use these methods to help grow an idea—for instance, a storyline on which you feel stuck. Juxtapose the elements you already have with the pictures you've gathered or the comments you've overheard and let that lead you to the next step. For example, in my play *Killing Mother*, I was stuck for a way to show the character's feelings when his cruel mother passed away. In a novel I could just reveal his thoughts, but on a stage it has to be translated into action. On a walk I photographed a series of storefronts, one of which was a dance studio. That suggested the solution: his mother had always made fun of his clumsiness; when she was gone, he did a dance around the room—still clumsy, but obviously now feeling free.

Another useful story-growing method is to imagine that you've finished writing the story and are being interviewed about it by someone who is very curious. Imagine them asking you about different aspects of the story—including the bits you don't know yet. You may be surprised at how solutions and story strands pop into your mind without any conscious effort on your part.

PART II
CHARACTERS COME TO LIFE

ow do the great writers get to know these products of their imagination so well that they seem to come alive? What are the essential attributes of a character who "jumps off the page"? And what's the secret of making them talk—that is, writing great dialogue?

In this section, Mark Twain, F Scott Fitzgerald, Patricia Highsmith, and many other masters of characterization reveal their secrets, and a variety of exercises show you how to apply these lessons to your writing.

5
Meeting your characters

or many authors, characters are the starting point and the plot flows from them. Hilary Mantel says:

If you aspire to a book that will last, that will be worth rereading, don't think about plot at all, think about your characters... If you make your characters properly they will simply do what is within them, they'll act out the nature you have given them, and there—you'll find—you have your plot.

The characters we remember long after we have forgotten the details of plot are as complex as the people we have in our own lives. Jane Gardam says:

If its characters (and that's what a novel is about, characters; the plot must look after itself except in thrillers and perhaps even then) are not contestable, arguable, differently interpreted by different readers, then the book has not been worth good money.

F Scott Fitzgerald advised:

Begin with an individual and you find that you have created a type; begin with a type and you find that you have created—nothing.

In a letter to his editor, Stieg Larsson, author of *The Girl with the Dragon Tattoo*, explained that he was consciously going against type in creating his investigative journalist protagonist and other characters:

I have tried to create main characters who are drastically different from the types who generally appear in crime novels. Mikael Blomkvist, for instance, doesn't have ulcers, or booze problems or an anxiety complex. He doesn't listen to operas, nor does he have an oddball hobby such as making model airplanes. He doesn't have any real problems, and his main characteristic is that he acts like a stereotypical "slut," as he himself admits. I have also deliberately changed the sex roles: In many ways Blomkvist acts like a typical "bimbo," while Lisbeth Salander has stereotypical "male" characteristics and values... A rule of thumb has been never to romanticize crime and criminals, nor to stereotype victims of crime.

Mark Twain said:

The test of any good fiction is that you should care something for the characters; the good to succeed, the bad to fail. The trouble with most fiction is that you want them all to land in hell, together, as quickly as possible.

Patricia Highsmith took the view that

PATRICIA HIGHSMITH (1921–95)

first, readers want to read about people, individuals whom they can believe in, and preferably like a little. A naïve, maybe careless but lucky hero or heroine would appeal to readers, I think, because we all worry about not doing the wise thing in a crisis; and if such a personage comes out alive and successful, the reader gets a lift from it. The reader has to identify—even slightly—with a character or two, otherwise he or she is not going to go on reading.

Highsmith's best-known works are *Strangers on a Train*, *The Talented Mr. Ripley*, and *Edith's Diary*. Her first writing job was scripting comic books for publisher Ned Pines. She wrote *The Prince of Salt* under a pen-name and did not acknowledge it as her own until decades later.

To create characters the reader will care about, first you have to get to know them: what drives them, what they would do in any given situation, and what they would say. As W Somerset Maugham pointed out:

You can never know enough about your characters.

Not everything you know will end up in the finished work. In her book *If You Want to Write*, Brenda Ueland noted:

Someone once asked Ibsen how he happened to name the heroine of A Doll's House Nora, and he said, "Well, her real name was Eleonora but they got to calling her Nora as a little girl." You see, he knew her whole life, everything about her, from earliest childhood, though in the play only a few hours of her life are shown.

The starting image

For many writers development is an organic process. It can start with just a single image of a character and grow from there, as Rose Tremain describes:

On a rainy afternoon in August 1983, I lay down in a hotel bedroom in Bourges and had a waking dream.

I imagined a middle-aged man standing by a low stone wall, somewhere in the countryside. He had thinning, sand-coloured hair. He appeared tired and melancholy. He looked up at the clear sky above him and saw an enormous bird circling there. He realized it was an eagle and his expression changed from sorrow to wonder. The eagle kept turning lower and lower. It landed on the wall right in front of the man and perched there, regarding him. Now, the man beamed. He felt violently happy. He understood that something miraculous had occurred.

This sequence of images, carrying in it the idea of a sudden transformation or transcendence, was the fragile foundation of my novel The Swimming Pool Season. *It was what I shall call the "first mystery" of the book, the thing that will—or might—contain the essence of what the book is going to be, provided the significance of the mystery is rightly interpreted. [It is] one part of the process of novel writing—that part in which the imagination conjures images and the controlling authorial mind gives them context and meaning.*

Thomas Fleming offers another example:

My latest novel, Hours of Gladness, *emerged as a single word: Mick. Then it became Mick O'Day. The name kept pushing against my consciousness. Slowly the character appeared: an Irish-American spiritually wounded by Vietnam, living with his fellow Irish-Americans in a New Jersey shore town, with the Vietnamese woman he loved now a refugee living nearby, untouchable, alienated forever.*

The kinds of fascinating people these authors mention are all around us, if we only pay attention to them. It's a matter of putting on the right filter. Perhaps you've noticed that if you are in the market for a new television set, suddenly the world seems to be full of ads for televisions. Once you've bought your new set, these ads disappear. Of course, they don't really go away, but since you're no longer in the market, your mind filters them out automatically.

Similarly, I've noticed that when I'm out and about with my camera, all kinds of people strike me as visually interesting; naturally they're there all the time, but with my camera in hand I'm looking for them. Sometimes it's possible to take their picture discreetly, other times it's not, but observing them closely burns them into my memory.

It's not just appearance but behavior that reveals character. I have an acquaintance who can't go for more than five minutes without checking her phone messages nor more than ten without looking at her Facebook page. It makes it very annoying to try to have a conversation with her, but it also gives me an excellent model should I want to create an insecure, narcissistic character.

Here is how Italo Calvino uses simple but vivid descriptions in telling us about some people who meet in *Invisible Cities*:

> *A girl comes along, twirling a parasol on her shoulder, and twirling slightly also her rounded hips. A woman in black comes along, showing her full age, her eyes restless beneath her veil, her lips trembling. A tattooed giant comes along; a young man with white hair; a female dwarf; two girls, twins, dressed in coral. Something runs among them, an exchange of glances link lines that connect one figure with another and draws arrows, stars, triangles, until all combinations are used up in a moment, and other characters come on to the scene: a blind man with a cheetah on a leash, a courtesan with an ostrich-plume fan, an ephebe, a Fat Woman. And thus, when some people happen to find themselves together, taking shelter from the rain under an arcade, or crowding beneath the awnings of the bazaar, or stopping to listen to the band in the square, meetings, seductions, copulations, orgies are consummated among them without a word exchanged, without a finger touching anything, almost without an eye raised.*

Let's take a look at two great examples of how classic authors—Charles Dickens and Robert Louis Stevenson—created characters that still live today.

Great Expectations

Great Expectations is the story of Pip, an orphan, and his quest to become a gentleman. Like many of Dickens's novels, it deals with class, crime, and ambition. It was published in serial form in

1860 and 1861 and written in the first person—Pip describing the remarkable events of his life. In this brief excerpt, notice how an item of clothing, Mrs. Joe's apron, holds a key to her character and how a vivid if improbable image (washing with a nutmeg grater) helps you picture her:

> My sister, Mrs. Joe, with black hair and eyes, had such a prevailing redness of skin that I sometimes used to wonder whether it was possible she washed herself with a nutmeg-grater instead of soap. She was tall and bony, and almost always wore a coarse apron, fastened over her figure behind with two loops, and having a square impregnable bib in front, that was stuck full of pins and needles. She made it a powerful merit in herself, and a strong reproach against Joe, that she wore this apron so much. Though I really see no reason why she should have worn it at all; or why, if she did wear it at all, she should not have taken it off, every day of her life.

Treasure Island

Treasure Island was originally serialized in the children's magazine *Young Folks* in 1881–82 and was Robert Louis Stevenson's first successful novel when it came out in book form in 1883.

Although conceived as a coming-of-age story for young readers, the novel was immediately admired by adult readers as well and is one of the most-often dramatized classics. Surely one of the reasons is Stevenson's ability to create characters who come alive on the page. In this excerpt, the opening of the book, Jim Hawkins, the young narrator, describes the arrival of Billy Bones at Jim's father's inn. Notice the details—the black, broken nails, the dirty, livid white scar, the tarry pigtail, the soiled coat—that all add up to an image of an unclean man from whom you'd probably want to keep your distance:

I remember him as if it were yesterday, as he came plodding to the inn door, his sea-chest following behind him in a hand-barrow—a tall, strong, heavy, nut-brown man, his tarry pigtail falling over the shoulder of his soiled blue coat, his hands ragged and scarred, with black, broken nails, and the sabre cut across one cheek, a dirty, livid white. I remember him looking round the cover and whistling to himself as he did so, and then breaking out in that old sea-song that he sang so often afterwards:

> *"Fifteen men on the dead man's chest—*
> *Yo-ho-ho, and a bottle of rum!"*

in the high, old tottering voice that seemed to have been tuned and broken at the capstan bars.

Already we can picture Billy Bones and imagine hearing him— two of our senses have been engaged. Of course, we also judge people by their actions and now we get some description of Bones's behavior as well:

Then he rapped on the door with a bit of stick like a handspike that he carried, and when my father appeared, called roughly for a glass of rum. This, when it was brought to him, he drank slowly, like a connoisseur, lingering on the taste and still looking about him at the cliffs and up at our signboard.

Another thing we pay attention to is what people say, so let's listen to Billy Bones's line of questioning:

"This is a handy cove," says he at length; "and a pleasant sittyated grog-shop. Much company, mate?"

My father told him no, very little company, the more was the pity.

"Well, then," said he, "this is the berth for me. Here you, matey," he cried to the man who trundled the barrow; "bring up alongside and help up my chest. I'll stay here a

bit," he continued. "I'm a plain man; rum and bacon and eggs is what I want, and that head up there for to watch ships off. What you mought call me? You mought call me captain. Oh, I see what you're at—there"; and he threw down three or four gold pieces on the threshold. "You can tell me when I've worked through that," says he, looking as fierce as a commander.

Comes across as rather a suspicious type, doesn't he? He wants to know if there are many visitors and is gratified to hear there are few, and he wants to see ships' movements—a man with something to hide, frightened as well as frightening.

It's all achieved in simple language that is still compelling almost two centuries after it was written.

Don't forget the supporting cast

While you will devote most of your time to your primary characters, Anton Chekhov pointed out the need to craft excellent secondary ones as well:

ANTON CHEKHOV (1860–1904)
Chekhov's best-known works are his plays *Uncle Vanya*, *Three Sisters*, and *The Cherry Orchard*. He also published many short stories and simultaneously practiced medicine. Chekhov was made to repeat a year of high school because he had failed a Greek test.

Like it or not, when you're putting a story together, you first worry about the framework: from a crowd of heroes and quasi-heroes you pick out a single figure—a wife or a husband—and you place that figure against a background and then you develop and accentuate it. The rest of the characters you scatter across the background like so much small change, and then you end up with something like a night sky: one big moon in the center of a crowd of very tiny stars. But the moon does not work because it can only make sense if the stars make sense, and meanwhile the stars are not clearly enough worked out.

Especially in films, the first character you introduce usually is assumed to be your protagonist. There are many exceptions, but be aware that your audience will form this impression and avoid starting with some minor character unless that person's action directly affects the introduction of your protagonist. Descriptions in film and television scripts and plays are more spare than in novels, so it becomes even more important to be selective about which ones you choose.

If you don't already have one, you can develop a writer's mindset. That is, continually be alert to provocative snatches of overheard speech, and people who do unexpected things. Some of the things you can be aware of:

- An unusual style of clothing or combination of clothes.
- A remarkable turn of phrase.
- Someone's distinctive posture or walking style and what they carry with them.
- How people interact with those serving them (waiters, cab drivers, etc.).
- How someone reacts to a compliment.
- Any strong smells associated with a person: perfume, cigar smoke, cleaning solutions, ripe fruit.

As well as being able to describe your characters, you need to know intimately what they would or would not do. That's the topic of the next chapter.

FROM ADVICE TO ACTION!

ACTION: The next time you go shopping or on some other errand, set the intention that you will notice at least one interesting person. Choose one detail about them: their scuffed shoes, the bulging oversize bag they're carrying, the multiple rings on their fingers.

Let your imagination spin that one detail into a bigger story about who they are. That man with the worn-out shoes—can't he afford a new pair? No, because he lost his job more than a year ago. He has the look of an office worker—where did he work? Was he fired? Why? An office romance that spiraled out of control?

If you are currently writing something, you can specify that you want to notice a detail that will fit into your project somehow. You may want to record this with your camera, discreetly, or by jotting it down in a notebook. If you do this once a day, soon you will find that the process becomes automatic.

6

What would they do?

Deborah Moggach applies the "what if?" test to her characters:

My test on whether they have worked is to imagine them in various situations—stuck in a lift, say, or riding a horse. Anything, really. And if they have gelled then I know exactly how they would behave. From then on I'm able to become them, and act them out to myself.

This conforms to André Gide's advice:

The bad novelist constructs his characters; he directs them and makes them speak. The true novelist listens to them and watches them act; he hears their voices even before he knows them.

I first encountered this in action in an interview with screenwriter Alvin Sargent, whose credits include *Ordinary People, Julia*, and, at the age of eighty-something, the Spiderman movies. I noticed a big pile of script pages on his desk and asked him what they were. He said they were for his next script. It looked like about 300 pages, so I asked whether it was going to be some kind of epic. No, he explained, he was getting into the characters by writing scenes in which they did various things, some having to do with the plot, some not. It was his way of getting to know them.

Sometimes the search for the right character can be like considering job candidates. Ann Cummins reveals:

Actually, for Yellowcake, I auditioned characters I thought it would be fun to embody. When I was a kid, I had very lively make-believe friends, all of whom I found much more inter-

esting than me. As a novelist, I just feed my childhood appetite for playing. I'm drawn to wicked types. I do find that in the process of developing characters, I always end up liking them, even the villains. They become very human to me.

Rick Moody says:

When stuck with trying to understand a character, I have in the past interviewed him or her. This works best if you then avoid using any of the material in the interview. Does he like area rugs or wall-to-wall? Has she ever tried to get a co-worker fired? To what extent is he willing to fudge numbers on his taxes? It's really fun to ask a character those sorts of questions, and the experience also helps you know well the idiosyncrasies of that person's voice. Voice is to character development what makeup and the outfit is to actors, the thing that legitimizes the intent to create, the thing that obliterates the artifice.

One of the things that becomes apparent when you get to know your characters well is that they will behave differently in different circumstances. As Tolstoy pointed out:

LEO TOLSTOY (1828–1910)

Tolstoy's novels include *War and Peace, Anna Karenina,* and *The Death of Ivan Ilyich.* He was excommunicated from the Russian Orthodox Church because of the radical views expressed in his novels. He found Shakespeare's writing boring and repulsive, and read all of Shakespeare's plays again as an old man to see if they would strike him differently. They didn't.

One of the most widespread superstitions is that every man has his own special, definitive qualities, energetic, apathetic, etc. Men are not like that... men are like rivers... every river narrows here, is more rapid there, here slower, there broader, now clear, now cold, now warm. It is the same with men. Every man carries in himself the germs of every human quality, and sometimes one manifests itself, sometimes another, and a man often becomes unlike himself, while still remaining the same man.

Do they change over time?

In screenplays there is an emphasis on what is called "the character arc," meaning the change in a character from one outlook or set of values to another over the course of the story. Transformation of the protagonist also is a feature of many novels. The classic example is Ebenezer Scrooge in *A Christmas Carol*, who starts out as a miser and misanthrope but, through the intervention of the Christmas ghosts, changes into a kindly and generous man by the end. We will return to this in a later chapter, but for now you may want to consider whether part of the story you want to tell is how your protagonist or other characters change. If so, "What would he or she do?" will have a different answer at the end of your novel, story, or screenplay than it does at the start.

Another way to get to know your characters well, considering what they want and what they need, is the topic of the next chapter.

FROM ADVICE TO ACTION!

ACTION: Imagine your character is open to being interviewed by you. Find a quiet place and a time when you won't be interrupted for about 15 or 20 minutes. Close your eyes and imagine your character sitting in front of you. Open your eyes long enough to look at the questions below, close them again, ask each question (either out loud or in your mind), and imagine the character answering. If they don't want to answer a particular question, move on (sometimes what they don't say is just as revealing as what they do say). You can jot down the answers as you go along or at the end.

✐ How would you describe your childhood?
✐ When you were a child, what did you want to be when you grew up?
✐ If there is a moral or lesson to be derived from your father's life, what is it? How about your mother's life?

- What do you think is the most important thing in life?
- What are you most proud of that you've done?
- What are you most ashamed of?
- What do you fear?
- How far would you go to defend the people most important to you?
- What is one thing you wish you could have done differently? How would you rather have done it?
- Who do you admire and why?
- Who do you despise and why?
- What's your best quality?
- What's your worst quality?
- When you die, what would you like people to say about you?

Naturally, you also can make up your own questions, especially ones relating to the specific story you are writing.

You also can imagine how a character would respond to various situations in the novels you read. For instance, in Gabriel García Márquez's *Love in the Time of Cholera* we read:

> At six that morning, as he was making his last rounds, the night watchman had seen the note nailed to the street door: "Come in without knocking and inform the police."

Would your protagonist follow those directions? Or would they tell someone else to go in, or ignore the note entirely, preferring not to get involved?

Again, the purpose isn't necessarily to generate material you will use directly, but rather to get a full sense of who these people are. You can select your own situations, but here are a few more to get you started. It may be easiest to imagine these situations with your eyes closed—visualize the character's response rather than deciding what it would be; if nothing comes to you, go on to the next one.

What would your character do if they:

- saw a teenager shoplifting at a department store?
- were approached for help by a homeless person?
- won a lot of money on the lottery?
- found a wallet or purse full of money (also containing the owner's ID)?
- saw an old person being mugged?
- had to choose between being injured or letting their best friend be injured?
- had to save just one thing from their house due to a fire?
- were asked to go on stage at a talent show?
- found a bug in their soup at a restaurant?
- met a famous actor they admired?
- were stuck in lift alone?
- were falsely accused of a crime?
- were told death would come calling in 90 days?

A more advanced version of the exercise is to imagine two of your characters encountering the same situation together. For instance, they find a wallet full of cash. Would they agree on what to do? If not, what arguments would each one have to justify their choice?

What they want, what they need, and why it's complicated

 useful question, and one that will suggest an action, is what your character wants. Kurt Vonnegut said:

> When I used to teach creative writing, I would tell the students to make their characters want something right away—even if it's only a glass of water. Characters paralyzed by the meaninglessness of modern life still have to drink water from time to time.

Josh Emmons agrees and provides some great examples:

> Most compelling characters want something. They want revenge against the white whale that took their leg. They want sex with nymphets. They want to get married. They want to destroy the round gold embodiment of all the world's evil. They want to find someone who isn't phoney. They want to live purely and adventurously as a knight errant. They want to be flattered by their dissembling daughters. They want to get back home from the war... In short, they want what they don't have (or think they don't have) and their efforts to attain that thing make them both interesting and sympathetic. While there are exceptions to this rule—characters content to stay where they are and do nothing whose fascinating reflections or other attributes make them compelling—it's generally true.

If your characters have wants that are easily satisfied, you don't have any conflict; without conflict, generally you don't have much of a story, or at least not one that will last through an entire book or screenplay (as opposed to a short story). If, however, there is something standing in the way of your characters' wants, and if the reader, as well as the characters, cares about those wants, there's a great chance you have a good story brewing.

The playwright David Mamet wrote a memo to the writers of the television series *The Unit*, for which he was executive producer. The memo later appeared on the website movieline.com. It was written all in capital letters, but I'll refrain from having it shout at you. Here is part of the memo regarding the definition of drama:

> *Every scene must be dramatic. That means: the character must have a simple, straightforward, pressing need which impels him or her to show up in the scene. This need is why they came. It is what the scene is about. Their attempt to get this need will lead, at the end of the scene, to failure—this is how the scene is over, this failure will, then, of necessity propel us into the next scene. All these attempts, taken together, will, over the course of the episode, constitute the plot.*

**AYN RAND
(1905–82)**

Rand's best-known works are *The Fountainhead, Atlas Shrugged*, and *We the Living*. As a teenager in the Crimea she worked with illiterate Red Army soldiers to teach them to read. Before selling any novels, Rand worked as an extra and then as a screenwriter in Hollywood; her first screenplay was sold in 1932, but was never produced due to its anti-Soviet leanings.

When a character goes beyond a stereotype, they may have competing impulses—in other words, they may want mutually exclusive things. Ayn Rand pointed out:

> *I want to emphasize that a character can have enormous conflicts and contradictions—but then these have to be consistent. You must select his actions so that the reader grasps: "This is what's the trouble with this character." For instance, there are contradictions in Gail Wynand's actions throughout The Fountainhead, but these contradictions are integrated to their ultimate root. If a character has contradictory premises, to say "I*

understand him" means: "I understand the conflict behind his actions."

Let's take a look at how Herman Melville's Captain Ahab reflects this kind of dilemma.

Moby-Dick

Captain Ahab is a prime example of a conflicted character. Basically a decent man, his obsession with the great whale overshadows everything else. Melville prepares us for encountering him by having Ishmael ask to meet him. He is told:

> *But I don't think thou wilt be able to at present. I don't know exactly what's the matter with him; but he keeps close inside the house; a sort of sick, and yet he don't look so. In fact, he ain't sick; but no, he isn't well either. Any how, young man, he won't always see me, so I don't suppose he will thee. He's a queer man, Captain Ahab—so some think—but a good one. Oh, thou'lt like him well enough; no fear, no fear. He's a grand, ungodly, god-like man, Captain Ahab; doesn't speak much; but, when he does speak, then you may well listen. Mark ye, be forewarned; Ahab's above the common; Ahab's been in colleges, as well as 'mong the cannibals; been used to deeper wonders than the waves; fixed his fiery lance in mightier, stranger foes than whales. His lance! aye, the keenest and the surest that out of all our isle! Oh! he ain't Captain Bildad; no, and he ain't Captain Peleg; HE'S AHAB, boy; and Ahab of old, thou knowest, was a crowned king!*

Notice all the contradictions—he's not sick, but he's not well, either. Ungodly but god-like, among cannibals but also among college students. Melville sets Ahab up as a man battling with himself as much as with the great whale.

Perhaps the ultimate in a character with competing impulses is Dr. Jekyll, who of course turns into Mr. Hyde. As was mentioned earlier, the story originated in a dream experienced by Robert Louis Stevenson. The tradition is that Stevenson's wife suggested he stress the allegorical nature of the tale, whereupon he burned the first draft and started over. He wrote it in under a week—some say with the aid of cocaine. He spent several weeks rewriting and polishing the novel, which was issued in book form in the US and the UK in 1886 and was an immediate success.

Wants versus needs

Frequently, there is a conflict between what characters want and what they need. Often we are blind to what we really need and instead exert all of our energy pursuing what we want. For instance, a middle-aged man may want to recapture his youth and spend money on a sports car, hair transplants, and a young mistress, when what he needs is to accept that he's getting older.

Or it may be that the character desires a relationship that is unattainable or unsuitable, as in *Great Expectations*. This is the first time Pip, the protagonist, meets Estella:

> *Though she called me "boy" so often, and with a carelessness that was far from complimentary, she was of about my own age. She seemed much older than I, of course, being a girl, and beautiful and self-possessed; and she was as scornful of me as if she had been one-and-twenty, and a queen.*

When Miss Havisham commands Estella to play with Pip, Estella says:

> *With this boy? Why, he is a common laboring boy!*

Pip notes:

I thought I overheard Miss Havisham answer,—only it seemed so Unlikely,—"Well? You can break his heart."

In a Hollywood film, these opposites would battle for 90 minutes, all the while falling in love, and end up together. In Dickens's perhaps more realistic world, the story ends just as badly as it starts. Pip should know that he needs a woman capable of loving him—but his want overshadows mere facts.

Similarly, a psychologist probably would argue that while Captain Ahab wants revenge, what he needs is to accept his injury and get on with his life. Although that may be a good prescription for a happy life, it's a terrible prescription for drama. Finding a juicy discrepancy between your protagonist's needs and wants and dramatizing these opposing forces is one path to a compelling story.

FROM ADVICE TO ACTION!

One way to explore your character's needs and desires is to use the hierarchy of needs. Developed by psychologist Abraham Maslow in his 1943 paper "A Theory of Human Motivation," this identifies several stages of growth in human beings, and what we seek at each level. Often represented as a pyramid, it starts with the most basic level at the base, the physiological needs. These include breathing, food, sex, sleep, and the other essential functions.

The next level represents safety—that is, basic security for the individual, their family, the home, and so on.

The next level up is about love and belonging, a good relationship with family, spouse or partner, and friends.

Above that are concerns relating to esteem: being respected and respecting oneself, having a sense of accomplishment, serving a valuable function.

At the top level, the tip of the pyramid, is what Maslow called self-actualization. This is the realm of creativity, spirituality, and morality. His belief was that the lower needs must be met before we have the ability to concern ourselves with the higher ones.

Many stories follow a character's travel up this hierarchy, threatening them at the level of sheer survival and then confronting them with more sophisticated challenges as they progress. That is true of many of Dickens's protagonists, for example. On the other hand, Kafka often liked to start with characters who were nearer the top and show how quickly and easily they could be cast down to the lowest levels without comprehending what they did to deserve such a fall (if deserving came into it at all).

ACTION: Consider the location of your protagonist on Maslow's hierarchy at the start of your story. How satisfied are they with their situation? Do they yearn for something higher on the scale? Also consider how the developments in the story affect them—is it a journey up the pyramid, or down? To what degree is your character responsible for these changes? How do they feel about them? What do they do to resist or enable this movement?

Complex characterization

While it's useful to consider characters in terms of what they want and need, and how those often clash, we can look deeper into their souls to find both the good and the bad of their natures.

Only in shallow fiction is the hero all good or the villain all bad. As Ben Nyberg points out:

> *Characters are sometimes forced into unnatural behaviour by writers who are out to prove a point, take revenge, or just vent frustrations… the godlike power to create people carries the equally large responsibility to understand them, to present them as fairly and compassionately as possible.*

A common "out" for a villain is the excuse of insanity. It's a solution novelist Nyberg rejects:

> [E]ven monsters need something driving them more than wicked hearts. However deep his profligates' or philanderers' villainy, a good writer will explain such behaviour well enough to "justify" it in human terms... Which leads to another all-too-common abuse of writer's "license": copping a plea on the basis of insanity. However fair a defense it may be in the real world, it's nothing but a dodge in fiction's court... fiction's "madness" always has a method.

Just to prove that there are exceptions to every rule, we have Mrs. Danvers, from Daphne du Maurier's *Rebecca*, published in 1938 to huge success. There's little ambiguity about Mrs. Danvers. Here is part of the account of Mrs. de Winter's first meeting with the housekeeper who was to torment her almost to the point of suicide:

> "This is Mrs. Danvers," said Maxim, and she began to speak, still leaving that dead hand in mind, her hollow eyes never leaving my eyes, so that my own wavered and would not meet hers, and as they did so her hand moved in mine, the life returned to it, and I was aware of a sensation of discomfort and shame.

Mrs. de Winter drops her gloves. Mrs. Danvers picks them up.

> As she handed them to me I saw a little smile of scorn upon her lips, and I guessed at once she considered me ill-bred.

Mrs. Danvers is obsessed with Maxim de Winter's first wife Rebecca to the point of mental illness, a situation brought home when we find out what a rotten person Rebecca really was, at least to her husband. Maybe she treated the servants well. The actress Anna Massey, who played Mrs. Danvers in a television adaptation, had the theory that perhaps the housekeeper was sexually obsessed with Rebecca. In an article in *The Guardian* she wrote:

> Whether Mrs. Danvers was a latent lesbian, I have no idea. But she was certainly in love, totally and utterly obsessed with Rebecca. The book is littered with sexual symbols—the hairbrush and the nightie laid out carefully on the bed.

Of course, it is Mrs. de Winter's insecurity—Maslow would say her lack of mastery of the level of esteem—that makes it easy for Mrs. Danvers to manipulate her emotions. It's a good example of the importance of matching the victim and the victimizer in a way that makes the relationship plausible.

Especially in the case of a protagonist, a character about whom we are ambivalent—who, like us, has a complex mix of good and bad qualities—frequently is the most interesting. Rosellen Brown says:

> [F]or me it's usually when a character begins to be thorny that he or she turns interesting. Do we reject Lear because he bungles his fateful moment? Do we condemn Gurov in Chekhov's Lady with Lapdog because he's a rake: philandering, insincere, guilty of seducing an innocent married woman into an affair that is probably going to cause many people a good deal of pain? Although Jane Austen's Elizabeth is a delight, her Emma is not.

No writer can afford to ignore the shadow side of life. As Chekhov said:

> To a chemist there is nothing impure on earth. The writer should be just as objective as the chemist; he should liberate himself from everyday subjectivity and acknowledge that manure piles play a highly respectable role in the landscape and that evil passions are every bit as much a part of life as good ones.

He went even further:

> Literature is accepted as an art because it depicts life as it actually is. Its aim is the truth, unconditional and honest… the writer is not a pastry chef, he is not a cosmetician and not an entertainer. He is a man bound by contract to his sense of duty and to his conscience. Once he undertakes this task, it is too late for excuses, and no matter how horrified, he must do battle with his squeamishness and sully his imagination with the grime of life. He is just like any ordinary reporter. What would you say if a newspaper reporter, as a result of squeamishness or a desire to please his readers, were to limit his descriptions to honest city fathers, high-minded ladies, and virtuous railroadmen?

Emma

Let's take a look at a protagonist who has a mix of the good and bad, Jane Austen's Emma. Jane Austen said of Emma:

> I am going to take a heroine whom no-one but myself will much like.

Austen introduces her this way, with a clear statement of the faults that will lead to the misunderstandings and heartbreaks to come:

> Emma Woodhouse, handsome, clever, and rich, with a comfortable home and happy disposition, seemed to unite some of the best blessings of existence; and had lived nearly twenty-one years in the world with very little to distress or vex her.

JANE AUSTEN (1775—1817)
Austen's novels include *Pride and Prejudice*, *Sense and Sensibility*, and *Emma*. The satirical style of her earliest work, compiled into the Juvenilia, has been compared to Monty Python. Only one man ever proposed marriage to her; she accepted, but rescinded her acceptance the following day.

She was the youngest of the two daughters of a most affectionate, indulgent father; and had, in consequence of her sister's marriage, been mistress of his house from a very early period. Her mother had died too long ago for her to have more than an indistinct remembrance of her caresses; and her place had been supplied by an excellent woman as governess, who had fallen little short of a mother in affection.

Sixteen years had Miss Taylor been in Mr. Woodhouse's family, less as a governess than a friend, very fond of both daughters, but particularly of Emma. Between them it was more the intimacy of sisters. Even before Miss Taylor had ceased to hold the nominal office of governess, the mildness of her temper had hardly allowed her to impose any restraint; and the shadow of authority being now long passed away, they had been living together as friend and friend very mutually attached, and Emma doing just what she liked; highly esteeming Miss Taylor's judgment, but directed chiefly by her own.

The real evils, indeed, of Emma's situation were the power of having rather too much her own way, and a disposition to think a little too well of herself; these were the disadvantages which threatened alloy to her many enjoyments. The danger, however, was at present so unperceived, that they did not by any means rank as misfortunes with her.

Emma does not have bad intentions. Her main fault is that she misjudges her own ability to matchmake or to read other people's emotions accurately. Rich and spoiled, without the need to marry for financial security, she is free to meddle in the romances of several other characters, as a result of which a number of hearts are broken. She is a delightfully complex character whose actions cause others pain. She is a good example of the fact that a protagonist doesn't have to be all good or even likeable all the time—just interesting enough to hold our attention. Often it's a character's faults that make them interesting.

Characterization in film and television

The difficulty with creating complex characters in film and television is that other than using voice-over narration, it's difficult to reveal their inner thoughts. When a talented writer's script is given to a talented director who then works with talented actors, this can be overcome, but it's a challenge. There's another issue with mainstream feature films, as screenwriter Paul Schrader points out:

> The weakest writing in America today is in the movies, the best writing is on TV, in series like The Sopranos. That's because scripts for TV are about human beings and human behaviour, not a journey to the centre of the earth. Movies have become less and less about good writing and more and more about spectacle, so the importance of the screenwriter has declined. The most spirited dialogues in spectacle films are lines like: "Look, it's coming" or "Run, run, run."

He adds, more hopefully:

> But as screen sizes become small—TV, cable, computers, mobile phones—spectacle will become less important, and the importance of the screenwriter will be re-established.

Especially in television, the definition of "villain" is changing. Referring to series like *Dexter* (featuring a serial killer) and *The Shield* (featuring a corrupt policeman), my screenwriting and teaching colleague Tony McNabb points out:

> We have always liked edgy characters such as maverick cops, spooks, and psychopaths—in fiction and in feature films. Ruthless and amoral characters are not new. But our complicity with them is. It's one thing to have someone like this as the hero of a novel or a movie. Quite another to make them the returning hero of a TV series... Now we want them in our living rooms, week after week, pursuing our enemies,

telling us we're as powerful and dangerous as our enemies are... They are not anti-heroes, ironic challenges to our moral certainties, but anti-anti-heroes, doing what has to be done in a dangerous new world where morality is being redefined and new myths constructed.

It has been said that writers who are not able to construct characters with a pronounced darkness may be afraid of their own shadow side, the more negative or destructive aspects of their personalities. Carl Jung wrote about that in these terms:

Unfortunately there can be no doubt that man is, on the whole, less good than he imagines himself or wants to be. Everyone carries a shadow, and the less it is embodied in the individual's conscious life, the blacker and denser it is.

Exploring this in fiction—writing it or reading it—is one of the safer ways to access and perhaps neutralize the darker parts of ourselves. Perhaps that's why crime novels about serial killers are so popular.

One rich area of characterization that is not often discussed in writing texts is the question of status. In the next chapter you'll see how that influences just about everything a character says and does.

FROM ADVICE TO ACTION!

If getting more in touch with the dark side of yourself is something you'd like to do, there are several useful exercises to get you started.

ACTION: Make a list of the 10 things that bother you most about other people. For instance, these might include selfishness, greed, rudeness, and arrogance. (Do that now, before reading on.)

Have you made the list? If so, now consider whether these might be the qualities you most dislike in yourself. Can you think of times when you exhibited any of the ones you listed? Psychologists say that it's quite common for us to dislike in others the negative qualities we fear we have ourselves.

Next, conjure up a character who embodies a number of these traits. What would they be like? What kind of story might feature such a person? Would this person make a good antagonist, if not a fully fledged villain for your story?

Also consider the negative aspects of the personality of your protagonist. Would it humanize them if these came out more? Are they something your protagonist struggles with and perhaps finds a hindrance to getting what they want or need?

8

What's their status?

inding where in society you belong, or trying to get to where you think you belong—your status—may be one of the most fundamental drives of human beings. In his book *Impro*, master improviser Keith Johnstone says that the quest for status is the key to human transactions. Some people want high status: to feel superior to others. Some are more comfortable feeling low status. In the previous chapter we met two people to whom status was significant: Mrs. Danvers, whose position as a housekeeper normally would render her low status, was able to cow her insecure new mistress Mrs. de Winter into feeling inferior.

Probably you've met some strong examples of both kinds of individuals. If you talk to colleagues about your last vacation, the high-status person will have been to the same place already and will imply that it was much better then. The low-status person will express envy that you can go to such a wonderful place.

Sometimes what sounds like a low-status statement is actually a desire to be on top by suffering more than anyone else. There's a classic Monty Python sketch in which several people try to get one up on each other with the dire circumstances of their youth. When one says that their roof was full of holes and allowed the rain to come in, another says: "You had a roof?"

Of course, status can change according to circumstance. A man may be high status at work but low status in relation to his spouse, for example.

We can even express status relative to an object like a ticket machine at a train station. If the ticket fails to come out, one person gives the machine a slap, another slinks away and hopes nobody noticed his embarrassment at having been defeated.

Furthermore, the objects with which people surround themselves give us a clue to their status, or at least to the status they are trying to project. Does your protagonist wear a Rolex or a Swatch? Does she drive a Porsche or a Smart Car?

Johnstone writes:

> Once you understand that every sound and posture implies a status, then you perceive the world quite differently, and the change is probably permanent. In my view, really accomplished actors, directors and playwrights are people with an intuitive understanding of the status transactions that govern human relationships. This ability to perceive the underlying motives of casual behavior can also be taught... A good play is one which ingeniously displays and reverses the status between the characters.

From Shakespeare to Basil Fawlty

Any Shakespeare play is worth studying in this light. For instance, in *Macbeth* it's the quest for higher status that takes Macbeth and his wife on their doomed path. When Macbeth hears the witches call him the thane of Cawdor (a title already taken) and king (a position held by Duncan), at first he doesn't dare to believe it, and asks them:

> Stay, you imperfect speakers, tell me more:
> By Sinel's death I know I am thane of Glamis;
> But how of Cawdor? the thane of Cawdor lives,
> A prosperous gentleman; and to be king
> Stands not within the prospect of belief,
> No more than to be Cawdor. Say from whence
> You owe this strange intelligence? or why
> Upon this blasted heath you stop our way
> With such prophetic greeting? Speak, I charge you.

They say no more, but when he finds out that the thane of Cawdor had turned traitor and the king has given Macbeth that

title, it seems more plausible to him that the witches' other pre-
diction may come true as well. But it's his wife who really warms
to the prospect of having her husband become king, whatever it
takes. Her fear is that he isn't up to taking the shortest course, the
murder of the current king. And indeed, Macbeth suggests that
having the king elevate his status to thane of Cawdor is enough:

> We will proceed no further in his business:
> He hath honour'd me of late; and I have bought
> Golden opinions from all sorts of people,
> Which would be worn now in their newest gloss,
> Not cast aside so soon.

Lady Macbeth isn't satisfied with that and by challenging her
husband's manhood, a definite affront to his status, gets him to
commit murder. As the story progresses their relative status shifts
and the treacherous actions they take to maintain Macbeth's new
position drive the play toward its violent conclusion.

In *King Lear* it's Lear's resentment that his daughter Cordelia
isn't willing to give him the same fulsome pledges of love he
receives from his other two daughters that leads him to disinherit
her. His other daughters flatter him, but privately consider him
old and foolish. As soon as they have what they want, they stop
their pretense of holding him in high regard and his former status plummets, and various other characters vie for supremacy.

The quest for higher status is at the heart of what many consider one of the greatest novels ever written, *Madame Bovary*.
Inspired by the romantic novels she reads, bored with provincial
routine and soon also with her marriage and motherhood,
Emma Bovary resorts to affairs and lavish spending in hopes of
having the dramatic life of which she dreams. Flaubert foreshadows this in his description of Emma as a young girl:

> Accustomed to calm aspects of life, she turned, on the contrary,
> to those of excitement. She loved the sea only for the sake of its
> storms, and the green fields only when broken up by ruins.

> She wanted to get some personal profit out of things,
> and she rejected as useless all that did not contribute to the
> immediate desires of her heart, being of a temperament
> more sentimental than artistic, looking for emotions, not
> landscapes.

A tragic modern example is found in Arthur Miller's *Death of a
Salesman*, in which Willie Loman gradually realizes that his style
of salesmanship has gone out of fashion and with it his dreams
of high status. His wife objects to the idea that he can be cast
aside now that he is old and no longer gets the results he used to.
She tells their son, Biff:

> I don't say he's a great man. Willy Loman never made a lot
> of money. His name was never in the paper. He's not the
> finest character that ever lived. But he's a human being, and
> a terrible thing is happening to him. So attention must be
> paid. He's not to be allowed to fall into his grave like an old
> dog. Attention, attention must finally be paid to such a per-
> son. You called him crazy... no, a lot of people think he's lost
> his... balance. But you don't have to be very smart to know
> what his trouble is. The man is exhausted. A small man can
> be just as exhausted as a great man. He works for a com-
> pany thirty-six years this March, opens up unheard-of terri-
> tories to their trademark, and now in his old age they take
> his salary away. Are they any worse than his sons? When he
> brought them business, when he was young, they were glad
> to see him. But now his old friends, the old buyers that loved
> him so and always found some order to hand him in a
> pinch—they're all dead, retired. He used to be able to make
> six, seven calls a day in Boston. Now he takes his valises out
> of the car and puts them back and takes them out again and
> he's exhausted. Instead of walking he talks now. He drives
> seven hundred miles, and when he gets there no one knows
> him anymore, no one welcomes him.

Status relationships also are at the core of the classic sitcom *Fawlty Towers*. John Cleese plays Basil Fawlty, the owner of a run-down hotel. He prides himself on being in charge, but is totally dominated by his wife. Unable to assert his status with her, he takes it out on poor Manuel, the waiter who is the lowest man on the totem pole. Much of the humor comes from Fawlty's delusions of high status for both himself and his pathetic establishment. On the other hand, when confronted by apparent aristocracy, he is quick to abase himself. In the "Touch of Class" episode, he is annoyed that a guest signs in with only one name, until the guest says: "I am Lord Melbury, so I simply sign myself 'Melbury.'" There is a long pause, then:

> BASIL: I'm so sorry to have kept you waiting, your
> lordship... I do apologise, please forgive me. Now,
> was there something, is there something, anything,
> I can do for you? Anything at all?

Melbury offers him the filled-in registration card.

> BASIL: Oh, please don't bother with that. (he
> takes the form and throws it away) Now, a special
> room?... a single? A double? A suite?... Well, we
> don't have any suites...

Raising yours by lowering theirs

Examples of someone elevating their status by lowering the other's can be found in Henrik Ibsen's *A Doll's House*. In one scene Nora is visited by an old friend who is now a widow, childless, and in desperate need of a job:

> NORA: So you are quite alone. How dreadfully sad
> that must be. I have three lovely children. You
> can't see them just now, for they are out with

their nurse. But now you must tell me all about
it.
MRS. LINDE: No, no; I want to hear about you.
NORA: No, you must begin. I mustn't be selfish
today; today I must only think of your affairs.
But there is one thing I must tell you. Do you
know we have just had a great piece of good luck?
MRS. LINDE: No, what is it?
NORA: Just fancy, my husband has been made manager
of the Bank!

Talk about rubbing it in!

Another of Ibsen's characters, Hedda Gabler, has an equal
talent for putting people in their (lower) place. Tesman,
Hedda's husband, compliments his kindly aunt Julia on her
new bonnet. She says she bought it so Hedda wouldn't be
ashamed of going out with her. She has also brought Tesman
his favorite slippers:

TESMAN: Yes, I missed them terribly. [Goes up to
her.] Now you shall see them, Hedda!
HEDDA: [Going towards the stove.] Thanks, I really
don't care about it.
TESMAN: [Following her.] Only think—ill as she
was, Aunt Rina embroidered these for me. Oh you
can't think how many associations cling to them.
HEDDA: [At the table.] Scarcely for me.

A moment later, Hedda says she can't get on with the servant, Berta:

HEDDA: [Pointing.] Look there! She has left her
old bonnet lying about on a chair.
TESMAN: [In consternation, drops the slippers on
the floor.] Why, Hedda—
HEDDA: Just fancy, if any one should come in and
see it!

TESMAN: But Hedda—that's Aunt Julia's bonnet.

HEDDA: Is it!

MISS TESMAN: [Taking up the bonnet.] Yes, indeed it's mine. And, what's more, it's not old, Madam Hedda.

HEDDA: I really did not look closely at it, Miss Tesman.

MISS TESMAN: [Trying on the bonnet.] Let me tell you it's the first time I have worn it—the very first time.

TESMAN: And a very nice bonnet it is too—quite a beauty!

MISS TESMAN: □Oh, it's no such great things, George. [Looks around her.] My parasol—? Ah, here. [Takes it.] For this is mine too—[mutters]—not Berta's.

TESMAN: A new bonnet and a new parasol! Only think, Hedda.

HEDDA: Very handsome indeed.

As you can see, assertions of status can be used for comic or dramatic effect and tell us a great deal about the characters without resorting to direct description.

Reversal of status

Many comedies and dramas have been based on a reversal of status; that is, putting a high-status person into a situation where they have low status or vice versa. In the film and television world this is often called the "fish out of water" situation.

The film *Trading Places* took this literally and put a rich man and a poor man in each other's places for comedic effect. This also works in drama, as in the classic film *The Servant*, in which Dirk Bogarde plays a scheming manservant who manages to take over his master's life.

The biblical story of Job is another example. To test his loyalty to God, poor Job is plunged from a normal existence to experiencing every trial and terror imaginable.

Many crime, mystery, and spy novels depend on reversal of status as well, when an upstanding citizen unjustly becomes a murder suspect or unwittingly becomes the possessor of a microdot or memory card containing valuable information.

One reason this kind of reversal is so appealing is that it allows us to discover, as God did with Job, what the character is really made of.

When accomplished writers create characters, how much do they draw on what they and the people they know are made of? That process and its advantages and possible dangers are examined in the next chapter.

FROM ADVICE TO ACTION!

Having considered your characters' wants and needs, also think about whether and how those relate to their desire to be high status or low status. Some questions to consider:

- What status do they think they are?
- What status do others think they are?
- If there's a discrepancy, do you use it to create a comic or a tragic effect?
- What are the status relationships of your main characters to each other? What impact does that have on the conflict between them?
- What possessions reflect their actual or desired status?
- Could adjusting the status levels of your characters make them more interesting or boost the tension and conflict in your story?
- Are there elements of role reversal in your story? Could there be? How would your characters react if it happened to them?

9

The character in the mirror

T wo questions every fiction writer encounters frequently are "Do you base your characters on real people?" and "Is your protagonist based on you?" Generally, the answer is "Not exactly," but of course one's experience is a crucial source.

The narrator in *The Unbearable Lightness of Being*, who is writing the book but may or may not be intended to be the actual author, Milan Kundera (who loves to play with identity), says:

> As I have pointed out before, characters are not born like people, of woman; they are born of a situation, a sentence, a metaphor containing in a nutshell a basic human possibility that the author thinks no one else has discovered or said something essential about. But isn't it true that an author can write only about himself?… The characters in my novels are my own unrealized possibilities. That is why I am equally fond of them all and equally horrified by them. Each one has crossed a border that I myself have circumvented. It is that crossed border (the border beyond which my own "I" ends) which attracts me most. For beyond that border begins the secret the novel asks about. The novel is not the author's confession; it is an investigation of human life in the trap the world has become.

Sara Paretsky says:

> I've written five novels, all of them featuring a woman named VI Warshawski, a detective who lives alone but whose close friend is a doctor some twenty years her senior named Lotty Herschel. People sometimes ask if VI is me, if Lotty is based on someone real. They're not: you can't put real people in a

book, at least I can't—if I try to describe a real person's idio-syncrasies and make a fictional character act the way that a real person would, everything becomes wooden. The action can't flow naturally because my imagination is penned in by how that living person would have acted.

Others admit a closer relationship between their characters and themselves. For instance, Roddy Doyle says:

Half of my books have been written in the first person, so, yes, I identify with the narrator. I have to, in order to find the language I need to drive the story, and the geography and humour, etc. My first book, The Commitments, was more of an ensemble piece, but I still let one character, Jimmy Rabbitte, do most of the seeing. It was his book.

Stephen King says:

Everything starts with me. Even if I'm trying to mimic some-one from real life—Dick Cheney… was a touchstone for one character—it obviously comes out of my imagination.

VS Naipaul admitted that his fictional creations are not that dif-ferent from himself:

Whenever I have to write a fiction, I've always had to invent a character who has roughly my background. I thought for many years how to deal with this problem. The answer was to face it boldly—not to create a bogus character but to cre-ate, as it were, stages in one's evolution.

Haruki Murakami is similar, as he explained in rather dramatic fashion:

Please think of it this way: I have a twin brother. And when I was two years old, one of us—the other one—was kidnapped. He was brought to a faraway place and we haven't seen each other since. I think my protagonist is him. A part of myself, but not me, and we haven't seen each other for a long time. It's a kind of alternative of myself. In terms of DNA we are the same, but our environment has been different, so our way of thinking would be different. Every time I write a book I put my feet in different shoes. Because sometimes I am tired of being myself. If you can't have a fantasy, what's the point of writing a book?

Tennessee Williams didn't say he wrote directly from himself, but that he was drawn to writing about certain types of people:

I have found it easier to identify with the characters who verge upon hysteria, who were frightened of life, who were desperate to reach out to another person. But these seemingly fragile people are the strong people really.

In an interview with the BBC, EM Forster said:

I am quite sure I am not a great novelist because I've only got down onto paper really three types of people. The person who I think I am, the people who irritate me, and the people I'd like to be. When you get to the really great people, like Tolstoy, you find they can get hold of all types.

Eudora Welty agreed:

Characters take on life sometimes by luck, but I suspect it is when you can write more entirely out of yourself, inside the skin, heart, mind, and soul of a person who is not yourself, that a character becomes in his own right another human being on the page.

EUDORA WELTY
(1909—2001)

Welty is best known for *The Optimist's Daughter*, *The Ponder Heart*, and the short story "A Worn Path." Her home state of Mississippi commemorates her with an annual Eudora Welty Day on May 2. She was inspired to begin writing by her experiences as a publicity photographer for the WPA during the Great Depression.

In the film world, too, some writers basically exploit their own personality. Woody Allen is the prime example, and the weakness of his later films may be due to the fact that he's no longer of an age to play the mid-life neurotic.

Is that me?

Authors sometimes worry about family or friends recognizing themselves. Carol Shields says:

> I made up my mind at the beginning of my writing life not to write about my family and friends, since I want them to remain my family and friends. Others, it seems, have come to a similar conclusion. The novelist Robertson Davies was once asked why he had waited until age sixty before writing his marvellous Deptford Trilogy. There was a long pause, and then he replied, haltingly, "Well, certain people died, you see."

Yet others feel it's more important to write what you want, and let the chips fall where they may. Bonnie Friedman says:

> The friend who shelved her worries so she could write her autobiographical novel told me, "I think it's essential to set yourself outside that sphere of personal consequence for the space of the writing, to free yourself, to forgive yourself, and write what's most true—what's so often both the ugliest and the most beautiful."

Ernest Hemingway had the rather unusual and perhaps dangerous (in terms of litigation) belief that if you use real people as models for your characters, you have to be true to every aspect of them. He took F Scott Fitzgerald to task for not doing this in *Tender Is the Night*:

It started off with that marvellous description of Sara and Gerald... Then you started fooling with them, making them come from things they didn't come from, changing them into other people and you can't do that, Scott. If you take real people and write about them you cannot give them other parents than they have (they are made by their parents and what happens to them) you cannot make them do anything they would not do. You can take me or Zelda or Pauline or Hadley or Sara or Gerald but you have to keep them the same and you can only make them do what they would do. You can't make one be another. Invention is the finest thing but you cannot invent anything that would not actually happen.

Memorable characters attain that status not only through what they do, but also through what they say and how they say it. The art of writing dialogue is the subject of the next chapter.

FROM ADVICE TO ACTION!

ACTION: To draw on yourself, consider these questions:

- What parts of yourself that don't come out in your real life would be interesting to explore in fiction?
- What are the formative experiences that shaped you, and how would you have been different if they had been otherwise?
- What do you think is the most interesting aspect of your personality?
- What is the most interesting experience you've had that you could explore further in fiction?

To draw on people you know, consider these questions:

- ✍ Who are the most memorable people you can think of that you've met? What made them so?
- ✍ What would happen if two of the memorable people you have in mind got together?
- ✍ What is the most dramatic incident you have witnessed? Would it be worth exploring further, perhaps via what happened to the people involved both before and after the incident?

10

Make them talk

Characters reveal themselves through dialogue as well as action. Eudora Welty advised:

Dialogue has to show not only something about the speaker that is its own revelation, but also maybe something about the speaker that he doesn't know but the other character does know.

She also said that dialogue may seem deceptively easy:

In its beginning, dialogue's the easiest thing in the world to write when you have a good ear, which I think I have. But as it goes on, it's the most difficult, because it has so many ways to function. Sometimes I needed to make a speech do three or four or five things at once—reveal what the character said but also what he thought he said, what he hid, what others were going to think he meant, and what they misunderstood, and so forth—all in his single speech. And the speech would have to keep the essence of this one character, his whole particular outlook, in concentrated form. This isn't to say I succeeded. But I guess it explains why dialogue gives me my greatest pleasure in writing.

If dialogue isn't good it undermines the reality of the characters. Some newer writers make the mistake of creating dialogue that is a logical exchange of information. Transcribing any real conversation reveals how chaotic it actually is, how often we interrupt ourselves and others, and how frequently we abandon a line of thought in mid-sentence. Writing dialogue too accurately would make all of your characters sound like blithering idiots, because we make allowances for real speech that we don't make for dialogue from fictional characters.

Hemingway pointed out that it's important that when characters are talking, it's really them talking, not the author:

ERNEST HEMINGWAY (1899-1961)
Hemingway's novels include *A Farewell to Arms*, *The Sun Also Rises*, and *For Whom the Bell Tolls*. He disliked his first name because of its associations with Oscar Wilde's *The Importance of Being Earnest*. He was close friends with Ezra Pound and James Joyce.

> *If the people the writer is making talk of old masters; of music; of modern painting; of letters; or of science then they should talk of those subjects in the novel. If they do not talk of those subjects and the writer makes them talk of them he is a faker, and if he talks about them himself to show how much he knows then he is showing off... For a writer to put his own intellectual musings, which he might sell for a low price as essays, into the mouths of artificially constructed characters which are more remunerative when issued as people in a novel is good economics, perhaps, but does not make literature.*

The better you know your characters, the easier it is to know what they would say and how. This is influenced by their age, their level of education, their work experience, whether they are trying to convince others they're higher or lower on the social ladder, their ethnicity, their values, and many other considerations.

Penelope Fitzgerald points to the possible debasing of dialogue by television:

> *TV probably conditions us too much to disagreements and insults, the staple of the comedy script. A novelist can allow time, if he wants to, for conversations which just tick over, the dialogue of contentment.*

Another danger that Ernest Hemingway warned against is over-use of slang:

> Never use slang except in dialogue and then only when unavoidable. Because all slang goes sour in a short time.

How does one develop an ear for dialogue? Hemingway suggested it's all in the listening:

> When people talk, listen completely. Don't be thinking what you're going to say. Most people never listen. Nor do they observe. You should be able to go into a room and when you come out know everything that you saw there and not only that. If that room gave you any feeling you should know exactly what it was that gave you that feeling. Try that for practice. When you're in town stand outside the theatre and see how the people differ in the way they get out of taxis or motor cars. There are a thousand ways to practice. And always think of other people.

One author who has practiced this is Annie Proulx:

> I listen attentively in bars and cafés, while standing in line at the checkout counter, noting particular pronunciations and the rhythms of regional speech, vivid turns of speech and the duller talk of everyday life. In Melbourne I paid money into the hand of a sidewalk poetry reciter to hear "The Spell of the Yukon," in London listened to a cabby's story of his psychopath brother in Paris, on a trans-Pacific flight heard from a New Zealand engineer the peculiarities of building a pipeline across New Guinea.

Plays, especially, are useful to study: they depend on excellent dialogue since they are denied the easy action sequences of films, television, or novels. When studying classic plays, however, you may find that they start with a big chunk of exposition, sometimes from the mouths of a couple of maids who helpfully explain the situation to each other while they dust. Needless to say, this is no longer advisable unless you're writing a parody.

Dialogue in context

While we have been talking about dialogue as a separate element of your fiction, of course in a story, novel, or screenplay it's an element that has to be well integrated with what the characters are doing. In the case of a novel, the author also has the option of commenting on all the other elements. The opening of DH Lawrence's *Women in Love* is a great blend of all of these:

> Ursula and Gudrun Brangwen sat one morning in the window-bay of their father's house in Beldover, working and talking. Ursula was stitching a piece of brightly-coloured embroidery, and Gudrun was drawing upon a board which she held on her knee. They were mostly silent, talking as their thoughts strayed through their minds. "Ursula," said Gudrun, "don't you REALLY WANT to get married?" Ursula laid her embroidery in her lap and looked up. Her face was calm and considerate.
>
> "I don't know," she replied. "It depends how you mean."
>
> Gudrun was slightly taken aback. She watched her sister for some moments.
>
> "Well," she said, ironically, "it usually means one thing! But don't you think anyhow, you'd be—" she darkened slightly—"in a better position than you are in now."
>
> A shadow came over Ursula's face.
>
> "I might," she said. "But I'm not sure."
>
> Again Gudrun paused, slightly irritated. She wanted to be quite definite.
>
> "You don't think one needs the EXPERIENCE of having been married?" she asked.
>
> "Do you think it need BE an experience?" replied Ursula.

"Bound to be, in some way or other," said Gudrun, coolly. "Possibly undesirable, but bound to be an experience of some sort."

"Not really," said Ursula. "More likely to be the end of experience."

Gudrun sat very still, to attend to this.

"Of course," she said, "there's THAT to consider." This brought the conversation to a close. Gudrun, almost angrily, took up her rubber and began to rub out part of her drawing. Ursula stitched absorbedly.

"You wouldn't consider a good offer?" asked Gudrun.

"I think I've rejected several," said Ursula.

"REALLY!" Gudrun flushed dark—"But anything really worth while? Have you REALLY?"

"A thousand a year, and an awfully nice man. I liked him awfully," said Ursula.

"Really! But weren't you fearfully tempted?"

"In the abstract but not in the concrete," said Ursula. "When it comes to the point, one isn't even tempted—oh, if I were tempted, I'd marry like a shot. I'm only tempted NOT to." The faces of both sisters suddenly lit up with amusement.

"Isn't it an amazing thing," cried Gudrun, "how strong the temptation is, not to!" They both laughed, looking at each other. In their hearts they were frightened.

It's brilliant orchestration: the homely atmosphere, the somewhat random but amusing dialogue, and then that one-sentence revelation, that in their hearts they were frightened, which suddenly changes the way we see them and the situation.

Subtext

The contrast between what is said (the text) and what is meant (the subtext) is an important tool for every kind of fiction writer.

You've already seen this at work in some of the statements in the section about status. For example, if you've bought a small new car someone might say, "What a practical little car! I do admire people who buy a vehicle based purely on utility." The text is a compliment; the subtext is that you've chosen an ugly car.

Another way to reveal subtext is by describing the difference between what is said and the accompanying action. For instance, someone might greet another person enthusiastically but maintain maximum distance between their bodies when they hug.

Since we all spend quite a bit of time saying things we don't mean, subtext can be an important way of revealing character.

Attribution

A reader of my book *Your Writing Coach* emailed me in response to my endorsement of author Elmore Leonard's advice to use "said" as the standard dialogue attribution, instead of options like "he laughed/chortled/exclaimed."

This reader wrote:

> I have been a primary school teacher for 33 years and over the last five, a supply (substitute) teacher. The interesting thing is that teachers are teaching children to always use something more interesting than "said." In fact anything other than said. Now obviously most of the children so taught will not end up writers, but some will. Did you know about this and could you comment on it, as I have found myself writing a whole variety of synonyms for "said" in my own writing.

No, I didn't know that, but it explains a lot! (That's me, exclaiming.) The thing is that most of the time, we just "say." And if we laugh, it's not exactly at the same moment that we're saying the words, so it's much more accurate to write, for example, "I hope you don't blame me," Lydia said, laughing, rather than, "I hope you don't blame me," Lydia laughed.

Most of the synonyms for said, such as asserted, babbled, croaked, divulged, hinted, insisted, pointed out, or snarled, call attention to themselves rather than to what was said. After three or four of them, we start to picture the author with a thesaurus in their hand.

While a flotilla of "saids" may stand out on the page, when we read they basically disappear. Most of the time they're attached to a name and that's really what we want to know: who is talking. Often that's clear without any attribution, and the best writers write dialogue that itself gives us a clue as to how the words were said.

Sometimes characters begin to tell you what they want to say or do. In the next chapter, find out which writers welcome this development, which scoff at it, and how to handle it if it happens to you.

FROM ADVICE TO ACTION!

ACTION: To sharpen your ear for dialogue, cultivate the art of discreet eavesdropping. When possible, watch a couple talking, but stay out of earshot. Make up dialogue in your mind that is what you think they might be saying. Then move close enough to hear them. How is the content of what they're saying different from what you imagined? How is the way they're saying it different from what you imagined? Do you discern any subtext? If so, was there any body language previously that could have given it away? When they are gone, mentally or on paper write a continuation of their conversation.

When you've written any dialogue, check it to see:

- Is it really something this character would say?
- Does it reveal more than just its literal content?
- If you're using slang, is it appropriate for the character and the time in which your work is based?

11
They're taking over!

Many writers have said that once they get to know their characters well, their creations take on a life of their own and sometimes pull the plot in directions the author didn't anticipate.

Here's how William Faulkner described it:

> It begins with a character, usually, and once he stands up on his feet and begins to move, all I can do is trot along behind him with a paper and pencil trying to keep up long enough to put down what he says and does.

Elie Wiesel likened the process to a kind of giving birth:

> These characters want to get out, to breathe fresh air and partake of the wine of friendship; were they to remain locked in, they would forcibly break down the walls. It is they who force the writer to tell their stories.

For Ray Bradbury, getting the characters to do the work for you is the key to creating worthwhile stories. In an interview with *Bookselling This Week* in 1997, he said:

> I was at a bookstore last night and a book clerk there said, "I'm having trouble with a novel I'm writing. I do this, I do that." I said, "Stop that"—no outlines, no plans. Get your characters to write the book for you. Ahab wrote Moby-Dick, Melville didn't. Montag wrote Fahrenheit 451, I didn't. If you let your characters live, and get out of their way, then you have a chance of creating something individual.

Talking to *Book Magazine*, he said:

> I never know from day to day which of my books I'll be work-
> ing on. I lie in bed at seven in the morning and the voices of
> my characters talk to me. They control everything. I write
> hurrying on, hoping to find out what will happen next.

Patricia Highsmith advised authors to be open-minded about
their characters' preferences:

> A recalcitrant character may veer the plot in a better direction
> than you had thought at the outset. Or he or she may have to
> be curbed, changed, or scrapped and rewritten entirely. Such
> a snag is worth a few days' pondering, and usually requires it.
> If the character is very stubborn and also interesting, you may
> have a different book from the one you set out to write, maybe
> a better book, maybe just as good, but different. You should
> not be thrown by this experience. No book, and possibly no
> painting, is ever exactly like the first dream of it.

Alan Gurganus says he's not really inventing characters:

> We are always surrounded by voices that are like and unlike
> our own and that are our own. And part of the joy of having
> written for twenty-odd years is that as I'm now sitting here,
> I seem to be alone but in fact I'm trailing about sixty people.
> They're people that I've created but also people that I've
> actually, to be more precise linguistically, discovered
> because they preexisted me. They've always been around
> and waiting to be heard.

Perhaps no author has given more control to her characters than
Alice Walker. She says that when she was writing *The Color
Purple* the characters were telling her where they wanted her to
live:

They also didn't like seeing buses, cars, or other people whenever they attempted to look out. "Us don't want to be seeing one of this," they said. "It makes us can't think."... Luckily I had found (with the help of friends) a fairly inexpensive place in the city. This too had been a decision forced by my characters. As long as there was any question about whether I could support them in the fashion they desired (basically an undisturbed silence) they declined to come out.

To me, letting your characters tell you where to live sounds like one step too far—but it did result in *The Color Purple*, so at least for Alice Walker it all worked out well. For the opposite viewpoint, we turn to Toni Morrison:

I take control of them [characters]. They are very carefully imagined. I feel as though I know all there is to know about them, even things I don't write—like how they part their hair. They are like ghosts. They have nothing on their minds but themselves and aren't interested in anything but themselves. So you can't let them write your book for you. I have read books in which I know that has happened—when a novelist has been totally taken over by a character. I want to say, You can't do that. If these people could write books they would, but they can't. You can. So, you have to say, Shut up. Leave me alone. I am doing this.

When the characters become real to you, it can be a wrench to leave them when the book or screenplay is finished. That was Charles Dickens's experience, as he related in his preface to the 1850 edition of *David Copperfield*:

I do not find it easy to get sufficiently far away from this Book, in the first sensations of having finished it, to refer to it with the composure which this formal heading would seem to require. My interest in it, is so recent and strong; and my mind is so divided between pleasure and regret—

pleasure in the achievement of a long design, regret in the separation from many companions—that I am in danger of wearying the reader whom I love, with personal confidences, and private emotions… It would concern the reader little, perhaps, to know, how sorrowfully the pen is laid down at the close of a two-years' imaginative task; or how an Author feels as if he were dismissing some portion of himself into the shadowy world, when a crowd of the creatures of his brain are going from him for ever.

Although few characters actually tell their authors where to live, where the *characters* live makes an important contribution to your fiction, as you'll see in the next chapter.

FROM ADVICE TO ACTION!

The main "trick" to getting to the point where your characters take over is to get to know them as well as possible, using the techniques suggested earlier in this section, and then get on with your writing. This phenomenon of the characters taking on a life of their own is very similar to what has been described by psychologist Mihaly Csikszentmihalyi as the "flow" state, when you are completely immersed in the task and all of your emotions are aligned with what you are doing. You feel joy and any sense of time disappears.

ACTION: While you can't command the condition of flow to appear, there are some things you can do, which the best authors may do instinctively, to make it more likely that you will enter this state:

- You must have a clear goal. For a writer, this would be writing a scene or chapter.
- You must have confidence that the task is within your ability, although it should also be challenging in order to engage

you. One of the key obstacles to flow is the "inner critic" that questions whether we have the skills required. Therefore, ignoring the inner critic is a requisite for getting into flow. Chapter 32 on writer's block gives suggestions for how to do this.

- There has to be a feedback mechanism that allows you to tell whether or not you are on the right track and, if not, to give you guidance to adjust what you are doing. For writing, this would be mostly instinctive. Your gut will tell you whether or not you are on target. Actually stopping to assess each sentence or paragraph, however, is more likely to prevent any chance of flow. That's why most writers suggest plowing on, not worrying about punctuation or grammar when you're in the heat of composition, and going back to edit and rewrite later.

12
Setting: Where and when?

ncluding a discussion of setting in a section about characters makes sense because the two are indivisible. Your characters exist in the world you create and in a way that world becomes another character. This world can be as small as a prison cell or as large as the entire globe or even outer space.

Mystery author Peter James told *Books Quarterly* that it was reading Graham Greene's *Brighton Rock* at the age of 14 that made him decide to be a writer and one day to write a novel set there, in his home town. He's carried that out in his Roy Grace novels. He said:

> The city of Brighton and Hove is as much a character in the books as Roy Grace and the members of his team. I have a theory that the common denominator between all the most vibrant cities of the world is a dark undertow of criminal activity. In the UK we have plenty of pleasant seaside resorts—but only one, Brighton, known for 70 years as the "crime capital of England"—has global iconic status. Graham Greene put it on the map. I guess I'm doing my best to keep it there!

For mystery writer Phillip Kerr it's 1930s Berlin that serves as the vital backdrop to many of his mystery novels featuring Bernie Gunther. For Martin Cruz Smith, author of *Gorky Park*, Moscow is the world within with Russian investigator Arkady Renko operates. A setting can take a leading role even in a television series, as demonstrated by *Sex and the City* for New York.

Aspects of setting include the day, month, season, and year in which the events take place, the weather, the influence of historical or current events, the natural surroundings, and details such as furnishings.

Let's look at how some masterful writers introduce us to where we are, and when.

To Kill a Mockingbird

In *To Kill a Mockingbird*, Harper Lee describes the town that Scout Finch lives in. Notice that she starts with the bigger picture and then moves in for a series of close-ups, and how she tells you not only what the setting looked like but also how it affected the people and animals in it:

> Maycomb was an old town, but it was a tired town when I first knew it. In rainy weather the streets turned to red slop; grass grew on the sidewalks, the courthouse sagged in the square. Somehow, it was hotter then: a black dog suffered on a summer's day; bony mules hitched to Hoover cars flicked flies in the sheltering shade of the live oaks on the square. Men's square collars wilted by nine in the morning. Ladies bathed before noon, after their three o'clock naps, and by nightfall were like soft teacakes with frostings of sweat and talcum.

In Lee's opening we're not told exactly when these events took place, but the fact that men had square collars tells us it's quite some time ago, and additional details soon make clear that it was during the Great Depression.

The things she points out and the way she describes them—comparing ladies to soft teacakes, for example—establish a gentle, lightly humorous tone. We don't expect a lot to happen right away, but we know we are going to enjoy this foray into a slower pace of life. Later, when dramatic events do take place, they gain strength by contrast to the easy-going feel of the first pages.

Crime and Punishment

In *Crime and Punishment*, Dostoyevsky begins outside and then
takes us into the protagonist's living space:

> On an exceptionally hot evening early in July a young man
> came out of the garret in which he lodged in S. Place and
> walked slowly, as though in hesitation, towards K. bridge.
>
> He had successfully avoided meeting his landlady on
> the staircase. His garret was under the roof of a high, five-
> storied house and was more like a cupboard than a room.
> The landlady who provided him with garret, dinners, and
> attendance, lived on the floor below, and every time he went
> out he was obliged to pass her kitchen, the door of which
> invariably stood open. And each time he passed, the young
> man had a sick, frightened feeling, which made him scowl
> and feel ashamed. He was hopelessly in debt to his land-
> lady, and was afraid of meeting her.

We learn relatively little about the setting, but what we do
know—it's hot, it's very small, and it was positioned so that he
had to pass his landlady every time he came in or went out—
helps to set up the feeling of claustrophobia and feverishness the
young man experiences. A bit later we hear about what it's like
outside, and find that he can't get any relief there, either:

> The heat in the street was terrible: and the airlessness, the
> bustle and the plaster, scaffolding, bricks, and dust all about
> him, and that special St. Petersburg stench, so familiar to all
> who are unable to get out of town in summer—all worked
> painfully upon the young man's already overwrought nerves.

Again, the details and the tone, in this case rather matter-of-fact
and without charm, support the nature of the story and very
quickly transport us into the psychological as well as the physical world of the character.

Babbit

The opening of Sinclair Lewis's *Babbit* describes a fictional city, Zenith. The setting immediately foreshadows the book's theme, that business is the new religion:

> *The towers of Zenith aspired above the morning mist; austere towers of steel and cement and limestone, sturdy as cliffs and delicate as silver rods. They were neither citadels nor churches, but frankly and beautifully office-buildings.*

The era's disdain for the traditional or the merely old is reflected in the next paragraph:

> *The mist took pity on the fretted structures of earlier generations: the Post Office with its shingle-tortured mansard, the red brick minarets of hulking old houses, factories with stingy and sooted windows, tenements colored like mud. The city was full of such grotesqueries, but the clean towers were thrusting them from the business center, and on the farther hills were shining new houses, homes—they seemed—for laughter and tranquillity.*

As often is the pattern in films as well, Lewis goes from long shot to medium shot:

> *Over a concrete bridge fled a limousine of long sleek hood and noiseless engine. These people in evening clothes were returning from an all-night rehearsal of a Little Theater play, an artistic adventure considerably illuminated by champagne.*

Then he goes in for a series of closer shots with more details:

> *In one of the skyscrapers the wires of the Associated Press were closing down. The telegraph operators wearily raised*

their celluloid eye-shades after a night of talking with Paris and Peking. Through the building crawled the scrubwomen, yawning, their old shoes slapping...

Having set the scene, Lewis then takes us into the life of his protagonist, George Babbit, and also tells us when all this is taking place:

His name was George F. Babbit. He was forty-six years old now, in April, 1920...

Connect the setting to the action

In classic literature it was not unusual to start with a long description of the town or countryside in which the story was set and often the next step was to give us a long history of the protagonist, perhaps going back several generations—all before the story kicked into action. Today's readers generally don't have the patience for that; now the convention is to integrate the description of the setting with the description of the characters.

Gabriel García Márquez achieves this in the opening of *Love in the Time of Cholera*. Notice how the details of the setting allow you to picture where the action occurs and also tell you a great deal about the character who is found dead by Dr. Juvenal Urbino:

It was inevitable: the scent of bitter almonds always reminded him of the fate of unrequited love. Dr. Juvenal Urbino noticed it as soon as he entered the still darkened house where he had hurried on an urgent call to attend a case that for him had lost all urgency many years before. The Antillian refuge Jeremiah de Saint-Amour, disabled war veteran, photographer of children, and his most sympathetic opponent in chess, had escaped the torments of memory with the aromatic fumes of gold cyanide.

He found the corpse covered with a blanket on the campaign cot where he had always slept, and beside it was a stool with the developing tray he had used to vaporise the poison. On the floor, tied to a leg of the cot, lay the body of a black Great Dane with a snow-white chest, and next to him were the crutches. At one window the splendour of dawn was just beginning to illuminate the stifling, crowded room that served as both bedroom and laboratory, but there was enough light for him to recognize at once the authority of death. The other windows, as well as every other chink in the room, were muffled with rags or sealed with black cardboard, which increased the oppressive heaviness. A counter was crammed with jars and bottles without labels and two crumbling pewter trays under an ordinary light bulb covered with red paper. The third tray, the one for the fixative solution, was next to the body. There were old magazines and newspapers everywhere, piles of negatives on glass plates, broken furniture, but everything was kept free of dust by a diligent hand.

Appeal to the senses

In the excerpt above, notice how we get information targeted at various senses, starting with the smell of bitter almonds from cyanide fumes. We see many details of the room, and we also feel the heavy, stifling atmosphere. Sound is missing, but we wouldn't expect there to be much sound in this cramped chamber occupied by a dead man.

When possible, allow readers to experience the setting via sight, sound, feeling (something like the oppressiveness of a room or the texture of a piece of clothing, for instance), and smell. Sometimes taste is appropriate as well.

Connect the setting to the character's motivation

In some works, the setting heavily influences the thoughts and actions of the protagonist or another character. The following example comes from Proust's *Swann's Way*. Following a long passage describing the torture of his insomnia, the narrator describes his bedroom. Notice how it becomes almost another character, an opponent:

> At Combray, as every afternoon ended, long before the time when I should have to go up to bed, and to lie there, unsleeping, far from my mother and grandmother, my bedroom became the fixed point on which my melancholy and anxious thoughts were centred. Some one had had the happy idea of giving me, to distract me on evenings when I seemed abnormally wretched, a magic lantern, which used to be set on top of my lamp while we waited for dinner-time to come: in the manner of the master-builders and glass-painters of gothic days it substituted for the opaqueness of my walls an impalpable iridescence, supernatural phenomena of many colours, in which legends were depicted, as on a shifting and transitory window. But my sorrows were only increased, because this change of lighting destroyed, as nothing else could have done, the customary impression I had formed of my room, thanks to which the room itself, but for the torture of having to go to bed in it, had become quite endurable. For now I no longer recognised it, and I became uneasy, as though I were in a room in some hotel or furnished lodging, in a place where I had just arrived, by train, for the first time.

How much description of setting is enough?

Again, tastes have changed. A couple of hundred years ago novelists usually gave extremely detailed descriptions of their settings; these days the norm is to do this more succinctly. Partly this is because modern readers will already be familiar with what many settings look like even if they've never been there, as a result of watching television and going to movies. For instance, whether or not you've been in a courtroom yourself you know what one looks like. You may never have visited the pyramids, but their appearance also is familiar to you. The challenge, then, is to find details and aspects of the setting that go beyond what everybody already knows but without going overboard. As Sol Stein points out in his book, *Stein on Writing*:

You're a story-teller, not an interior designer.

Screenwriters have the easiest ride in this regard. If they want to set a scene in a typical courtroom, they just write, "INT. COURTROOM – DAY" and get on with the scene. However, even in a screenplay, it pays to consider how the setting can convey something about the character or the mood. If the scene is set in the protagonist's living room, describing the décor, whether the room is large or small, and whether the curtains are always open or always closed can help give a specific impression of the person who lives there, without a word being spoken.

The amount of description used by playwrights tends to fall somewhere in between the conventions of prose and screenplays. Usually it's quite functional, designed to accommodate the comings and goings of the characters, but it can also offer clues to the theme or feel of the piece. For instance, here's JB Priestley's description of the set of the Birling household in *An Inspector Calls*:

```
SCENE: The dining room of the Birlings' house in
Brumley, an industrial city in the North Midlands.
An evening in Spring, 1912.
    It is the dining room of a fairly large sub-
urban house, belonging to a prosperous manufac-
turer; a solidly built square room, with good
```

```
solid furniture of the period. There is only one
door, which is up stage in the left wall. Up stage
centre, set in an alcove, is a heavy sideboard
with a silver tantalus, silver candlesticks, a
silver champagne cooler and the various oddments
of a dinner. The fireplace is on the right wall.
Below the door is a desk with a chair in front of
it. On the wall below the fireplace is a tele-
phone. Slightly upstage of centre is a solid but
not too large dining table, preferably oval, with
a solid set of dining-room chairs round it. The
table is laid with a white cloth and the closing
stages of a dinner. Down stage of the fireplace is
a leather armchair. A few imposing but tasteless
pictures and large engravings decorate the walls,
and there are light brackets above and below the
fireplace and below the door. The former are lit,
but the latter is not. The general effect is sub-
stantial and comfortable and old-fashioned, but
not cosy and home-like.
```

In the 1992 National Theatre production of the play, directed by Stephen Daldry with set design by Ian McNeil, the set became the star of the show. The story concerns how the Birling household is turned upside down when a police inspector calls on them to inquire about the death of a young woman. The National Theatre set was like a giant doll's house on stilts and it collapsed as more family secrets were revealed. The production also incorporated dramatic lighting and music and sound effects to create a film noir feeling.

Getting it right

If you get something wrong about the setting, the flow of emails and letters correcting you, often replete with disparaging remarks, will make you wonder whether there are people out there who live to highlight such errors. Dan Brown found this out when angry Parisians pointed out that the getaway routes Robert Langdon took in *The Da Vinci Code* aren't feasible.

The best solution is to research your settings carefully. It's ideal if you can visit the location, but now the internet offers a great second best. I'm not talking about the official websites that cities and countries put up, although those can be useful. They tend to stick to describing the most obvious tourist locations, not necessarily the offbeat or minor details that make a place come alive on the page.

The resource I'm recommending is personal blogs. Millions of people chronicle their daily lives on the internet. Most of the time their only readers are their relatives and friends, but there's nothing to stop you from having a look, too. They'll talk about the restaurants they went to, the weather, their parking problems, and lots of other details that can be extremely helpful to getting a sense of a place.

How to find them? Try searching for the name of the city or town or even the neighborhood. Also use Google Alerts—you type in a term, and Google sends you a daily email roundup of websites and blogs in which that term was mentioned. When you find a relevant blog, follow it for a while. Leave some comments and if you have a question about the location just email the person—most likely they'll be delighted to help you.

For visual references, www.Flickr.com is an excellent resource.

If your story is set in the past, memoirs and autobiographies of people alive at the time can be a boon. Even then, though, it pays to double-check any facts, because many such books rely on the authors' fallible memories. Some magazines and newspapers, including the *New York Times*, have archives going back many years that you can access online for free or a nominal fee.

The internet also allows you to find and consult historians and other experts easily and you may be surprised to discover that many of them are happy to help you without charge. If you receive this help, it's proper to mention it on an acknowledgments page.

Beware of relying on other novels for information; their authors may have made mistakes or intentional distortions. Especially beware of getting your facts from movies. They are notorious for changing elements to improve the pace of the story, to create a romantic element where none existed, or to serve a limited budget.

As an author of fiction, you do have leeway denied to historians. For instance, it may not be known whether two historical figures ever met, but you may choose to create such a meeting in your novel. There is also the option of speculative fiction, such as Robert Harris's novel *Fatherland*, based on the premise that Germany won the Second World War.

For science fiction authors the guideline is that you can make up things that don't exist, but readers expect you to get right the things that do exist. Many of them also expect you to stay true to the known laws of physics when creating the devices of the future. The realm of fantasy writing is less encumbered by today's facts. What's the difference? Miriam Allen deFord said that science fiction consists of improbable possibilities, fantasy of plausible impossibilities. It's not a neat divide, though; something like HG Wells's *The Time Machine* probably falls right in the middle.

Beyond mere facts

As you can tell from the examples I've given, when you're describing the setting and the time in which your characters move, you are not only giving the reader factual information, you're also establishing a tone for your entire story, book, or script, and you may also be reflecting the book's theme. In *Babbit*, the wry descriptions of the setting—the mist taking pity on structures not as magnificent as the office buildings—match the tone of the entire book.

The meticulous description of the room in which the man has killed himself in *Love in the Time of Cholera* parallels the way in which Márquez will throughout the book examine the many facets of love. To cite a personal example, my play, *Living Skills*, is about a woman who realizes that the dreams she had for her life have faded away. I felt that making her a teacher and setting the action in the school was a good choice, because there she would be surrounded by youngsters whose dreams were still untarnished by reality, providing a sharp contrast to her situation.

FROM ADVICE TO ACTION!

The same setting can be described in many different ways, and the choices you make will lead to different effects on the reader.

ACTION: To experiment with this, imagine a typical room in a grand old hotel and prepare to describe it three times. The furniture, view, and décor will be exactly the same, but you can choose what to describe and how to describe it.

How would you describe it if your story is about a depressed salesman who has decided to kill himself in this room if he fails to make a big sale at his next appointment?

How would you describe it if your tale concerns a happy couple who are spending their first night together here?

What description would you employ if you are writing about a child who has never stayed in a hotel before?

In your own writing, take a look at your descriptions of the setting, including the weather, any period details, objects, and how the setting affects your characters. Imagine you knew nothing else about the plot or the feel of the book or script. What impression would the description of the setting give you? Is it the one you intended? If not, what would work better?

Next, check whether you have appealed to all the senses. Is there scope for broadening the description to include more?

Finally, ascertain whether you have integrated your descriptions with the action rather than in a block of exposition. If not, see how you can combine them to improve the pace of the prose.

PART III
SHAPING THE STORY

Characters don't come alive until they do something, and the something they do ends up being your plot. Certain genres of writing, such as whodunits, come with a traditional structure—which you may choose to follow or to break. Whatever structure you use, it has to be such that readers keep on reading and at the end feel they have been on a worthwhile journey with your characters.

Many of the most successful authors admit that while coming up with characters is a delight, working out the plot seems more like hard work.

Of course, it's not just what the characters do that counts, it's the manner in which the story is told—the elusive quality of style.

In this section we'll find out how authors approach constructing their stories as well as how they make the way they tell them so special.

13

POV: Who's telling the story?

our story can be told from several perspectives. Which narrative point of view you choose has a huge effect and each option has advantages and disadvantages.

First person

One of the quickest ways to establish an intimate bond between the reader and the character is to let the latter tell the story in their own words. One of the most influential examples of this is Mark Twain's *The Adventures of Huckleberry Finn*. Here is the opening paragraph, with Huck talking to us:

> *You don't know about me without you have read a book by the name of* The Adventures of Tom Sawyer; *but that ain't no matter. That book was made by Mr. Mark Twain, and he told the truth, mainly. There was things which he stretched, but mainly he told the truth. That is nothing. I never seen anybody but lied one time or another, without it was Aunt Polly, or the widow, or maybe Mary. Aunt Polly—Tom's Aunt Polly, she is—and Mary, and the Widow Douglas is all told about in that book, which is mostly a true book, with some stretchers, as I said before.*

Right away Twain establishes a humorous tone and a character we will enjoy joining on his journey.

Ernest Hemingway said:

> *All modern American literature comes from one book by Mark Twain called* Huckleberry Finn.

It's an opinion that is confirmed when you read the opening of JD Salinger's *Catcher in the Rye*:

> *If you really want to hear about it, the first thing you'll probably want to know is where I was born, and what my lousy childhood was like, and how my parents were occupied and all before they had me, and all that David Copperfield kind of crap, but I don't feel like going into it, if you want to know the truth. In the first place, that stuff bores me, and in the second place, my parents would have about two hemorrhages apiece if I told anything pretty personal about them. They're quite touchy about anything like that, especially my father. They're nice and all—I'm not saying that—but they're also touchy as hell. Besides, I'm not going to tell you my whole goddam autobiography or anything.*

Generally the narrator tells the story in the past tense, but there are occasional exceptions, like Haruki Murakami's *Kafka on the Shore*, parts of which are written in the present tense:

> *He takes a small box of lemon drops out of the glove compartment. He pops one into his mouth. He motions for me to take one, and I do.*

Sometimes the person is telling someone else's story. That's the case with Ishmael in *Moby-Dick*, for instance, and Nick Caraway in *The Great Gatsby*. In the film *Citizen Kane*, it's reporter Jerry Thompson who narrates the search for the truth behind "rosebud" and the life of Charles Foster Kane.

Whoever your narrator is, their prose has to fit their background, their personality, and their level of education; an uneducated handyman who has just fallen in love wouldn't write his story in the same language used by a neurotic psychotherapist.

As already mentioned, the key advantage of using the first-person point of view is that it quickly establishes a connection between the character and the reader. The downside is that you can't reveal anything the character doesn't know.

In films, a first-person viewpoint can be established by having the protagonist narrate the story in voice-over or, less commonly, having him address the audience directly (to camera). Strictly speaking, this means we should see only those things the protagonist does, but if the voice-over establishes that we are seeing events that happened in the past, he might say something like, "Of course, I didn't know at that point that my brother was planning to double-cross me," and then the action switches to a scene of the brother plotting the betrayal.

If you elect to use a voice-over narration, it's important that it's not telling us things we already know from the other elements of the film. In other words, if the scene shows the family having fun on the beach, it's not necessary for the narrator to say, "We had fun on the beach." The voice-over narration should be used to tell us things we can't know from the on-screen action. As the scene on the beach plays, he might say, "That was the last day I saw my father alive," which affects the way we experience the scene.

Multiple first-person narrators

Some authors let more than one person tell the story from their perspective. A modern example is Kathryn Stockett's *The Help*, which is narrated by Aibileen and Minny, two black servants, and Miss Skeeter, the college-age daughter of the white household. The first two chapters are in Aibileen's voice, the next two in Minny's, and the next two in Miss Skeeter's. Thereafter it changes less predictably. A switch is signaled simply by using the name of the viewpoint character as the heading of the chapter.

The unreliable narrator

Authors often use what has come to be known as the "unreliable narrator." That's someone who tells the story, but for various reasons may not be telling it accurately or truthfully, or just may not know the complete or true story. For the reader, part of the enjoyment is realizing that what actually happened is different from what has been described.

One example of an unreliable narrator is "Chief" Bromden in *One Flew Over the Cuckoo's Nest*, whose mental illness leads him to relate several fantastic events. In the film *Rashomon*, multiple narrators tell their own differing versions of the same event. In the movie *The Usual Suspects*, the narrator lies to protect himself from the police and also fools the audience until the final moment.

In some cases the truth is revealed at the end, in others it's left up to the reader or audience to decide which, if any, of the versions are correct.

Second-person

In second-person narrative the narrator addresses "you" or characterizes himself or herself as "you." An early example is Nathaniel Hawthorne's story "The Haunted Mind," from his *Twice-Told Tales*:

> By a desperate effort, you start upright, breaking from a sort of conscious sleep, and gazing wildly round the bed, as if the fiends were any where but in your haunted mind. At the same moment, the slumbering embers on the hearth send forth a gleam which palely illuminates the whole outer room, and flickers through the door of the bed-chamber, but cannot quite dispel its obscurity. Your eye searches for whatever may remind you of the living world. With eager minuteness, you take note of the table near the fire-place, the book with an ivory knife between its leaves, the unfolded letter, the hat and the fallen glove. Soon the flame vanishes, and with it the whole scene is gone, though its image remains an instant in your mind's eye, when darkness has swallowed the reality.

Another example comes from Jay McInery's *Bright Lights, Big City*:

You are not the kind of guy who would be at a place like this at this time of the morning. But here you are, and you cannot say that the terrain is entirely unfamiliar, although the details are fuzzy. You are at a nightclub talking to a girl with a shaved head.

This approach is trying to make you experience the action as though you were the narrator. Many readers find the second-person point of view tiresome after a while and they may resist continually being told what is happening to them; they're perfectly happy to read about someone talking to a girl with a shaved head, but they know they're not doing so themselves.

Second-person narratives usually are written in the present tense: you are walking rather than you walked, for instance.

Third-person limited

The most commonly used narrative voice is third person, a description in past tense of the characters' actions. The person telling the story is not identified, and in the "limited" version knows the thoughts and feelings of only one of the characters; the actions of other characters are described, of course, but we don't get into their heads.

This excerpt from Nathanael West's dark look at Hollywood, *The Day of the Locust,* is an example of the third-person limited point of view:

She invited him into her room for a smoke. She sat on the bed and he sat beside her. She was wearing an old beach robe of white towelling over her pajamas and it was very becoming. He wanted to beg her for a kiss but was afraid, not because she would refuse but because she would insist on making it meaningless.

West shares with us the feelings of the protagonist, Tod, but not the other character.

The reader gets insight into the viewpoint character—not quite as much as in a first-person narrative, but it does give you the chance to reveal things a first-person narrator doesn't experience or wouldn't know.

Sometimes an author will use multiple third-person points of view by shifting the viewpoint character from chapter to chapter or even scene to scene.

Patricia Highsmith said:

> I prefer two points of view in a novel, but I don't always have them… Using two points of view—as I did in Strangers on a Train, the two young men protagonists who are so different, and in The Blunderer, Walter and Kimmel, again vastly different people—can bring a very entertaining change of pace and mood.

The third-person limited viewpoint is the most popular one among novelists and sometimes it's mixed with the first person. For instance, if you were writing a novel about a kidnapping, you might have a chapter in the first person told by the young victim's mother, and alternate that with chapters in the third person that reveal what the kidnappers are doing.

The film version would follow only one character or a limited number of characters throughout the film. For instance, it might show a kidnapping story from the perspective of the parents of the kidnapped child, the child, and the lead police officer, but not the kidnapper (although we'd see him any time he was in a scene with any of the three).

Third-person omniscient

In third-person omniscient novels, the narrator can reveal what's going on in the minds of several characters within the same chapter or scene. While this allows the author to impart more information, it makes for a less intimate relationship with the reader and can also be confusing. However, it has been used in some of the greatest works of literature.

Tolstoy was a master of shifting viewpoints. As Ursula Le Guin says of *War and Peace*:

> it's almost miraculous the way it shifts imperceptibly from the author's voice to the point of view of a character, speaking with perfect simplicity in the inner voice of a man, a woman, even a hunting dog, and then back to the thoughts of the author… till by the end you feel you have lived many lives: which is perhaps the greatest gift a novel can give.

In the first chapter of *War and Peace*, Anna Pavlovna is talking with the Prince. Tolstoy tells us not only what the Prince does, but the thought or feeling behind the action:

> "If they had known that you wished it, the entertainment would have been put off," said the prince, who, like a wound-up clock, by force of habit said things he did not even wish to be believed.

A little later Tolstoy tells us:

> Prince Vasili always spoke languidly, like an actor repeating a stale part. Anna Pavlovna Scherer on the contrary, despite her forty years, overflowed with animation and impulsiveness. To be an enthusiast had become her social vocation and, sometimes even when she did not feel like it, she became enthusiastic in order not to disappoint the expectations of those who knew her. The subdued smile which, though it did not suit her faded features, always played round her lips expressed, as in a spoiled child, a continual consciousness of her charming defect, which she neither wished, nor could, nor considered it necessary, to correct.

By telling us the characters' motives as well as their actions, he is taking us into their psychological as well as their physical world, but it's all done so smoothly that we hardly notice.

Third-person omniscient is especially useful for epic tales that involve many characters over a long period.

In a movie, the equivalent is having the camera being able to go anywhere at any time. Treatments and screenplays are written in third-person omniscient, present tense ("George opens the cabinet and is surprised to find it empty").

It takes time

Mastering the use of points of view that best serve your story is something that takes time and practice. John Irving points out:

> Voice is a technical thing; the choice to be close to this character, distant from that character—to be in this or that point of view. You can learn these things; you can learn to recognize your own good and bad habits, what you do well in the first-person narrative voice, and what you do to excess, for example; and what the dangers and advantages are of a third-person narrative that presumes historical distance (the voice of a biographer, for example). There are so many stances involved, so many postures you can assume while telling a story; they can be much more deliberate, much more in a writer's control, than an amateur knows. The reader, of course, shouldn't be aware of much of this. It's brilliant, for example, how Grass calls Oskar Matzerath "he" or "Oskar" at one moment, and then—sometimes in the same sentence—he refers to little Oskar as "I"; he's a first-person narrator and a third-person narrator in the same sentence. But it's done so seamlessly, it doesn't call attention to itself; I hate those forms and styles that call great attention to themselves.

You will need to know from whose perspective we are seeing or experiencing the story, but how many other elements of the story do you have to plan before you start writing? In the next chapter you'll discover how noted authors answer this question.

FROM ADVICE TO ACTION!

ACTION: In deciding which point of view to employ, consider the following:

- How important is it to establish a close bond quickly between the reader and the protagonist?
- What personal qualities of your protagonist would come out more strongly if they narrated the story? If another character were doing the describing? If you used the omniscient narrator mode?
- Are there events crucial to your story that your protagonist would not be privy to? If there are, but you want to use first-person narration, are there other ways of revealing those events? For instance, someone else could tell your protagonist about them, but that puts the incidents in the past and takes them off stage, which diminishes their dramatic impact.
- What would be the advantages to your story of mixing points of view? What would be the disadvantages?

When you've answered these questions, choose the viewpoint you feel would work best for your story. If in the course of writing you feel too constrained by your choice, you can always add another perspective.

Alternatively, you could try writing your opening in the first person and the third-person limited and omniscient to help you decide with which one you feel most comfortable and which one best serves your story.

14

To plan or not to plan?

There are two extreme schools of thought about planning: that you should know everything about the plot before you put pen to paper; and that knowing anything about the story makes it predictable and less enjoyable to write.

The planners

Edgar Allen Poe could be the poster boy for planning. He said:

Nothing is more clear than that every plot, worth the name, must be elaborated to its denouement before anything be attempted with the pen. It is only with the denouement constantly in view that we can give a plot its indispensable air of consequence, or causation, by making the incidents, and especially the tone at all points, tend to the development of the intention.

PG Wodehouse described what form this took for him:

Oh well, that's just a matter of patience. I just sit down, I put down notes after notes, about 400 pages of them, practically all of them utterly valueless, and then eventually one scene would clip onto another scene. It's a bit like doing a crossword puzzle, you get the clue down and then you have to get the one across and unless the two fit in you can't get any further... I have to know exactly where I'm going before I start a novel, I have the complete scenario.

The spontaneists (yes, I know that's not a word—it is now)

In contrast to Poe and Wodehouse, Shelley Jackson said she knows "not a thing" about the plot before she starts writing, adding:

> I would have very little interest in writing a book if I knew what I was going to say ahead of time.

Top crime writer George Pelecanos is not quite as extreme. He knows "very little" before he starts, but he does have a situation and a vague idea of where he wants to end up. He says:

> I'm much more focused on finding the characters. Once you do that, the book begins to write itself.

Another author who counts on the characters to lead him to the story is playwright Edward Albee. He describes his process:

> When I sit down I don't know what the first line of the play is going to be. I know what the destination is, but I don't have any idea necessarily how I am going to get there. I believe in letting the characters determine that in their situation. How they behave determines where it goes.

Stephen King also says he knows "almost nothing."

Starting with a totally or nearly blank slate sounds scary, but EL Doctorow says:

> Writing is an exploration. You start from nothing and learn as you go... Writing is like driving at night in the fog. You can only see as far as your headlights, but you can make the whole trip that way... Writing is a socially acceptable form of schizophrenia.

Sometimes when the plot reveals itself to the writer it has a surprising effect. Playwright John Guare says:

I can still remember throwing up when I realized what the ending of The House of Blue Leaves would be—that after the songwriter realized the true worth of his work he would have to kill his wife because she saw him as he was.

The in-betweeners

Paul Auster is one of the many authors who falls somewhere between the two extremes. He says he starts with

a general sense of the shape of the story, a feeling for the beginning, middle and end, but once I begin working, things always change and the book I thought I was going to write when I started often turns out to be a different book.

Michael Chabon outlines,

but not at first. And never with a whole lot of detail. And usually about three-fifths of the way in I start to go off the plan and never entirely get back to it. Often I end up hating the person who wrote the damn outline.

Asked whether she outlines, Amy Tan says:

I used to say no and I think that's a lie. I outlined in certain ways—not the outline that your third-grade teacher taught you to do. Sometimes I write down in a flash form what I think is the overall story structure. They're cryptic notes to myself. Or I'll sit down and write a summary—three to ten pages of what I think it's about. Or I'll write down the movement of a particular chapter. It's good to have that because I can then move to the next part and say, Oh, I needed to include this or that.

Gabriel García Márquez suggests that one strategy works when you're starting out, but may not be the best for the long run:

> *In the first stories I wrote I had a general idea of the mood, but I would let myself be taken by chance. The best advice I was given early on was that it was all right to work that way when I was young because I had a torrent of inspiration. But I was told that if I didn't learn technique, I would be in trouble later on when inspiration had gone and technique was needed to compensate. If I hadn't learned that in time, I would not now be able to outline a structure in advance. Structure is purely a technical problem, and if you don't learn it early you'll never learn it.*

With films you can just start writing without any kind of plan if it's a spec script; that is, one you are writing for yourself. If you expect someone to commission a script from you, they will probably want a complete outline of the plot before they part with any money. This usually takes the form of a treatment written in the present tense and it can be divided into three acts (you'll find more about these acts in Chapter 17).

Whether you work out your story in advance or discover it as you go along, what will emerge is the marriage of your characters and the story you want to tell. This relationship is explored in the next chapter.

FROM ADVICE TO ACTION!

Most writers find their preferred level of planning through trial and error. However, there are some steps you can take, especially at the beginning of your writing career, that can save you some time and effort.

ACTION: If you're not sure how much planning you want to do before you start writing, answer these questions:

- In general, how comfortable are you with being spontaneous? If you aren't comfortable with it in life, you may not be comfortable with it in writing, either.
- Try writing without planning. If you soon hit a block or dead end, that's a good signal that you're a planner.
- As you write, periodically stop and jot down your thoughts about what you think should happen next. Notice how far ahead in the story your mind tends to travel.
- If you decided to plan your story in detail in advance but find you're getting bored writing it, feel free to tear up the outline and let your characters and your instincts guide you.

15

Characters become plots
(and vice versa)

The much-debated question of what comes first, characters or story, probably never will be decided. Anyway, it's almost a moot point, because a story requires characters (which may not always be human, of course), and as soon as characters begin to interact there is at least the possibility of a story.

EM Forster gets us off to a quick start:

> Let us define a plot. We have defined a story as a narrative of events arranged in their time-sequence. A plot is also a narrative of events, the emphasis falling on causality. "The King died and then the Queen died," is a story. "The king died, and then the Queen died of grief," is a plot.

What is certain, however, is that the two must respect each other. Just as letting characters act logically can ease the job of plotting, letting the demands of a plot overwhelm the reality of a character can take you in the opposite direction. Ben Nyberg says:

> most dishonest plot-planning comes down to thinking up adventures that overtax a character's ability or will to accomplish what's asked of him. He must do what he can't (in some cases, what nobody could) or what no one of sound mind would agree to do.

In certain kinds of genre fiction, this is accepted—for instance, the vulnerable young woman in the horror story who ventures into the cellar when she hears strange noises. Generally, however, it can ruin the credibility of the character and the plot.

The plot and the character arc

As we discussed in the section on characters, novels and films often feature a "character arc," a transformation of some kind.

In most Hollywood films the change is from some kind of negative state (self-centeredness, insensitivity, greed) to a positive one (concern for others, ability to love, generosity). That's true in novels as well—for instance, Sinclair Lewis's *Dodsworth* tells the story of George Dodsworth, who starts as a typical 1920s American businessman, an automobile executive devoted to progress, but ends up appreciating European history and culture, a change paralleled by the disintegration of his marriage.

At times the shift is from positive to negative values, as exemplified by the arc of *Macbeth* or of Michael Corleone in the Godfather film trilogy. When the arc is handled well, it seems natural. However, there are three common problems that can make a character arc seem clumsy.

When the size of the change doesn't match the size of the incidents that supposedly cause it

If a character is consumed by greed, one conversation with a beggar isn't likely to make him suddenly become altruistic. We know from our own experience and observation that it usually takes a big event to cause a big change. If you've ever seen that list of the things that cause the most stress, it's a pretty good guide: a near death experience, losing a loved one, a serious illness, divorce, losing your job. If you want your character to undergo a major transformation, your story has to give him a big kick up the backside, or usually several. Remember, Scrooge required three ghosts, not just one.

Sometimes the motivation goes missing entirely. In the case of the film *Dead Poets Society*, the teacher played by Robin Williams is an eccentric character who teaches the boys in his charge to challenge convention, take risks, and choose self-expression over societal norms. Makes you wonder why he was ever hired by the conservative school. It turns out that in the original script, written by Tom Schulman, the teacher is conventional, but then finds out that he's terminally ill. Realizing that he's never seized the day, he decides to make teaching his students not to make the same mistake his last act. Director Peter Weir thought this would be too downbeat and the script was changed to allow a happier ending. It didn't seem to hurt the project, as the screenplay won an Oscar. Nonetheless, Bookrags.com reported that Peter Weir has since said he wished he'd used the original ending.

If not the dictates of a director, it can be the reactions of focus groups or test audiences that lead to a change of plot and a corresponding lack of motivation. In the film *Pretty in Pink*, Molly Ringwald plays a poor girl who falls in love with a rich boy. The latter's best friend tells him she's not the right kind of girl and he dumps her. At the school prom, the rich boy realizes the error of his ways and tells the girl he wants her back. In the meantime, she has discovered that her eccentric best friend, a boy called Duckie, is in love with her and she falls for him. She tells the rich boy to get lost.

Well, she did, until test audiences of young girls, the movie's target market, declared that they wanted her to end up with the rich boy. So, although it's rather difficult to buy in terms of character motivation, a new ending was shot in which the rich boy apologizes to her, she takes him back, and her friend Duckie rather randomly ends up attracting the kind of girl who would never have given him a second look in the movie up until then.

I wish it were otherwise, but once again the box office take ($40.5 million domestic, not at all bad for 1986) proves that character and story flaws don't necessarily doom a movie to poor returns.

When the change is one-dimensional

Let's take a male mid-life crisis as an example. Yes, one obvious change might be that the man in question buys a red sports car, but it will also be reflected by all kinds of little changes as well. These might be getting a new hairstyle (or a toupee, or hair implants), a change in what he wears, joining a gym, and so on. I'm not suggesting that you have to include all of these; that would be overkill. But you'd definitely want to have this change reflected in several ways, and if you can find some more subtle ones, so much the better. Each of these would also have an effect on the character's relationships, so it's helpful to show those ripples as well.

When the path of change is too smooth

We humans have a hard time changing. Seldom is the path smooth (and smooth paths don't make for interesting drama in any case). There should be setbacks, unintended and unanticipated by-products of the change, and retreats.

While many fine works of fiction do feature such a change, Diane Lefer says:

> My objection is that life experience teaches us an equally dramatic (if frustrating) truth: In spite of conflict, confrontation and crisis, people often don't, can't or won't change.

Even in Hollywood, not every story has a protagonist who undergoes such a change. James Bond doesn't change much. Neither does the killer (or the others) in *No Country for Old Men*, or Butch Cassidy and the Sundance Kid, or Charles Foster Kane as an adult. Currently I'm writing a young adult novel in which a teenager is the only one who really knows what is happening (bad things), but nobody believes him. The story is about his determination to be heard, even when telling the truth could destroy his father. Although he doesn't change much other than becoming a bit less naïve than he is at the beginning, I still think the story works.

Bottom line: If a character arc for your protagonist isn't a natural part of the story you want to tell, don't feel that you have to shoehorn it in.

The temptation of comedy

Especially in the realm of comedy, there is a temptation to make a character do something because it serves your purpose—in this case, getting a laugh—rather than because it's actually something they would do. My mentor in this field was Danny Simon, known to his chagrin mainly as Neil Simon's brother even though he had a successful comedy writing career in his own right. His motto was "never sacrifice the reality of the character for the sake of a joke." And indeed, of the shows for which I wrote early in my time in Hollywood, the ones that are still remembered or at least still rerun are the ones, like *Benson* and *Family Ties*, where the characters were taken seriously even though the object was comedy.

In creating a plot for a comedy, I usually begin with a story that could work just as well as a drama; it's the attitudes of the characters that ultimately turn it into a comedy. Imagine *Hamlet* as written by Woody Allen—it would still work, although as a rather black comedy. Master farceur Ray Cooney said much the same in an interview in *The Times*:

> The plot in a good farce should be able to be transplanted into a stark tragedy. Most tragedies have as their theme the struggle of the individual against forces that are overwhelming and the individual's efforts to combat those forces as the tide runs stronger against him. Also, the individual is usually tortured because of his own character flaws and his inability to control those flaws under stress. Well, that sums up most of my farces.

When I was story editing comedy scripts, I always found that the way to make a script funnier was to make it more real. Not more conventional, but more in tune with the characters and the situation that had been established. That surprised a lot of newer writers, who thought that the way to a funnier script was more punch lines or more outrageous behavior.

In both comedy and drama the point is the same: character and plot must be joined in a happy marriage in which they stay true to each other.

The types of story

In a talk Kurt Vonnegut gave on writing, he pointed out the universality of fairy tales and used the structure of the folk tale *Cinderella* as an example of a story shape that everyone can relate to. Cinderella starts out as the underdog, suffering at the hands of her stepmother and stepsisters. Suddenly, with the invitation to the ball, things look up. But there's an obstacle—the stepsisters forbid her to go. Hope reappears in the form of the fairy godmother, who makes a beautiful dress and glass slippers for Cinderella and provides her with a coach. At the ball, everything goes well and it looks like Cinderella will triumph. But disaster strikes at midnight and she has to rush away, in the process leaving behind one of her glass slippers. Having glimpsed happiness, she now is even sadder than at the beginning. Fortunately, the Prince loves her so much that he doesn't give up looking for her and when he finds her, via the proper fit of the glass slipper, they go off and live happily ever after.

KURT VONNEGUT (1922–2007)
Vonnegut's novels include *Slaughterhouse-Five*, *Cat's Cradle*, and *Mother Night*. Vonnegut appears briefly in several of the film adaptations of his books and played himself in the 1986 film *Back to School*. Before his novels became well known he had an unsuccessful career as a sports journalist.

In some versions the stepsisters beg for forgiveness and Cinderella grants it. In other versions their eyes are pecked out by pigeons. In more gruesome versions, they also hack off part of their feet in order to try to fit the glass slipper. You can see why Disney went with the milder variation.

This story of the underdog who wins out in the end is a universal pattern and still works today. *Rocky* fits the pattern perfectly, and even a movie like *The King's Speech* has elements of it.

The King was not an underdog socially, but his stutter is a hindrance he has to overcome. These days usually the character overcomes the oppression or disability through their own efforts rather than just by being beautiful, but otherwise the structure is the same as for *Cinderella*.

There are other universal plots found in mythology and folk and fairy tales that continue to serve as the basis of modern novels, films, plays, and short stories. Experts differ on the number of such story patterns; some have claimed there are 7, some that there are 36, but trying to define an exact number probably is a waste of time. Here are some examples.

The quest

This was written about at length in Joseph Campbell's book *The Hero with a Thousand Faces* and is also known as the hero's journey. The protagonist is dedicated to finding and bringing back some kind of prize—golden treasure, the love of a princess, or a magic talisman. It has become well known in the film world because George Lucas used it as the foundation for *Star Wars*.

The quest includes a number of elements that mythologist Campbell found to be common in the myths of many cultures, for instance the appearance of a mentor to inspire and instruct the hero. There are several different versions of the hero's journey available in various books and courses, including one that claims there are more than 500 steps or elements to the journey.

Rebirth

The protagonist is affected by some kind of dark spell or personal limitation and must find redemption through love or acts of unselfishness. This is the foundation of *A Christmas Carol*.

Overcoming the monster

The protagonist must defeat a force that is endangering people. *Frankenstein* is a classic example, *Erin Brockovich* is a modern version in which the monster is a deadly form of pollution.

The journey and return

The story pattern here is the protagonist going on a journey to another world, learning things while there, and returning to their own world a changed person. This is the structure of *The Wizard of Oz* and *Avatar*.

Rags to riches

The protagonist starts with nothing, then is elevated to a position of wealth or power, but loses it and then must act in order to return to the elevated status. This is the basis for *Cinderella* as well as *Great Expectations*, among many others.

A story may combine elements of several types of plots. For instance, in *Citizen Kane* Charles Foster Kane goes from rags to riches, but finds that wealth doesn't help him on his other quest—it can't buy him love. In *Lord Jim*, the protagonist imagines himself the kind of hero who could overcome the monster that threatens the people, in this case the sea, but finds himself lacking. While he goes on a journey of redemption, he ultimately finds that the best he can do is accept his fate. *Star Wars* combines the hero's journey with the need to destroy the monster as represented by Darth Vader.

Regardless of which type of story you want to tell, there will be some kind of conflict at the heart of it. In the next chapter we look at the types of conflict and how they function in shaping your story.

FROM ADVICE TO ACTION!

ACTION: If you find that you are having trouble working out the plot of your story, the first place to look is at your characters. Have you given them the kind of background that makes it likely—or at least possible—that they will perform the actions you'd like to feature in your story? For instance, many thrillers, both films and novels, lose credibility by having an average person suddenly turn into a James Bond type. While this may be accepted by the undemanding reader who just wants a quick read on the beach or on an airplane, it's not the prescription for a work that lasts.

As you develop your story, keep checking to make sure your characters are acting in a way that's consistent with their values and experience or, if you need them to behave uncharacteristically, that you have created circumstances strong enough to warrant that kind of change.

If you have an arc of transformation for any of your characters, consider:

- What are they like at the start?
- What are they like at the end?
- What are the crucial events that cause the change?
- What are the setbacks along the way?

If you are not sure what kind of plot your story should have, consider which fairy or folk tales or myths have stuck in your mind or had the most impact on you.

- What is their story pattern?
- What relevance do they have to your experience?
- Are you drawn to finding a modern way of telling a story with that foundation?

16
Conflict

The heart of most plots is conflict. Spy thriller writer John Le Carré put it most simply:

As a rough principle I always begin with one character and then perhaps two, and they seem to be in conflict with each other. "The cat sat on the mat" is not a story. "The cat sat on the dog's mat" is a story.

The level of conflict can vary greatly. Some authors are drawn to heightening it as much as possible, for instance Ayn Rand, who wrote:

I believe with Victor Hugo that the more melodramatic the action in which one can express the drama, the better the story. If you can unite the two—if you can give a relevant and logical physical expression to the spiritual conflict you present—then you have high-class drama.

Sometimes the conflict is the starting point of the story, if not necessarily the start of the book. Elizabeth Bowen gave an example:

I think of the situation first, so often. Some instance, an extreme one. Somebody throwing somebody else over a cliff. And I think who is the person who went over the cliff and why is the other one angry... you think who are the kind of people to whom this incident or action or catastrophe would be most likely to happen and why would it happen, and the character shapes itself around.

Types of conflict

One of the crucial questions about any story is: What is at stake for the characters? What do they want and what are the forces of conflict that get in their way?

There are several types of conflict; one or a combination of two or more usually are the drivers of the plots of novels and films and an element of short stories. Because short stories frequently are more like a snapshot than a film, sometimes their conflict is implied and we see only the consequence of the conflict or one moment in its development.

One way to look at the variety of conflicts is to return to Maslow's hierarchy of needs.

At the most basic level, physiological needs may be threatened in a conflict between man and nature. This is explored in works like Defoe's *Robinson Crusoe*, Jack London's *The Call of the Wild* (although there it's dogs versus nature and humans), and Hemingway's *The Old Man and the Sea*.

At the level of safety, there may be a conflict between man and man. This is the most common in films and in crime and spy novels: the criminal versus the cop, the gang leader versus a rival, James Bond versus Dr. No. This is a strong element of *Les Misérables*, *The Man in the Iron Mask*, the tales of Sherlock Holmes, and countless others.

Raymond Chandler advised:

RAYMOND CHANDLER (1888–1959)
Chandler's famous works include *The Big Sleep*, *The Long Goodbye*, and *The Lady in the Lake*. He was born in America, but moved to England when he was 2, becoming a British subject at age 19 and resuming his American citizenship at age 49. The locations in his novels are real places in Los Angeles under altered names.

When in doubt, have a man come through the door with a gun in his hand.

In other words, if you want to interest the reader, create a threat to your protagonist.

There can also be conflict between people at the psychological level, such as parents vying for custody of a child, or two women in love with the same man, or a battle for power between a father and son.

In situations relating to esteem, being respected and respecting oneself, having a sense of accomplishment, or serving a valuable function, there can be competition in sports or academia or the world of work, as exemplified in David Mamet's play *Glengarry Glen Ross*.

Man against society is a conflict in which the protagonist is up against a strong element of his social world, which could be in the arena of politics, business, or general morality. For instance, Hester in *The Scarlett Letter* confronts her society with her status as an adulteress rather than trying to hide it or run away from it. Ralph Ellison's *The Invisible Man* and Harper Lee's *To Kill a Mockingbird* both are about someone confronting societal racism.

At the top level of the hierarchy of needs, self-actualization, the conflict is man against himself. Internal conflict occurs when someone is pulled in two or more directions that are mutually exclusive. Sometimes the conflict develops between what the character wants at the beginning of the story and what he begins to realize he needs. For instance, in the classic comedy film *Tootsie*, Michael Dorsey is driven by his desire to be a successful actor, and meaningful relationships don't seem to be important to him. He gets his wish by pretending to be a woman and, in that guise, landing a plum role in a soap opera. Then he falls in love with his female co-star, but he can't tell her his feelings without also revealing that he's really a man, which would lead to his losing the role.

Internal conflict may involve someone striving to overcome some kind of addiction or fear or obsession or other illness or weakness. One example is *Under the Volcano*, Malcolm Lowry's semi-autobiographical novel. It chronicles the impact of the protagonist's alcoholism on his relationships and his desire to write a book.

Some critics have added more categories of conflict, including man vs. God, man vs. supernatural forces (ghosts, vampires, werewolves, aliens), and man vs. technology (robots, for instance).

The divisions seldom are neat and most stories of any complexity involve several levels of conflict. For instance, in *Don Quixote* the protagonist is the victim of his delusions as well as coming into conflict with various people who humiliate and beat him.

Often one kind of conflict leads to another. In *Lord of the Flies*, initially Ralph is in conflict with Jack one to one, but later, when the boys have accepted Jack as their leader, Ralph comes into conflict with the society that has developed.

In the next chapter we'll look at some of the story structures available to you as you develop the conflicts your characters are experiencing into a plot.

FROM ADVICE TO ACTION!

Great books have been written about epic conflicts (*War and Peace*) and about small domestic conflicts (the works of Jane Austen). As long as you get the reader to care about your characters and what happens to them, the scale of the conflict in their situation is up to you and the type of story you want to tell.

ACTION: When you are planning your story, it can be helpful to answer these questions:

- What is the core conflict? Is your protagonist up against nature, another person, society, themselves, or some combination of these?
- What will make readers care about the outcome of this conflict? Have you given them characters they can identify with or find fascinating?
- Does the conflict change over time? What causes the change?

17

Building the plot

f you have interesting characters and a conflict, you have the basic building blocks of a plot. As we've seen, some authors don't believe in pinning down the plot ahead of time, but often these are accomplished writers who through experience or superior intuition are aware of how to structure a story effectively.

There are a number of traditional story forms, most notably what is often called the "three-act structure." At its simplest, it's just the beginning, about a quarter of your story; the middle, which is about half; and the end, which is the final quarter.

In Act One, you establish your character and their world and introduce an inciting incident—something new that will set your character on their journey to achieve some kind of goal.

In Act Two, your protagonist encounters many obstacles and setbacks. Some versions of this model suggest that there must be a major reversal or change in the middle of Act Two that alters the way your protagonist sees the quest and goes about seeking the goal. The goal itself may change over the course of this journey, as we discussed in the reference to wants and needs. The quest culminates in a decisive moment at the end of Act Two, at which point the outcome could go either way, for or against your protagonist. Often this is also the highest point of danger. Failure could mean losing everything, including life itself.

In Act Three you play out the consequences of this moment of truth and reveal the fate of the protagonist.

This construction was suggested by Aristotle in his Poetics. Of course, today there is no actual division into acts; even in the theatre typically there is only one break, roughly in the middle.

Some screenwriters prefer to think of a four-act structure, with the traditional Act Two divided in half, often with a game-changing event taking place at the mid-point.

My teaching colleague, Michael Hauge, says that all successful Hollywood movies fit into a six-stage plot structure, with the traditional Act One consisting of the Setup and the New Situation, the traditional Act Two comprising Progress & Complications and Higher Stakes, and Act Three consisting of the Final Push and the Aftermath. Even if that's true, though, you may not want to write a traditional Hollywood movie.

The many options of the writer

Especially for novels, there are so many options you have for how to structure your plot that it's impossible to list them all. You may want to tell the events chronologically from the viewpoint of one character, or you could have that person remembering past events but intermingle them with an account of what is happening to her now.

Or you can have multiple narrators—and not all of them have to be human.

You can stick to the rules of life as we know it, or you can use magical realism to have something fantastic happen to a character living an otherwise normal life.

It's liberating, but also daunting to have so many choices. If in doubt, especially when you are starting out, consider using a traditional structure, and vary it only when you are convinced that this will improve the story.

In films the scope is not as wide, but pictures like *Memento*, *Pulp Fiction*, *Donnie Darko*, and many others, especially European films, prove that there are exceptions to traditional structure in that field as well.

Find your path and your method

Many authors have a specific method for developing a story. Emma Tennant says:

I had many years of stuffing large, unfinished manuscripts under my bed until finally I met the science-fiction writer Michael Moorcock who told me, "You don't understand how to structure things. You have 160 pages divided into four parts, labelled 'introduction of characters,' 'development of characters,' and so on." He wrote it all out for me with coloured pens and I'm eternally grateful, and always try to tell people that you have to become very humble and think: here are my 160 pages, I'm going to split it into parts, and then it's not so frightening. If you tell yourself, "Here are my first ten pages, and in my first ten pages I must introduce, say, half my characters," then you've already got something to do, introducing your characters in situations which show what they're like. This will then automatically lead you to think about the development of what's going to happen. Although this sounds so crass and crude, and as if it only belonged to a rather child-like science fiction, it can get a writer going, and away from that inchoate terror of a mountain of white paper. It's a general formula which makes you do it.

Orhan Pamuk says:

The division of a book into chapters is very important for my way of thinking. When writing a novel, if I know the whole story line in advance—and most of the time I do—I divide it into chapters and think up the details of what I'd like to have happen in each. I don't necessarily start with the first chapter and write all the others in order. When I'm blocked, which is not a grave thing for me, I continue with whatever takes my fancy. I may write from the first to the fifth chapter, then if I'm not enjoying it I skip to number fifteen and continue from there.

FROM ADVICE TO ACTION!

ACTION: Regardless of when you decide to consider the structure of your story, it's useful to answer the questions below. They reflect the traditional structure of plots. While many writers violate the rules of structure, most of them agree that it's useful to know them and, if you do violate them, to have a story-based reason for doing so.

- Does the opening scene or chapter hook the reader?
- Is the progression of events in your plot logical—or at least believable?
- Does the action escalate, driving the conflict and tension higher and higher (with some pauses to give readers time to catch their breath)?
- Does the action reach a point of resolution at which the main conflict is resolved?
- If you've featured subplots, are they also resolved—unless, of course, you make the decision consciously to leave them open?
- Reverse engineer the books you like in order to figure out how they were structured. Outline the key developments of the plot, notice how they were broken into chapters or sections, and be aware of how the author motivated you to keep reading.

The index card method

The index card method is a useful tool for structuring your plot. First, use index cards to take notes on anything that occurs to you about your writing project as you go through your daily life. This is how author and writing teacher Anne Lamott uses them:

I have index cards and pens all over the house—by the bed, in the bathroom, in the kitchen, by the phones, and I have them in the glove compartment of my car. I carry one with me in my back pocket when I take my dog for a walk. In fact, I carry it folded lengthwise, if you need to know, so that, God forbid, I won't look bulky. You may want to consider doing the same. I don't even know you, but I bet you have enough on your mind without having to worry about whether or not you look bulky. So whenever I am leaving the house without my purse—in which there are actual notepads, let alone index cards—I fold an index card lengthwise in half, stick it in my back pocket along with a pen, and head out, knowing that if I have an idea, or see something lovely or strange or for any reason worth remembering, I will be able to jot down a couple of words to remind me of it. Sometimes, if I overhear or think of an exact line of dialogue or a transition, I write it down verbatim. I stick the card back in my pocket. I might be walking along the salt marsh, or out at Phoenix Lake, or in the express line at Safeway, and suddenly I hear something wonderful that makes me want to smile or snap my fingers—as if it has just come back to me—and I take out my index card and scribble it down.

The other way to use index cards is to jot down the individual moments of your story on them and then lay them out in order. You can see whether the flow makes sense, where there are things missing, and where there may be material you don't need. Vladimir Nabokov used this method to write most of his novels, including *Lolita*. It took more than 2000 cards to create *Ada*. As well as using the method himself, he had John Shade, his fictional poet in *Pale Fire*, employ it to compose his masterwork.

In his novel *Lila*, Robert Pirsig also has a protagonist who uses this method to write his book. In this extract, Pirsig describes the advantages of index cards over traditional outlines:

The reason Phaedrus used slips rather than full-sized sheets of paper is that a card-catalog tray full of slips provides a more random access. When information is organized in small chunks that can be accessed and sequenced at random it becomes much more valuable than when you have to take it in serial form. It's better, for example to run a post office where the patrons have numbered boxes and can come in to access these boxes any time they please. It's worse to have them all come in at a certain time, stand in a queue and get their mail from Joe, who has to sort through everything alphabetically each time and who has rheumatism, is going to retire in a few years, and who doesn't care whether they like waiting or not. When any distribution is locked into a rigid sequential format it develops Joes that dictate what new changes will be allowed and what will not, and that rigidity is dead.

Hilary Mantel describes her method of using the cards:

The little words breed—sometimes several hundred offspring. I keep them on the board, in any order, until one day I see a sequence, a logic, begin to emerge. Then I repin them, very approximately, very roughly, in the order in which I think the narrative will shape. A few weeks on, all these bits of paper—the original cards and anything that has accumulated behind them—go into a ring-binder. With a ring-binder you can easily swap the papers around—you're still not committing yourself to an order of events. You can add pages, transpose pages. But now you can begin to see how much of your book you have written. Some incidents… will be fully described, and some characters will come complete with their biographies, snatches of dialogue, their appearance and way of talking. Other parts of the book will not have "written themselves" at all—they await focused attention. But you know—indeed, you can see—how much work you have to do…

   This method is soothing. Its virtue is that you never write yourself into a cul-de-sac; you have flexibility. Until *you sit down to write your first draft sequentially, you have not committed yourself to linear narrative. I am amazed at how easily ideas fall into place, how they multiply, if you give them a chance, and if you don't close off their possibilities too early. This is really a method of growing a book, rather than writing one.*

The actions/reactions grid

Another way to plot your story is to use a chart I developed that I call the actions/reactions grid. In the first column on the left is the action a character takes, in the columns to the right are the reactions (when appropriate) of the other characters. Here's an example—the explanation follows the chart:

Action	George	Mary	Son	Daughter	George's mother
George loses job		Berates him	Is happy—more time with Dad	Worries about not getting presents	Sympathizes
Mary berates George	Gets drunk, spends night with another woman		Hides in room	Sides with Mary	Warns Mary that she's endangering marriage
George, drunk, cheats on wife				Sees him coming out of house	
Daughter tells Mary	Furious with daughter	Goes home to her mother	Sides with father		Disappointed in George
Mary goes home to her mother	Drinks more		Tells teacher	Blames George	Assumes control of the household

This chart assumes we want to write a short story or even a novel that tells what happens to a man's family when he loses his job. That's the first action, indicated in the top of the first column. To the right we see the other characters in our story: his wife Mary, their son, their daughter, and George's mother, who lives with them. We have the choice of which of these reactions to focus on.

Let's say that it's Mary's reaction that we want to feature because she's the one he tells first and she's the one most affected (this assumes that we are writing in the third-person omniscient or third-person limited, not first person). The other responses are there for us to portray as well, of course, but the next scene centers on Mary, who berates her husband for losing his job.

To the right of that we see how the others react to that event: their son hides in his room during the argument, their daughter sides with Mary, George's mother warns Mary she's endangering the marriage, and George gets drunk and ends up spending the night with a sympathetic woman he meets at the bar.

Clearly, George's response is the most drastic and interesting one, so we make that the next scene. The process continues all the way through the story. Not only does this allow you to construct the plot, it helps you to get to know the characters really well, because you have to identify how they feel about all of the major events of the story, even the ones that are not directly about them.

If you're a planner, you can use this to build your story; if not, you can use it to diagram the first draft, which will give you alternatives if some parts of the plot seem to veer off the story's spine or are not interesting enough. In the latter case, focusing on the reaction of one of the other characters may give you a richer scene or sequence.

In the next three chapters we take a closer look at how to construct the beginning, middle, and end of your story.

FROM ADVICE TO ACTION!

ACTION: These are the steps to the index card method:

- During the time you are planning the story, jot down ideas, character traits, lines of dialogue, and anything else pertinent that occurs to you. Use one index card for each idea.
- When you're ready, sort the cards into categories such as plot points, character traits, lines of dialogue, and miscellaneous.
- Pin the plot-related cards to a corkboard or lay them out on a flat surface in the order in which you think the events described on the cards will occur. It may help to organize them into events in Acts One, Two, and Three.
- Analyze what's missing and brainstorm how to fill those gaps. Write your ideas on index cards and fit them where they belong.
- Analyze whether there are cards with events you don't need. Remove those cards.
- Go through the character-related cards and notice what gaps there might be in your understanding of the characters. Use the methods described in the creating characters section of this book to flesh them out. Put your new ideas onto cards and keep those with the others.
- Decide how detailed you want your planning to be before you start writing. Obviously, Nabokov's 2000 cards represent an extremely detailed version of the story. Other writers might be happy with only a few dozen cards, and yet others might aim for a hundred.
- When you're about to write a scene or a chapter, review the cards relating to the people and the action and the dialogue in that scene.

You may also want to experiment with the action/reaction grid both before and after you use the index card approach, to find out which one works better for you or how you can get the two to support each other.

18

Openings, foreshadowing and Act One

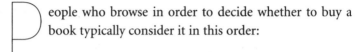

People who browse in order to decide whether to buy a book typically consider it in this order:

- The cover
- The back cover
- The opening

If the opening doesn't hook them, they go no further—and that's true whether they've picked up the book in a store or use the "look inside" feature online.

What's the secret of a good opening? Alexandre Dumas *père* advised:

> *Begin with something interesting rather than beginning with something boring; begin with action rather than beginning with background information; speak about the characters after they have appeared rather than having them appear after having spoken about them.*

Some classic fiction does begin with a leisurely description of the weather, the landscape, the building, and finally the protagonist or another character. Today's readers are too impatient for that; in fact, even Chekhov warned a fellow author about this:

> *The story should begin with the sentence, "Somov, it seems, was upset." Everything that comes before—that stuff about the cloud prostrating itself, about the sparrows, the field stretching out into the distance—all these elements are just so much tribute paid to routine.*

Sometimes writers are petrified to write their first sentence, even though it's easy to go back later and change it. Openings bother Philip Roth:

PHILIP ROTH (b 1933)
Roth's novels include *Goodbye, Columbus*, *Portnoy's Complaint*, and *American Pastoral*. He frequently writes himself and his friends and family into his novels. He believes that novel reading will become a "cultic" practice within the next 25 years.

I type out beginnings and they're awful, more of an unconscious parody of my previous book than the breakaway from it that I want. I need something driving down the center of a book, a magnet to draw everything to it—that's what I look for during the first months of writing something new. I often have to write a hundred pages or more before there's a paragraph that's alive. Okay, I say to myself, that's your beginning, start there; that's the first paragraph of the book. I'll go over the first six months of work and underline in red a paragraph, a sentence, sometimes no more than a phrase, that has some life in it, and then I'll type all these out on one page. Usually it doesn't come to more than one page, but if I'm lucky, that's the start of page one. I look for the liveliness to set the tone. After the awful beginning comes the months of freewheeling play, and after the play come the crises, turning against your material and hating the book.

Another writer who struggles with openings is Gabriel García Márquez:

One of the most difficult things is the first paragraph. I have spent many months on a first paragraph, and once I get it, the rest just comes out very easily. In the first paragraph you solve most of the problems with your book. The theme is defined, the style, the tone. At least, in my case, the first paragraph is a kind of sample of what the rest of the book is going to be.

There is no all-purpose rule for what the opening should be. As Diane Lefer points out:

> *Kafka began* The Metamorphosis *with the most dramatic moment: "As Gregor Samsa awoke one morning from uneasy dreams he found himself transformed in his bed into a gigantic insect." I can just imagine a modern-day workshop leader telling Kafka that this transformation is clearly the climactic moment and must happen near the end.*

It's also an excellent example of how the first sentence immediately lets the reader know what kind of story is in store, a blend of the magical and the mundane.

George Pelecanos summarizes what the first chapter must do for the writer as well as for the reader:

> *From the author's standpoint, reading it should inspire you to continue writing and to push on. You should look at it and say, I've got something here. I'm not talking about that the-first-paragraph-of-the-novel-should-hook-the-reader bullshit. I'm saying, the voice should be strong and it should be compelling.*

The opening of one of Conan Doyle's Sherlock Holmes tales shows that you don't need to jump into the action of the plot right away; if you have an interesting enough character you can start with him or her. By the way, note how timely the story seems—Dr. Watson has just come back from combat in Afghanistan and Holmes is in need of an intervention.

The Sign of Four

Sherlock Holmes took his bottle from the corner of the mantel-piece and his hypodermic syringe from its neat morocco case. [Immediately, we wonder what he's doing with a hypodermic syringe] *With his long, white, nervous fingers he adjusted the delicate needle, and rolled back his left shirt-cuff. For some little time his eyes rested thoughtfully upon the sinewy forearm and wrist all dotted and scarred with innumerable puncture-marks. Finally he thrust the sharp point home, pressed down the tiny piston, and sank back into the velvet-lined arm-chair with a long sigh of satisfaction.* [This probably isn't what we expected, so it's intriguing]

Three times a day for many months I had witnessed this performance, but custom had not reconciled my mind to it. [Now we wonder who this "I" is and his relationship to Holmes] *On the contrary, from day to day I had become more irritable at the sight, and my conscience swelled nightly within me at the thought that I had lacked the courage to protest. Again and again I had registered a vow that I should deliver my soul upon the subject, but there was that in the cool, nonchalant air of my companion which made him the last man with whom one would care to take anything approaching to a liberty. His great powers, his masterly manner, and the experience which I had had of his many extraordinary qualities, all made me diffident and backward in crossing him.* [We suspect that the confrontation he's been avoiding may be coming and wonder how it will work out]

Yet upon that afternoon, whether it was the Beaune which I had taken with my lunch, or the additional exasperation produced by the extreme deliberation of his manner, I suddenly felt that I could hold out no longer. [Great, here it comes!]

"Which is it to-day?" I asked,—"morphine or cocaine?"

He raised his eyes languidly from the old black-letter volume which he had opened. "It is cocaine," he said,—"a seven-per-cent. solution. Would you care to try it?"

"No, indeed,'" I answered, brusquely. "My constitution has not got over the Afghan campaign yet. I cannot afford to

throw any extra strain upon it." [We have another interesting clue about the person narrating the story]

When Watson further rebukes him, Holmes explains:

> *"My mind," he said, "rebels at stagnation. Give me problems, give me work, give me the most abstruse cryptogram or the most intricate analysis, and I am in my own proper atmosphere. I can dispense then with artificial stimulants. But I abhor the dull routine of existence. I crave for mental exaltation. That is why I have chosen my own particular profession,—or rather created it, for I am the only one in the world."* [Now we know we are reading about a unique and fascinating character]

This pattern of raising questions in the mind of the reader, answering some of them at the same time as you create more, is an excellent model to follow all the way through your story. Your goal is to get people to start reading and keep reading. You can do that by continually stimulating their curiosity and also partly satisfying it so that they don't feel confused or frustrated.

Is your writing short fuse or long fuse?

As we have seen, some stories start with a bang, some take a while to get going but gain impact from the run-up to the point of ignition.

These days in both films and novels, the trend is toward starting with a big dramatic incident. Sometimes a book uses a prologue to expose you to that kind of scene and then the first chapter goes back in time. The prologue is the promise of action and intensity to come and it buys your patience.

Both types of openings have pitfalls.

The risk with a long-fuse story is that you will lose the interest of the reader before you ignite the central conflict. This means that, as with Holmes, your characters have to be fascinating and you have to foreshadow some of the more active elements to come.

The risk with a short fuse is that a big opening will make your reader eager for more of the same. If you give in to that, you may find yourself losing your grip on the more personal aspects of the story, or you may even write yourself into a corner, as happened with the television series *Lost*. There was so much high-profile mysterious action that ultimately there was no way the writers could pay it off in a satisfying manner.

Some authors like to consider this issue before they start writing, others just write and think about these things when they get into the rewriting phase. But sooner or later, you have to consider what kind of fuse will serve your story best and how to make sure you hold the reader's attention.

There are many ways to capture the reader's interest right from the first sentence. What is important is to find one that is consistent with the tone and intent of your story.

Opening sentences

Below are some opening sentences that have stood the test of time. The first three rely on paradox or apparent contradiction to arouse our interest:

> *It was the best of times, it was the worst of times, it was the age of wisdom, it was the age of foolishness, it was the epoch of belief, it was the epoch of incredulity, it was the season of Light, it was the season of Darkness, it was the spring of hope, it was the winter of despair. (Charles Dickens,* A Tale of Two Cities)

As well as making us curious about the contradictions, this sentence establishes right away that this is a book with a big sweep.

> *I am an invisible man. (Ralph Ellison,* Invisible Man)

From this opening we know that we are about to hear one man's personal story.

> *I had the story, bit by bit, from various people, and, as generally happens in such cases, each time it was a different story. (Edith Wharton, Ethan Frome)*

This line suggests that we are going to hear a tale from several different perspectives and perhaps will have to come to our own conclusions about the truth.

The next one creates curiosity about what explains the strange situation described:

> *Someone must have slandered Josef K., for one morning, without having done anything truly wrong, he was arrested. (Franz Kafka, The Trial)*

From this opening we understand that we are going to read the story of a wronged man and his battle against unknown forces.

And, finally, a first line that creates curiosity on the literal level and perhaps echoes as a metaphor, at least for the reader who has reached middle age:

> *Midway in our life's journey, I went astray from the straight road and woke to find myself alone in a dark wood. (Dante Alighieri, The Divine Comedy, Inferno)*

FROM ADVICE TO ACTION!

ACTION: You can choose whether to write an opening spontaneously or plan what it should contain. Whichever approach you use, sooner or later it is useful to do an analysis of it. For these purposes you might want to think about the first line, the first paragraph, the first page, and the first chapter. Consider the following questions about your opening:

🖉 Does it introduce one of the key characters? If so, what do you reveal about them that makes the reader curious to know more?

🖉 Does it promise conflict of some kind?

🖉 Does it hint at the important elements of the story to come?

🖉 Does it raise any questions in the mind of the reader? Does it answer some and raise more?

🖉 Are its tone and style consistent with the rest?

🖉 If it doesn't take us directly into the story, what will compel the reader to keep reading?

Foreshadowing

Foreshadowing is giving a clue or hint as to the important developments to come. Like a good first sentence, it captures our curiosity and makes us want to keep reading. It also means that when the development comes to pass, although it may surprise us, on some level we have been prepared for it. For instance, in a ghost story there will be some hint of the presence of the ghost long before it appears, even if at that point there is also another possible explanation.

Mary Shelley opens her novel *Frankenstein; or, The Modern Prometheus* with a letter from R Walton to his sister. Walton is the one who first catches sight of Dr. Frankenstein's creation. The opening letters are rather leisurely by modern standards, but notice how from the very first sentence the author suggests that all will not end well.

Letter 1
St. Petersburgh, Dec. 11th, 17–
TO Mrs. Saville, England
You will rejoice to hear that no disaster has accompanied the commencement of an enterprise which you have regarded with such evil forebodings. [The notion that somebody had "evil forebodings" is interesting and we also

wonder who this person is] *I arrived here yesterday, and my first task is to assure my dear sister of my welfare and increasing confidence in the success of my undertaking.* [Now we know it's the letter writer's sister who had the forebodings]

I am already far north of London, and as I walk in the streets of Petersburgh, I feel a cold northern breeze play upon my cheeks, which braces my nerves and fills me with delight. Do you understand this feeling? This breeze, which has travelled from the regions towards which I am advancing, gives me a foretaste of those icy climes. Inspirited by this wind of promise, my daydreams become more fervent and vivid. ["fervent and vivid" makes it sound like he's almost feverish, a nice taste of what is to come] *I try in vain to be persuaded that the pole is the seat of frost and desolation; it ever presents itself to my imagination as the region of beauty and delight.* [This sets up the contrast we will encounter eventually between Dr. Frankenstein's idealistic vision of what he wants to create and its cruel reality] *There, Margaret, the sun is forever visible, its broad disk just skirting the horizon and diffusing a perpetual splendour. There—for with your leave, my sister, I will put some trust in preceding navigators—there snow and frost are banished; and, sailing over a calm sea, we may be wafted to a land surpassing in wonders and in beauty every region hitherto discovered on the habitable globe.* [We're being told that anything can happen in this setting] *Its productions and features may be without example, as the phenomena of the heavenly bodies undoubtedly are in those undiscovered solitudes. What may not be expected in a country of eternal light?*

None of these references is obvious if you don't know what is coming, but like all the best foreshadowing, they operate at the subconscious level.

In movies it's not unusual for there to be an early line of dialogue that foreshadows the core conflict or issue of the film. For instance, in an early scene in *Tootsie*, Michael Dorsey, an aspiring actor who is working as a waiter, is asked by his roommate why, instead of trying to be Michael Dorsey the best actor or Michael Dorsey the best waiter, he doesn't just try to be the best Michael Dorsey. That's what the whole movie is about: Michael's quest to connect to people, especially women, on a real level. Of course, these lines should not stand out; they work best when they are subtle.

FROM ADVICE TO ACTION!

ACTION: Look at your opening pages to determine whether they foreshadow one of the following:

- The appearance of a key character who doesn't show up until later (if this is applicable to your story).
- The key events of the later parts of the book. You may paint a picture of a happy family, but if you are eventually going to immerse them in some kind of terror you may want to hint at that. For instance, if later there is going to be a home invasion, one of the family members might notice something out of place (later you will reveal that the robbers had been inside the house when nobody was there).
- The tone of the later parts of the book. Again, a ghost story may start out with everything normal, but perhaps one of the characters has a nightmare that unsettles her, which brings some anxiety into an otherwise upbeat ambiance.

The beginning

So far we have looked only at the openings. Now let's consider the entire first section, the equivalent of Act One, and see how it was handled by Joseph Conrad in *Lord Jim*.

Lord Jim: The beginning

Joseph Conrad's *Lord Jim* is the story of a young British seaman, a moment in time that affects his entire life, and his search for redemption. The book begins in a third-person omniscient voice that describes Jim and some of his circumstances. This is the first paragraph:

> He was an inch, perhaps two, under six feet, powerfully built, and he advanced straight at you with a slight stoop of the shoulders, head forward, and a fixed-from-under stare which made you think of a charging bull. His voice was deep, loud, and his manner displayed a kind of dogged self-assertion which had nothing aggressive in it. It seemed a necessity, and it was directed apparently as much at himself as at anybody else. He was spotlessly neat, appareled in immaculate white from shoes to hat, and in the various Easter ports where he got his living as ship-chandler's water clerk he was very popular.

Having piqued our interest with that comment about self-assertion, Conrad goes on to describe what Jim's job is and by the second page he hints at an event that forms the center of the story:

> To the white men in the waterside business and to the captains of ships he was just Jim—nothing more. He had, of course, another name, but he was anxious that it should not be pronounced. His incognito, which had as many holes in it as a sieve, was not meant to hide a personality but a fact. When the fact broke through the incognito he would suddenly leave the seaport where he happened to be and go to another—generally farther east. He kept to seaports because he was a seaman in exile from the sea.

Having aroused our curiosity and thereby bought our patience, Conrad describes Jim's childhood, his fantasies, and his first sea-going experiences, including an incident in which he narrowly misses the chance to be the hero he dreams of being. We hear that he stays on the move, trying to stay incognito, and apparently running away from something in the past.

Then the book relates how he became first mate on the ship, the *Patna*, a steamship that carries pilgrims to Mecca. The ship experiences a strange vibration, the crew believe it has struck something and is about to go down, and we wonder how Jim will react.

Chapter 4 starts a month later, with an official inquiry at which Jim reveals that he believed the *Patna* had been in a collision and that there would be panic among the passengers of the apparently doomed ship. Consistent with the omniscient view, we are told what Jim is thinking and feeling as he testifies. Looking at the people watching his testimony, Jim notices Marlow and feels he has some sense of connection with him.

From Chapter 5 on, Marlow takes over telling the story, sitting on a verandah with a group of people eager to hear what happened. It's an unusual shift, but one that flows smoothly.

Marlow is fascinated by Jim and tells how when they met later he invited him to dinner and Jim related his experience the night of the incident, including the moment the crew decided to abandon ship and leave the passengers to their fate. The light of the ship disappeared and the crew assumed that the vessel had gone down. They concocted a story to justify their actions. In fact, the ship had only turned and was rescued with all of the passengers (except for one white man) alive and well.

Marlow tells how the inquiry cancels Jim's certificates, meaning that he can no longer work as a seaman.

This occurs about one third of the way through the novel and represents the end of the beginning, the end of what we could consider Act One. It sets up that Jim has his honor in tatters and his dreams of a life of glory on the sea dashed, and his way of making a living taken away from him.

Conrad's methods

Conrad piques our curiosity about Jim and what he's trying to escape. This curiosity also drives Marlow, the narrator as of Chapter 5, who feels some kind of affinity with Jim, declaring at several points that he is "one of us." One of the reasons we keep reading is to find out what happened to the *Patna*, but Conrad stretches out the revelation, an excellent example of using what is in part a mystery story as a framework within which to explore character and a number of more abstract issues, such as the nature of honor and self-image.

FROM ADVICE TO ACTION!

In addition to having a strong opening and foreshadowing elements of your larger story, you can check your first chapters to make sure that they:

- Introduce your major characters.
- Establish or at least hint at their relationships.
- Establish the setting (which may be the place your protagonist leaves in order to fulfill their journey, or it may be where the entire action takes place).
- Establish or hint at the theme (this may come later if you're not consciously dealing with the theme as you write the first draft).
- Reveal the incident or action that will set the protagonist on a new course.

19

The troublesome middle

The middle of the story usually is the part that gives authors the most trouble. How can you sustain readers' interest as the story develops? Creating the action/reaction grid should be a big help with this, as it will offer you additional subplots or story strands to follow, based on the actions and reactions of secondary characters.

More generally, there are three strategies that are useful:

- *Avoid predictability.* If we have the feeling we know exactly what is going to happen and find that we are right, we lose interest and stop reading.
- *Hold back information.* If we are getting to know the characters better as we go along, we will continue reading.
- *Have some variety.* Don't make all the chapters the same length. The surprise element doesn't have to be restricted to the content, it can also come from the way the content is related. If it fits, include a letter or a newspaper article or a sequence of tweets, or some other way to impart information.

As suggested in the first point above, creating some surprises for readers keeps them reading. Naturally, these must make sense within your story, but here are four examples of twists that fit any genre.

The person who is not who they seem to be

Sometimes a friend turns out to be an enemy, sometimes an enemy ends up being a friend. For example, in a thriller, the person who seems to be working for the CIA is actually a double agent. In a romance, the friend who is advising your heroine on her courtship actually wants the guy for herself. In a science fiction story, the apparently hostile alien's hidden motive is to save the human race from itself.

Sometimes a character's loyalty changes and then reverts. This can come about when two people who are enemies face a third enemy and they combine to defeat that person and then become enemies themselves again.

The unexpected complication

One good way to come up with one of these is to ask yourself: "At this moment, what's the worst thing that could happen?" It's all right to use coincidence to get your protagonist *into* trouble, it only feels like a cheat when you use it to get them *out of* trouble. So, for example, in a thriller, your hero is being chased by the bad guys. He falls and breaks his leg. In a romance, your rich heroine is pretending to be poor in order to find out whether men just want her for her money, but while she's on a date she runs into her banker who starts talking about her investment fund. In a science fiction plot, the alien who has the answer the human world needs catches a cold—which can kill that particular life form.

The downside of the upside

Your character has a win, but there's a cloud to the silver lining. This often is the "out of the frying pan into the fire" effect. For instance, your thriller's protagonist gets proof that exonerates her from a murder—but this puts her into the sights of the real killer. Or you romance's lead character finds her perfect love— but then discovers that he's terminally ill. Or the alien threat to humankind is overcome by an alliance of previously warring countries—but once the common threat is gone, they go back to fighting each other with the more powerful weapons they used to vanquish the aliens.

The terrible dilemma

This is similar to the downside of the upside, but in this case your protagonist has a choice. She can achieve something she desperately wants or needs, but only by giving up something equally valuable or putting another person at risk. Your thriller's protagonist realizes that the document everyone is after is hidden at a kids' summer camp, but going after it could lead the bad guys there and endanger the youngsters. Your romance's lead character is offered the job she wants, but it would mean relocating far away from the man she thinks she loves. Your science fiction scientist discovers a drug that can extend his life by 50 years, but it would mean outliving everyone he knows and loves.

When there is a problem in the middle, the place to look for a solution is the first section. That's where you need to plant the seeds that will flower in the second act. Chekhov famously said that if you show a gun in the first act, someone had better fire it in the second. Conversely, if someone fires it in the second, it should have been foreshadowed in the first.

Let's see how Joseph Conrad structured the middle of *Lord Jim*.

Lord Jim: The middle

Marlow feels a sense of responsibility for Jim, as well as kinship, and arranges for the disgraced former seaman to take a job at a rice mill. Jim accepts, but six months later leaves when another of the crew of the *Patna* takes a job there. He finds a new job, although he leaves that one as well when there is talk of the sinking ship he abandoned. Further similar incidents happen, until Marlow manages to place Jim in a position with Marlow's friend Stein, who also has a tragic past. Jim takes up the position of manager of a trade post on the remote island of Patusan, where his past is unlikely to catch up with him.

The story leaps forward to when Jim has made a success of the job and Marlow visits him. It appears that Jim has overcome the burden of his past and made a new life for himself. He has bravely confronted armed men and escaped when taken prisoner by the Rajah, who wants to control the trade. Here, for the natives, he has become "Lord Jim."

Another development is Jim's relationship with a woman he calls Jewel, the daughter of the wife of Cornelius, whom Jim replaced. Jewel helps him escape assassination by thugs sent by an ally of the Rajah.

Just as he had responsibility for the passengers of the *Patna*, he now has responsibility for the natives who look up to him. Marlow notes:

> *Jim the leader was a captive in every sense. The land, the people, the friendship, the love, were like the jealous guardians of his body. Every day added a link to the fetters of that strange freedom.*

Marlow leaves, Jim pledges to remain to help the natives although (or, given his past, perhaps because) he knows it is very dangerous, and it is understood that Jim and Marlow will never see each other again.

That is the end of what we could consider Act Two, and it finds Jim at a high point of redemption, yet with plenty of fore-shadowing that this story will not have an entirely happy ending and that Jim's enemies are preparing to challenge him one last time.

Conrad's methods

Like many novels of the era, *Lord Jim* was published in install-ments in a magazine, and sometimes that led to middles that were rambling and episodic. This charge was leveled at Conrad's novel, too. He addressed this in his Author's Note for a later edition:

> *When this novel first appeared in book form a notion got about that I had been bolted away with it. Some reviewers maintained that the work starting as a short story had got beyond the writer's control... The truth of the matter is, that*

my first thought was of a short story concerned only with the pilgrim ship episode; nothing more. And that was a legitimate conception. After writing a few pages, however, I became for some reason discontented and I laid them aside for a time. I didn't take them out of the drawer until the late Mr. William Blackwood suggested I should give something again to his magazine. It was only then that I perceived that the pilgrim ship episode was a good starting-point for a free and wandering tale; that it was an event, too, which could considerably colour the whole "sentiment and existence" in a simple and sensitive character.

It's certainly true that Conrad lets Marlow go off on quite a few digressions along the way, but he always brings us back to the central story, and in retrospect it's easier to see the thematic relationship of these episodes to Jim's story.

One outstanding aspect of Conrad's handling of the story is that he balances the negative developments with elements of the positive, and vice versa. In Conrad's world as in ours, clouds and silver linings don't exist without each other. What in one way is a straightforward story of redemption from a cowardly act thereby becomes a much more complex exploration of the nature of romantic dreams and the realities that undo them.

Subplots

A subplot is another story strand that runs parallel to your main story. Often it focuses on a different character from your main plot, but there's some relationship in terms of theme, setting, or emotion. While it would have its beginning in Act One, it's in the middle that a subplot is most useful as a way to offer variety and sustain interest.

Usually there is a contrast between the main plot and the subplot. If the main plot is serious, a subplot may provide comic relief. If the main plot is full of action, the subplot may concern the protagonist's more sensitive side. Or the subplot may focus on a character who is the opposite of the protagonist, to show another path a life can take.

Sometimes a subplot just sets up a plot device to move the main plot forward. In *Hamlet*, Rosencrantz and Guildenstern are minor characters summoned by the King to investigate Hamlet's strange behavior and then to escort him to England where he will be executed. However, Hamlet turns the tables and arranges for them to be killed instead. Playwright Tom Stoppard cleverly came up with an absurdist variation, *Rosencrantz and Guildenstern Are Dead*, in which they are the major characters, and Hamlet and the others are the minor characters.

In George Bernard Shaw's *Pygmalion*, the main plot concerns the relationship between Henry Higgins and Eliza Doolittle and a subplot is Freddy's wooing of Eliza. Freddy provides a contrast to the arrogant Henry, and Eliza's decision to leave Doolittle and her announcement that she will marry Freddy underscore the theme that you cannot command love, only win it through kindness and genuine caring.

If a subplot seems at first not to be connected to the main plot, it may eventually unite with it in some way and the reader's attention may be held by creating curiosity about how the two will tie up.

The subplot will have its own beginning, middle, and end and be interwoven with the main plot. Often an author will bring the plot to a high point of tension and then switch to the subplot, keeping the reader wondering and reading to find out how that part of the main plot is resolved.

In film and television the subplot sometimes is referred to as the "B" story and there may also be a "C" story, a more minor subplot. Typically in an action film the subplot will be the romance. In a television crime drama, the main plot may concern the murder or other crime and the subplot may be something happening in the personal life of one of the lead characters. Sometimes a subplot is concocted to give the characters who are not so heavily involved in that episode's main plot something to do, to keep the characters alive in the minds of the audience and to keep the actors happy.

FROM ADVICE TO ACTION!

If you are considering having a subplot in your book or screen-play, consider these questions:

- What does it reveal that isn't revealed by the main plot?
- How does it add to our understanding of the main characters?
- Does it vary the pace or tone of the main plot?
- If it seems unrelated, does it eventually come together with the main plot?

20
The end and the theme

The most common mistake writers make with endings, both in novels and in screenplays, is to let the key situation be resolved by coincidence or by forces that have not figured in the story so far, instead of by the actions of the protagonist. That feels like a cheat and it leaves the reader with the impression that they needn't have bothered to read the first two-thirds of the book. Agatha Christie may not have been the best stylist, but one thing she did well in her mysteries was to set up solutions that you don't see coming but that, once you do see them, are totally plausible. The same should be true of the endings of any type of fiction.

The mood of the ending, happy or unhappy, depends on the story you want to tell, but a survey done for World Book Day a few years ago found that readers prefer a happy ending by 50 to 1.

That's not a new development, however. When *Pygmalion* was first produced in London's West End, the producers changed the ending to suggest that Eliza would end up with Professor Higgins rather than Freddy. The producer told the author, George Bernard Shaw, "My ending makes money, you ought to be grateful."

Similar pressure caused Charles Dickens to alter the ending of *Great Expectations*. Originally, after Pip has seen the error of being ashamed of his father and has gone into business overseas, he returns to London and runs into Estella, the girl whom Miss Havisham had trained to be heartless as the old lady's revenge on men. It's not an entirely unhappy ending; it leaves both Pip and Estella having learned and changed for the better. However, it suggests that they will never get together.

Dickens's good friend, novelist Wilkie Collins, felt that the story deserved a happier resolution, so Dickens wrote another version. In the new ending, Pip and Estella meet again at the ruins of Satis House, Miss Havisham's estate:

"We are friends," said I, rising and bending over her, as she rose from the bench. "And will continue friends apart," said Estella. I took her hand in mine, and we went out of the ruined place; and, as the morning mists had risen long ago when I first left the forge, so the evening mists were rising now, and in all the broad expanse of tranquil light they showed to me, I saw no shadow of another parting from her.

Only this ending was published in Dickens's lifetime. Critics including George Bernard Shaw and George Orwell felt that the first ending was better, but Dickens apparently had no qualms about the change. He wrote to a friend that he thought the new version would be more acceptable and was for the best.

The end of the plot is not necessarily the end of the book. Many novels feature some kind of coda, and one of the most powerful is the ending of *The Great Gatsby*:

And as I sat there brooding on the old, unknown world, I thought of Gatsby's wonder when he first picked out the green light at the end of Daisy's dock. He had come a long way to this blue lawn, and his dream must have seemed so close that he could hardly fail to grasp it. He did not know that it was already behind him, somewhere back in that vast obscurity beyond the city, where the dark fields of the republic rolled on under the night.

Gatsby believed in the green light, the orgastic future that year by year recedes before us. It eluded us then, but that's no matter—tomorrow we will run faster, stretch out our arms farther... And one fine morning—

So we beat on, boats against the current, borne back ceaselessly into the past.

The last section generally is not the place to introduce major new characters unless they have been well foreshadowed or represent some kind of culmination of elements that have been covered before. Just as problems in the middle often have their origin in the beginning, problems in the end frequently have their origin in the middle. You can't effectively pay off a story that hasn't been set up well. If you are at a loss for how to end the story, or you get feedback that the ending is implausible, you will have to go back to the middle and make adjustments there.

One of the most satisfying aspects of a good ending is that it gives us the feeling that we have completed a journey and ended up where we started, although with greater understanding. This is a component of many examples of the hero's journey—the hero returns home, having gained the prize, and in the process changed for the better. In fact, that change may be the real prize and the treasure merely a way to get him to undertake the journey in the first place.

Let's see how that is reflected in the way that Conrad constructed the ending of *Lord Jim*.

Lord Jim: The ending

After Marlow leaves Jim for the last time, the narrative returns to the omniscient viewpoint with which it started. Two years later, one of the people who had been on the veranda listening to Marlow's tale gets a package from him that includes a letter telling what happened after he left Jim, as well as something Jim had started to write, and a letter to Jim from his father written before Jim took his post on the *Patna*.

Marlow's written narrative tells the rest of the story, as he was able to piece it together: he had visited Jim's employer and found Jewel and Jim's servant there. Jewel felt that Jim betrayed her.

Brown, a latter-day buccaneer, and his men had landed on the island looking for provisions while Jim was away in the interior. They were fired on by the locals and a fight broke out. Brown schemed to get on the Rajah's side and defeat the villagers, but then to betray the Rajah as well. He has enlisted Jim's enemy, Cornelius, to help him.

Jim returns and meets Brown. He seems to find in Brown a distressing picture of who he might have become, and something Brown says reminds Jim of his greatest moment of shame. Jim says he will give Brown and his men clear passage. However, Brown kills the local leader's son and Jim is discredited. He could escape with Jewel and his servant, but instead chooses to stay, knowing what will happen—the local leader shoots him. The story ends with a very brief view of Stein, the man who had given Jim the position on the island, old and approaching death, and Jewel, mute and broken.

Conrad's method

Surprisingly, none of the people who listen to Marlow's tale press him to reveal whatever happened to Jim; they leave with the story incomplete. Conrad tries to explain this at the beginning of Chapter 36:

> With these words Marlow had ended his narrative, and his audience had broken up forthwith, under his abstract, pensive gaze. Men drifted off the veranda in pairs or alone without loss of time, without offering a remark, as if the last image of that incomplete story, its incompleteness itself, and the very tone of the speaker, had made discussion vain and comment impossible.

With all due respect to the great man, this does sound a bit suspicious: these people have spent a very long time listening to the story and yet not one asks how it ends. One might be justified in guessing that their state of stunned silence owed more to the author's desire to tell the story a certain way than to a plausible illustration of human nature.

The concluding chapters of the novel echo the opening ones in that in both there is a mystery: in the first section it is what really happened to the *Patna*, in the last what happened to Jim after Marlow left. It also returns to the point of view that starts the novel, another example of bringing a story full circle.

One could make the case that Brown appears rather late in the story, but he is merely a catalyst for the forces that were already in place. The fact that Jim felt Brown was a kind of shattered mirror version of himself shows that Jim will never be able to escape his nature and his previous acts.

The plot is complete, but the novel leaves the reader with a lot to think about in terms of fate, choice, the nature of courage, illusions, and other complex facets of our lives.

FROM ADVICE TO ACTION!

When you construct your ending, ask yourself:

- Is this ending logical, perhaps even inevitable, given what has gone before?
- Did it come from the actions and choices of the protagonist, rather than from coincidence?
- Does it also wrap up the subplots?
- Did it bring together the main plot and the subplots? (Not essential, but desirable.)
- Does it leave the reader with something to think about?

About the theme

When we have finished reading a book we may think about its theme. By theme, I mean what the story is really about. On one level *Moby-Dick* is about a man trying to kill a whale, but that plot is used to explore a lot more, including the price of obsession. As we've seen, *Lord Jim* explores the themes of romantic illusions and harsh reality, fate, and what it means to be a hero or a coward.

It may emerge that although your plots vary, your stories consistently exemplify the pointlessness of trying to avoid your fate, or the inherent darkness of the human soul, or the essential wonder of being human (probably not all of those at once).

There are people who will tell you that you should know your theme in advance. Lajos Egri, who wrote the influential text *The Art of Dramatic Writing*, was one of them. He believed that before you write you should have what he called a premise, like "Jealousy results in tragedy," or "Pride results in downfall."

In my view, starting with a premise like that tends to lead to sermons, not great novels or screenplays. In fact, writers, including very good ones, sometimes are the last to know the theme of their work. They write what they are passionate about, they tell stories they feel they have to tell, and only later do they realize the deeper levels of what they've created.

Flannery O'Connor wrote:

> People have a habit of saying "What is the theme of your story?" and they expect you to give them a statement: "The theme of my story is the economic pressure of the machine on the middle class"—or some such absurdity. And when they've got a statement like that, they go off happy and feel it is no longer necessary to read the story… But for the fiction writer himself the whole story is the meaning, because it is an experience, not an abstraction.

Write a story with heart and soul and it will have a theme, whether you know it or not, and readers will absorb it and may well talk about it, but only the ones taking literature classes will feel compelled to analyze it.

Trying to prove a premise rather than letting it emerge sounds like trying to turn a novel into an instrument of the intellect and that's not the point, as Conrad pointed out poetically:

> But the artist appeals to that part of our being which is not dependent on wisdom: to that in us which is a gift and not

an acquisition—and, therefore, more permanently enduring. He speaks to our capacity for delight and wonder, to the
sense of mystery surrounding our lives; to our sense of pity,
and beauty, and pain; to the latent feeling of fellowship with
all creation—and to the subtle but invincible, conviction of
solidarity that knits together the loneliness of innumerable
hearts: to the solidarity in dreams, in joy, in sorrow, in aspi-
rations, in illusions, in hope, in fear, which binds men to
each other, which binds together all humanity—the dead to
the living and the living to the unborn.

Furthermore, should the theme or premise be too obvious, it can
kill the book, according to DH Lawrence:

Once a book is fathomed, once it is known, and its meaning
is fixed or established, it is dead. A book only lives while it
has power to move us, and move us differently; so long as we
find it different every time we read it.

FROM ADVICE TO ACTION!

Regarding your theme, ask yourself:

- Has the theme been "buried" deeply enough in the action
  so that it doesn't come across as a sermon?
- Would someone be able to enjoy the story just at the level
  of the plot, without necessarily discerning the theme?
- Have you left some ambiguity so that the story can be
  enjoyed even by someone who disagrees with your take on
  the theme?

21

Rewriting

Roald Dahl said, "Good writing is essentially rewriting." While there are a few writers who say they do very little rewriting, most of us find it necessary. Some enjoy the process, others compare it to having a root canal operation.

Let's start with an overview of the process as described by author and professor Jacques Barzun:

> Rewriting is called revision in the literary and publishing trade because it springs from re-viewing, that is to say, looking at your copy again—and again and again. When you have learned to look at your own words with critical detachment, you will find that rereading a piece five or six times in a row will each time bring to light fresh spots of trouble. The trouble is sometimes elementary: you wonder how you can have written it as a pronoun referring to a plural subject. The slip is easily corrected. At other times you have written yourself into a corner, the exit from which is not at once apparent. Your words down there seem to preclude the necessary repairs up here—because of repetition, syntax, logic, or some other obstacle. Nothing comes to mind as reconciling sense with sound and with clarity in both places. In such a fix you may have to start farther back and pursue a different line altogether. The sharper your judgment, the more trouble you will find. That is why exacting writers are known to have rewritten a famous paragraph or chapter six or seven times. It then looked right to them, because every demand of their art had been met, every flaw removed, down to the slightest.

A little rhyme from Jonathan Swift suggests that the process is not without stress:

Blot out, correct, insert, refine
Enlarge, diminish, interline;
Be mindful, when invention fails,
To scratch your head, and bite your nails.

A roll call of rewriters

If you are a writer who sometimes despairs of their first drafts and can't imagine not doing several drafts, you are in good company. Here are a few of your compatriots and their statements:

I have never thought of myself as a good writer... But I'm one of the world's great rewriters. (James Michener)

JOYCE CAROL OATES (b 1938)

Oates's books include *Black Water, What I Lived For,* and *Blonde.* Her favorite book as a child was *Alice's Adventures in Wonderland,* and she considers it to be the greatest influence on her writing. While a student at Syracuse University she wrote a series of novels, each of which she discarded as soon as she had finished it.

The pleasure is the rewriting: The first sentence can't be written until the final sentence is written. This is a koan-like statement, and I don't mean to sound needlessly obscure or mysterious, but it's simply true. The completion of any work automatically necessitates its revisioning. (Joyce Carol Oates)

When I say writing, O believe me, it is rewriting that I have chiefly in mind. (Robert Louis Stevenson)

For some writers, like Susan Sontag, it's the prospect of rewriting that takes some of the pressure off writing the first draft:

although this, the rewriting—and the rereading—sound like effort, they are actually the most pleasurable parts of writing. Sometimes the only pleasurable parts. Setting out to write, if you have the idea of "literature" in your head, is formidable, intimidating. A plunge in an icy lake. Then comes the warm part: when you already have something to work with, upgrade, edit.

Hemingway built a system for rewriting via his use of his writing tools:

After you learn to write your whole object is to convey every-thing, every sensation, sight, feeling, place and emotion to the reader. To do this you have to work over what you write. If you write with a pencil you get three different sights at it to see if the reader is getting what you want him to. First when you read it over; then when it is typed you get another chance to improve it, and again in the proof. Writing it first in pencil gives you one-third more chance to improve it. That is .333 which is a damned good average for a hitter. It also keeps it fluid longer so that you can better it easier.

As we have seen in some of the earlier chapters, writers vary greatly in how they edit. Some bash out a first draft as quickly as possible and then start rewriting; others, like Joyce Carol Oates, rewrite as they go along:

My method is one of continuous revision. While writing a long novel, every day I loop back to earlier sections to rewrite, in order to maintain a consistent, fluid voice. When I write the final two or three chapters of a novel, I write them simultaneously with the rewriting of the opening, so that, ideally at least, the novel is like a river uniformly flow-ing, each passage concurrent with all the others.

A needed break

One of the challenges of rewriting is the difficulty of being objec-tive about one's own work. Taking some time away from the project and coming back to it with a fresh eye is helpful, as EB White described:

> When I finished Charlotte's Web, I put it away, feeling that something was wrong. The story had taken me two years to write, working on and off, but I was in no particular hurry. I took another year to rewrite it, and it was a year well spent. If I write something and feel doubtful about it, I soak it away. The passage of time can be a help in evaluating it.

Hemingway liked to do the same, as he related in a letter to his editor and friend, Maxwell Perkins:

> Would like to finish this [A Farewell to Arms] down here if possible, put it away for a couple or three months and then rewrite it. The re-writing doesn't take more than six weeks or two months once it is done. But it is pretty important for me to let it cool off well before re-writing.

An outside eye

Often it falls to others to notice our mistakes, as Mark Twain described:

> And then there is that other thing: when you think you are reading proof, whereas you are merely reading your own mind; your statement of the thing is full of holes and vacancies but you don't know it, because you are filling them from your mind as you go along. Sometimes—but not often enough—the printer's proof-reader saves you—and offends you—with this cold sign in the margin: and you search the passage and find that the insulter is right—it doesn't say what you thought it did: the gas-fixtures are there, but you didn't light the jets.

Some authors have colleagues on whom they rely for feedback. Hemingway liked to have Gertrude Stein critique his work. The online Hemingway Resource Center notes:

> She urged him to give up journalism completely and con-centrate on his writing, explaining to him about the rhythm of prose and the power of the repetition of words. When she was dissatisfied with some of his early work, she made him start over and to concentrate more intensely. Hemingway felt so indebted to her that he made her the godmother of his first son and had some of her work published in one of the little magazines he was helping to edit.

Another of Hemingway's mentors was F Scott Fitzgerald. The website notes:

> Fitzgerald did some really important things for Hemingway's career... he introduced Hemingway to his publisher, Scribners, and helped in the editing of his first major novel The Sun Also Rises, which was published to great critical acclaim.

Of course, we can't all count on getting a stellar personal mentor, but these days the ability to gain feedback on your writing online has made it much easier to obtain external input before you rewrite.

F SCOTT FITZGERALD (1896–1940)

Fitzgerald is known for *The Great Gatsby*, *This Side of Paradise*, and *The Beautiful and the Damned*. He was the first to describe the 1920s as "The Jazz Age." His turbulent relationship with his wife, Zelda, has been depicted in movies and musicals in both America and Japan.

Murder your darlings

Another problem is that we can become fond of certain passages that may be very good on their own, but not in the context of the greater story. I encountered something similar while on a paint-ing holiday in Italy some years ago. I had painted a building and done a superb job on the doorway, but the rest of the building wasn't up to the same level. Our painting teacher came along and asked whether I minded if she made a small change. I said no, assuming that with a deft stroke or three she would bring up the level of the rest of the painting. Instead, to my initial horror, she dipped the brush in white paint and painted out my brilliant doorway. She was right. When I redid it, the doorway was not as good, but the painting was better.

Samuel Johnson's prescription for this situation:

> Read over your compositions and, when you meet a passage which you think is particularly fine, strike it out.

This is also what Sir Arthur Quiller-Couch meant when he suggested that you "murder your darlings."

Roddy Doyle offers further advice on what to cut:

> Clutter. Signposts. Bad writing. The hardest thing to cut is a good piece of writing that actually serves no real purpose in the novel or story. It always seems a shame, but I always feel somehow virtuous when I do it.

In screenwriting you have free rein until someone buys the script, but then they may ask you to rewrite it to fit a particular star, or to make the film easier to produce on a budget, or to accommodate the input of a director or producer. At this point you become a writer for hire and although you can argue against any changes you don't find acceptable, if the producer wants those changes he or she can fire you and hire someone else to make them. Indeed, in Hollywood it's usual for a script to be rewritten by several writers other than the original ones.

One tip for dealing with suggestions you find unacceptable is to discover what the person thinks the problem is that they are solving with the changes they are suggesting. Often they may be right that there is a problem, but their solution is not a good one.

If you can come up with a better one they will accept it and you will be able to live with the changes.

FROM ADVICE TO ACTION!

Someone said, "In life there are no second chances." Whether or not that's true, fortunately in writing there are second, third, and fourth chances to improve your first pass at your book or screenplay.

ACTION: If you are a planner, now compare what you've written to what you outlined and determine what needs to change. If you write more spontaneously, this will be the time to determine whether your structure needs to be tightened up. It's a good idea to start with the big questions that relate to your story's structure:

- Does the story grab the reader early enough?
- Do the characters come to life?
- Does the story develop logically—or at least plausibly?
- Does the story adhere to your central theme? (And if you wrote without one in mind, has one emerged?)
- Does the story maintain enough tension throughout, but also with enough variation in mood to give the reader some breaks?
- Will the ending satisfy the reader?

It can be a good idea to get some trusted colleagues to read your work and ask them these questions. Once you've fixed the big things, you can consider the more detailed ones that address the style of the book. That's the topic we look at in the next section.

PART IV
FINDING YOUR STYLE

Style is what distinguishes one author's writing from another's. As Diane Lefer notes, it comes from within:

> I won't deny that if you hope to be a popular author and even make money at it, you probably stand a better chance if you can write like Stephen King rather than Virginia Woolf. But I don't believe that's a matter of choice. Most writers create out of a personal vision; we each have a particular way of seeing the world.

It's also an integral part of the writing. EB White said:

> Young writers often suppose that style is a garnish for the meat of prose, a sauce by which a dull dish is made palatable. Style has no such separate entity; it is nondetachable, unfilterable.

A closer look reveals that indeed there are some elements of style on which many of the master writers agree; we explore these in this section.

22

Clarity, simplicity

Some writers feel that either you have a distinctive style or you don't. However, Robert Louis Stevenson believed that style is something you can learn, at least up to a point:

Style is the invariable mark of any master; and for the student who does not aspire so high as to be numbered with the giants, it is still the one quality in which he may improve himself at will. Passion, wisdom, creative force, the power of mystery or colour, are allotted in the hour of birth, and can be neither learned nor simulated. But the just and dexterous use of what qualities we have, the proportion of one part to another and to the whole, the elision of the useless, the accentuation of the important, and the preservation of a uniform character from end to end—these, which taken together constitute technical perfection, are to some degree within the reach of industry and intellectual courage. What to put in and what to leave out; whether some particular fact may be organically necessary or purely ornamental; whether, if it be purely ornamental, it may not weaken or obscure the general design; and finally, whether, if we decide to use it, we should do so grossly and notably, or in some conventional disguise: are questions of plastic style continually rearising.

Simplicity

Simplicity is one of the elements of style on which many authors are agreed. Mark Twain complimented a fellow writer in these terms:

I notice that you use plain, simple language, short words and brief sentences. That is the way to write English—it is the modern way and the best way. Stick to it; don't let fluff and flowers and verbosity creep in.

Willa Cather compared the appeal of simplicity in writing and painting:

Art, it seems to me, should simplify. That, indeed, is very nearly the whole of the higher artistic process; finding what conventions of form and what detail one can do without and yet preserve the spirit of the whole—so that all that one has suppressed and cut away is there to the reader's conscious-ness as much as if it were in type on the page. Millet had done hundreds of sketches of peasants sowing grain, some of them very complicated and interesting, but when he came to paint the spirit of them all into one picture, The Sower, the composition is so simple that it seems inevitable. All the discarded sketches that went before made the picture what it finally became, and the process was all the time one of simplifying, of sacrificing many conceptions good in them-selves for one that was better and more universal.

Metamorphosis

Notice in this opening of Kafka's novel *Metamorphosis* how sim-ple and straightforward are the descriptions of a very bizarre situation.

One morning, when Gregor Samsa woke from troubled dreams, he found himself transformed in his bed into a hor-rible vermin. He lay on his armour-like back, and if he lifted his head a little he could see his brown belly, slightly domed and divided by arches into stiff sections. The bedding was hardly able to cover it and seemed ready to slide off any moment. *His many legs, pitifully thin compared with the size of the rest of him, waved about helplessly as he looked.*

"What's happened to me?" he thought. It wasn't a dream. His room, a proper human room although a little too small, lay peacefully between its four familiar walls. A collection of textile samples lay spread out on the table—Samsa was a travelling salesman—and above it there hung a picture that he had recently cut out of an illustrated magazine and housed in a nice, gilded frame. It showed a lady fitted out with a fur hat and fur boa who sat upright, raising a heavy fur muff that covered the whole of her lower arm towards the viewer.

Gregor then turned to look out the window at the dull weather. Drops of rain could be heard hitting the pane, which made him feel quite sad. "How about if I sleep a little bit longer and forget all this nonsense," he thought, but that was something he was unable to do because he was used to sleeping on his right, and in his present state couldn't get into that position. However hard he threw himself onto his right, he always rolled back to where he was. He must have tried it a hundred times, shut his eyes so that he wouldn't have to look at the floundering legs, and only stopped when he began to feel a mild, dull pain there that he had never felt before.

More recently, Hemingway's pattern of short declarative sentences inspired a raft of imitators to the point where his own prose now sometimes seems a parody of itself. Raymond Carver took this style and made it his own. For instance, take this excerpt from the short story "Why Don't You Dance?" from the collection *What We Talk About When We Talk About Love*:

The man came down the sidewalk with a sack from the market. He had sandwiches, beer, whiskey. He saw the car in the driveway and the girl on the bed. He saw the television set going and the boy on the porch.

"Hello," the man said to the girl. "You found the bed. That's good."

"Hello," the girl said, and got up. "I was just trying it out." She patted the bed. 'It's a pretty good bed."

That's not to say that simplicity and clarity require a totally sparse style. Graham Greene's style was more mainstream, but still admired for its efficiency. The notoriously waspish Evelyn Waugh considered this trait a negative, saying that Greene's was "not a specific literary style at all." However, most critics and millions of readers disagreed. To give you a sample, this is the opening of Greene's novel *The Comedians*, which is set in Haiti:

When I think of all the grey memorials erected in London to equestrian generals, the heroes of old colonial wars, and to frock-coated politicians who are even more deeply forgotten, I can find no reason to mock the modest stone that commemorates Jones on the far side of the international road which he failed to cross in a country far from home, though I am not to this day absolutely sure of where, geographically speaking, Jones's home lay. At least he paid for the monument—however unwillingly—with his life, while the generals as a rule come home safe and paid, if at all, with the blood of their men, and as for the politicians—who cares for dead politicians sufficiently to remember with what issues they were identified?

Greene could be waspish as well, but on Waugh's death credited him with being the best writer of their generation. Critic Clive James called Waugh's style "unaffectedly elegant." Here is a sample, the opening of *Brideshead Revisited*:

"I have been here before," I said; I had been there before; first with Sebastian more than twenty years ago on a cloudless day in June, when the ditches were white with fool's-parsley and meadowsweet and the air heavy with all the scents of summer;

it was a day of peculiar splendour, such as our climate affords once or twice a year, when leaf and flower and bird and sun-lit stone and shadow seem all to proclaim the glory of God; and though I had been there so often, in so many moods, it was to that first visit that my heart returned on this, my latest.

The point is that you have wide stylistic leeway without losing the qualities of simplicity and clarity.

The need for these qualities is even more true in screenplays. Agents, producers, and others who read screenplays are used to relatively brief narrative descriptions. That doesn't mean that they can't have a style. For instance, here is a description from the script *Midnight Run*, by George Gallo:

```
INT. OLDSMOBILE — NIGHT
The driver taps a Camel cigarette. Raises it to
his lips. Lights it with his Zippo. The flame
reveals the face of JACK WALSH. Strong. Haggard. A
killer stare. Pressure-cooker of a man. Always
about to explode. The flame dances. Blue smoke
swirls. The flame fades.
```

Naturally, he doesn't include so many details throughout the script, but this is our first view of Walsh, and Gallo is establishing a film-noir feeling for this character.

By way of contrast, here is how screenwriter Charles Burnett introduces his character Gideon, in *To Sleep with Anger*:

```
INT. ROOM — DAY
GIDEON, a strong but elderly black man, is sitting
at a table, on which is a large bowl of fruit. A
crocheted tablecloth hangs over its side. Gideon
is dressed in a white suit and wears a pair of
well-polished wingtip shoes. His hat almost covers
his eyes, which are two points of greenish coals.
The fruit in the bowl is engulfed in flames.
```

In each case, the tone of the description fits the tone of the overall story and, while retaining clarity, manages to suggest the individual author's style.

FROM ADVICE TO ACTION!

ACTION: When you review a piece of your own writing, among the factors to assess are whether you're making clear:

- Where the action is taking place.
- When it's taking place.
- Who is talking. Unattributed dialogue can be confusing, so can characters with very similar names or too many characters (with regard to the latter, readers make allowances for the Russian masters that they won't necessarily make for you).

This doesn't mean you have to spell out everything, but you do have to give the reader enough clues to figure these elements out.

There is a danger that things that seem totally clear to you may be confusing to readers. That's why it's important to have a trusted colleague or friend who will give you feedback. This doesn't have to be a fellow writer. In fact, sometimes it's better if it's not, because a writer tends to try to tell you how to fix things they perceive to be wrong, when often all they mean is that they'd write it differently. A more typical reader will often give you straightforward feedback, especially if there are aspects of the story that they don't follow or understand.

23

Conciseness

Chekhov had strong opinions on conciseness (as on many other things):

I think descriptions of nature should be very short and always be à propos. Commonplaces like "The setting sun, sinking into the waves of the darkening sea, cast its purple gold rays, etc.," "Swallows, flitting over the surface of the water, twittered gaily"—eliminate such commonplaces. You have to choose small details in describing nature, grouping them in such a way that if you close your eyes after reading it you can picture the whole thing. For example, you'll get a picture of a moonlit night if you write that on the dam of the mill a piece of broken bottle flashed like a bright star and the black shadow of a dog or a wolf rolled by like a ball, etc.

He criticized Maxim Gorky on this issue:

I will begin with what in my opinion is your lack of restraint. You are like a spectator in a theatre who expresses his enthusiasm so unrestrainedly that he prevents himself and others from hearing. That lack of restraint is particularly noticeable in the descriptions of nature with which you interrupt dialogues; when one reads them, these descriptions, one wishes they were more compact, shorter, say two or three lines.

Mark Twain states it—well, concisely:

A successful book is not made of what is in it, but of what is left out of it.

Ernest Hemingway made a distinction about what to leave out:

> *If a writer of prose knows enough about what he is writing about he may omit things that he knows and the reader, if the writer is writing truly enough, will have a feeling of those things as strongly as though the writer had stated them. The dignity of movement of an ice-berg is due to only one-eighth of it being above water. A writer who omits things because he does not know them only makes hollow places in his writing.*

Specifically, one thing to cut is suggested by EL Doctorow:

> *Writers today derive all sorts of effects from scanting the interstitial explanations or transitions that get their story from one character to another, or their characters from one place to another, or from yesterday to next year.*

EL DOCTOROW (b 1931)
Doctorow novels include *Ragtime*, *The Book of Daniel*, and *The March*. His first novel, *Welcome to Hard Times*, was inspired by the many Westerns he read while working for a film studio. He served briefly in the US Army during the occupation of Germany.

Not everyone agrees. Stanley Elkin says:

> *I believe that more is more. I believe that less is less, fat FAT, thin thin, and enough enough. There's a famous exchange between Fitzgerald and Thomas Wolfe in which Fitzgerald criticizes Wolfe for one of his novels. Fitzgerald tells him that Flaubert believed in the mot précis and that there are two kinds of writers—the putter-inners and the taker-outers. Wolfe, who probably was not as good a writer as Fitzgerald but evidently wrote a better letter, said, "Flaubert me no Flauberts. Shakespeare was a putter-inner, Melville was a putter-inner." I can't remember who else was a putter-inner, but I'd rather be a putter-inner than a taker-outer.*

Since Chekhov's advice plays a large role in this chapter, it seems appropriate to look at the skillful and elegant way he used descriptions to set the scene in this opening of his short story "The Cook's Wedding." Notice that he tells us not only what's happening but also the effect it is having on various participants:

> Grisha, a fat, solemn little person of seven, was standing by the kitchen door listening and peeping through the keyhole. In the kitchen something extraordinary, and in his opinion never seen before, was taking place. A big, thick-set, red-haired peasant, with a beard, and a drop of perspiration on his nose, wearing a cabman's full coat, was sitting at the kitchen table on which they chopped the meat and sliced the onions. He was balancing a saucer on the five fingers of his right hand and drinking tea out of it, and crunching sugar so loudly that it sent a shiver down Grisha's back. Aksinya Stepanovna, the old nurse, was sitting on the dirty stool facing him, and she, too, was drinking tea. Her face was grave, though at the same time it beamed with a kind of triumph. Pelageya, the cook, was busy at the stove, and was apparently trying to hide her face. And on her face Grisha saw a regular illumination: it was burning and shifting through every shade of colour, beginning with a crimson purple and ending with a deathly white. She was continually catching hold of knives, forks, bits of wood, and rags with trembling hands, moving, grumbling to herself, making a clatter, but in reality doing nothing. She did not once glance at the table at which they were drinking tea, and to the questions put to her by the nurse she gave jerky, sullen answers without turning her face.

There are lots of details, such as the drop of perspiration on the nose, that help us to create a vivid mental picture, yet we never feel overloaded with description. Chekhov picks out the most telling images to give us a sense of the emotions swirling in this kitchen.

Go short on description

There's no doubt that tastes have changed in terms of the amount of description that novels feature.

EL Doctorow ascribes this partly to the influence of films:

> *The effect of a hundred years of filmmaking on the practice of literature has been considerable. As more than one critic has noted, today's novelists tend not to write exposition as fully as novelists of the nineteenth century. Where the first chapter of Stendahl's Red and the Black (1830) is given over to the leisurely description of a provincial French town, its topographic features, the basis of its economy, the person of its Mayor, the Mayor's mansion, the mansion's terraced gardens and so on, Faulkner's Sanctuary (1931) begins this way: "From beyond the screen of bushes which surrounded the spring, Popeye watched the man drinking."... The twentieth-century novel minimizes discourse that dwells on settings, characters' CVs and the like. The writer finds it preferable to incorporate all necessary information in the action, to carry it along in the current of the narrative, as is done in movies.*

James Patterson, one of the world's bestselling authors, took this tendency to heart. He told *Success* magazine:

> *I leave out a lot of detail. Like if you were telling me a story—and we were any good at it—we wouldn't go on and on and on with the kind of detail that is in a lot of non-fiction and even a lot of fiction... So my fiction tends not to have all that in it, and the plots really tumble forward.*

In this regard Chekhov was ahead of his time. The short excerpt opposite could just as easily have been the description of the series of shots a film director would choose in order to bring the audience into that kitchen and its fraught atmosphere.

Are you joining the story at the right time?

It's helpful to take a giant step back to make sure that you're not entering the story too early. If you're writing about a blind date, it might make sense to show each character preparing, talking to their friends about the date, arriving at the restaurant, looking around, perhaps initially approaching the wrong person. However, it could have much greater dramatic impact if your story starts with two strangers sitting across a restaurant table from each other, not knowing what to say. Who they are and why they are there will come out naturally through the interaction.

In film and theater, the rule is to enter the scene as late as possible, and that applies to books and short stories as well.

FROM ADVICE TO ACTION!

As you've seen, conciseness is not about sentence length or the length of the book itself, it's about the ability to discern and include only the essential, whether that's description, action, or dialogue.

ACTION: First check whether you are entering the story as late as possible. Experiment with starting later than you had in mind. What do you lose? What do you gain?

One you have a first draft, consider each sentence in terms of its function—for instance, revealing character, moving the plot along, or introducing a new story strand. Ask yourself:

- What does it achieve?
- Is it necessary?
- Does it create the emotional response you want in the reader?
- Is there a way to combine two or more into one? For instance, if a line of dialogue clearly reveals that the character is angry, do you also need to describe him as such?

24
It's in the details

Show, don't tell, is one of the standard directives that writing teachers impart. CS Lewis advised:

> Don't say it was "delightful"; make us say "delightful" when we've read the description. You see, all those words (horrifying, wonderful, hideous, exquisite) are only like saying to your readers "Please will you do my job for me?"

CS LEWIS (1898–1963)
Lewis is best known for *The Chronicles of Narnia*, *The Screwtape Letters*, and *The Space Trilogy*. He was close friends with JRR Tolkein, with whom he taught at Oxford University. Though he is known as a Christian novelist, he was an atheist and occultist in his teens and 20s.

Similarly, Mark Twain instructed:

> Don't say the old lady screamed—bring her on and let her scream.

One more, from Chekhov:

> Don't tell me the moon is shining; show me the glint of light on broken glass.

That quote points to the key to showing instead of telling: selecting vivid, specific details.

Gabriel García Márquez wrote:

> That's a journalistic trick that you can also apply to literature. For example, if you say that there are elephants flying in the sky, people are not going to believe you. But if you say that there are four hundred and twenty-five elephants flying in the sky, people will probably believe you. One Hundred Years of Solitude is full of that sort of thing.

Chekhov pointed out:

> In the realm of psychology you also need details. God pre-
> serve you from commonplaces. Best of all, shun all descrip-
> tions of the characters' spiritual state. You must try to have
> that state emerge clearly from their actions. Don't try for too
> many characters. The center of gravity should reside in two:
> he and she.

Let's see how Jane Austen used details in her description of
Catherine Morland in *Northanger Abbey*. It's more description
than we might encounter on the introduction of a character in a
modern novel, but it's done with such wry humor and deftness
that it doesn't wear out its welcome.

Northanger Abbey

> *A family of ten children will be always called a fine family,*
> *where there are heads and arms and legs enough for the*
> *number; but the Morlands had little other right to the word,*
> *for they were in general very plain, and Catherine, for many*
> *years of her life, as plain as any. She had a thin awkward fig-*
> *ure, a sallow skin without colour, dark lank hair, and strong*
> *features—so much for her person; and not less unpropitious*
> *for heroism seemed her mind. She was fond of all boy's*
> *plays, and greatly preferred cricket not merely to dolls, but*
> *to the more heroic enjoyments of infancy, nursing a dor-*
> *mouse, feeding a canary-bird, or watering a rose-bush.*
> [Notice the specific activities listed, that are indicative of
> the interests of a sensitive country girl—and play no role in
> the life of the girl being described] *Indeed she had no taste*
> *for a garden; and if she gathered flowers at all, it was chiefly*
> *for the pleasure of mischief—at least so it was conjectured*
> *from her always preferring those which she was forbidden to*
> *take. Such were her propensities—her abilities were quite as*

extraordinary. [You'll notice a fair amount of sarcasm in this excerpt] *She never could learn or understand anything before she was taught; and sometimes not even then, for she was often inattentive, and occasionally stupid. Her mother was three months in teaching her only to repeat the "Beggar's Petition"; and after all, her next sister, Sally, could say it better than she did. Not that Catherine was always stupid—by no means; she learnt the fable of "The Hare and Many Friends" as quickly as any girl in England. Her mother wished her to learn music; and Catherine was sure she should like it, for she was very fond of tinkling the keys of the old forlorn spinnet; so, at eight years old she began. She learnt a year, and could not bear it; and Mrs. Morland, who did not insist on her daughters being accomplished in spite of incapacity or distaste, allowed her to leave off. The day which dismissed the music-master was one of the happiest of Catherine's life. Her taste for drawing was not superior; though whenever she could obtain the outside of a letter from her mother or seize upon any other odd piece of paper, she did what she could in that way, by drawing houses and trees, hens and chickens, all very much like one another. Writing and accounts she was taught by her father; French by her mother: her proficiency in either was not remarkable, and she shirked her lessons in both whenever she could.* [The delicacy with which the author destroys this character is delicious: we might consider it a hatchet job done with a scalpel] *What a strange, unaccountable character!—for with all these symptoms of profligacy at ten years old, she had neither a bad heart nor a bad temper, was seldom stubborn, scarcely ever quarrelsome, and very kind to the little ones, with few interruptions of tyranny; she was moreover noisy and wild, hated confinement and cleanliness, and loved nothing so well in the world as rolling down the green slope at the back of the house.*

Such was Catherine Morland at ten. At fifteen, appearances were mending; she began to curl her hair and

long for balls; her complexion improved, her features were
softened by plumpness and colour, her eyes gained more
animation, and her figure more consequence. [Now our
hopes rise for this poor girl—we imagine her features
improving one by one, things are looking up!] *Her love of*
dirt gave way to an inclination for finery, and she grew clean
as she grew smart; she had now the pleasure of sometimes
hearing her father and mother remark on her personal
improvement. "Catherine grows quite a good-looking girl—
she is almost pretty today," were words which caught her
ears now and then; and how welcome were the sounds! To
look almost pretty is an acquisition of higher delight to a girl
who has been looking plain the first fifteen years of her life
than a beauty from her cradle can ever receive. [We are
brought back down to a less hopeful level, and a girl who
delights in being called almost pretty gains our sympathy, no
matter how untalented or uneducable she may be]

Austen achieves her effect by being specific. It would have been
easy to say that Catherine had no talent for drawing, but she tells
us where Catherine gets the paper and what she tries to draw,
and only then mentions that her hens and her houses looked
pretty much alike. The same is true of her other shortcomings.
These specifics make amusing a description that otherwise could
have been brutal.

This extract is also a good example of covering a long sweep
of time, summarizing without losing the power of the specific.
We never feel that we're being rushed through the decade.

Flannery O'Connor, author of the dark comic classic *Wise
Blood*, noted:

The beginning of human knowledge is through the senses,
and you cannot appeal to the senses through abstractions. It
is a good deal easier for most people to state an abstract idea
than to describe and thus re-create some object that they
actually see. But the world of the fiction writer is full of mat-

ter, and this is what the beginning fiction writers are very loath to create. They are concerned primarily with unfleshed ideas and emotions. They are apt to be reformers and to want to write because they are possessed not by a story but by the bare bones of some abstract notion. They are conscious of problems, of questions and issues, not of the texture of existence, of case histories and of everything that has a sociological smack, instead of with all those concrete details that make actual the mystery of our position on earth.

Metaphors and similes

Newer writers often are drawn to similes, comparing two things by saying one was like the other, and metaphors, vivid comparisons not meant to be taken literally. Many are found in literature, such as:

A hot wind was blowing around my head, the strands of my hair lifting and swirling in it, like ink spilled in water. (Margaret Atwood, The Blind Assassin)

Elderly ladies leaning on their canes listed toward me like towers of Pisa. (Vladimir Nabokov, Lolita)

But soft, what light through yonder window breaks? It is the east, and Juliet is the sun. (William Shakespeare, Romeo and Juliet)

All the world's a stage, and all the men and women merely players. (William Shakespeare, As You Like It)

While a well-chosen simile or metaphor can be powerful, using too many of them or reaching too far for a comparison can sound ridiculous or break the reading trance.

Jorge Luis Borges said:

When I was a young man I was always hunting for new metaphors. Then I found out that really good metaphors are always the same. I mean you compare time to a road, death to sleeping, life to dreaming, and those are the great metaphors in literature because they correspond to something essential. If you invent metaphors, they are apt to be surprising during the fraction of a second, but they strike no deep emotion whatever… I think that's better than the idea of shocking people, than finding connections between things that have never been connected before, because there is no real connection.

Something to avoid, unless you're using it for comic effect, is a mixed metaphor; that is, one that draws on two different elements of comparison in the same phrase. Examples are "a heart as big as gold," or "I could hear the handwriting on the wall."

If you review the excerpts of great books I've featured so far, you'll notice that the authors use similes and metaphors sparingly. Far more often they employ straightforward descriptions of precise details. Their example suggests that we should do the same.

In films the maxim "show don't tell" is even more important, because generally you don't have the option of telling what the character is thinking and you need to find ways to show it. Much of the responsibility will ultimately fall on the director and actor, of course, but you have to give them the blueprint that allows them to make their contribution.

However, there's a distinction between a reading script and a shooting script, and sometimes you will choose to put in directions to make a script easier to read. This will not endear you to the actors, however. One of my first script-doctoring jobs was on the movie *Mannequin,* and because it was being read piecemeal by the producer, I attached quite a few parentheticals, like (angrily), to the dialogue so that he could easily imagine what I had in mind. On the first day of the cast's read-through, Kim Cattrall used a big black marker to strike all of these out.

Someone asked what she was doing. Glaring at me, she said, "Crossing out all the places where the writer told me how to act!"

Whatever words you choose, the goal is to make the reader *feel* something. As EL Doctorow said:

> Good writing is supposed to evoke sensation in the reader, not the fact that it's raining, but the feeling of being rained upon.

FROM ADVICE TO ACTION!

ACTION: When reviewing your first draft, make a list of the details you have included about each character and setting. Ask yourself:

- Have you appealed to a variety of senses, describing not only what things look like but also how they sound, smell, and taste?
- Have you selected details beyond the obvious?
- Have you used language that makes the detail come alive?
- Have you used similes and metaphors sparingly but powerfully?
- Have you avoided mixed metaphors?
- Have you selected details that will influence the reader to have the impression you want of the person or object?
- Have you integrated description with action and dialogue rather than putting it into a large lump?

As an exercise, picture a homeless man sleeping in a doorway. Write three descriptions of him, each with a different intention:

- To awaken the reader's sympathy for him.
- To make the reader dislike or feel contempt for him.
- To evoke in the reader a neutral curiosity about him.

You can choose different details for each description, but only drawing from the same image. In other words, don't make him filthy and snoring loudly in one version and clean and issuing gentle sighs in another.

25

The right word and some wrong ones

ark Twain wrote this in an essay admiring the writing of William Dean Howells:

A powerful agent is the right word. Whenever we come upon one of those intensely right words in a book or a newspaper the resulting effect is physical as well as spiritual, and electrically prompt: it tingles exquisitely around through the walls of the mouth and tastes as tart and crisp and good as the autumn-butter that creams the sumac-berry.

Twain's summing up was succinct:

The difference between the right word and the almost right word is the difference between lightning and the lightning bug.

What is the right word? Naturally there is no formula, but these guidelines from George Orwell might help. In his essay, "Politics and the English Language," he wrote:

A scrupulous writer, in every sentence that he writes, will ask himself at least four questions, thus:
> *What am I trying to say?*
> *What words will express it?*
> *What image or idiom will make it clearer?*
> *Is this image fresh enough to have an effect?*
And he will probably ask himself two more:
> *Could I put it more shortly?*
> *Have I said anything that is avoidably ugly?*

One can often be in doubt about the effect of a word or a phrase, and one needs rules that one can rely on when instinct fails. I think the following rules will cover most cases:

Never use a metaphor, simile, or other figure of speech which you are used to seeing in print.

Never use a long word where a short one will do.

If it is possible to cut a word out, always cut it out.

Never use the passive where you can use the active.

Never use a foreign phrase, a scientific word, or a jargon word if you can think of an everyday English equivalent.

Break any of these rules sooner than say anything outright barbarous.

GEORGE ORWELL (1903–50)

Orwell's best-known works are *1984* and *Animal Farm*. He was born Eric Arthur Blair and at Eton his French teacher was Aldous Huxley. Orwell was a volunteer for the Republican side during the Spanish Civil War.

The opening of Orwell's famous novel *1984* is written in language as simple as that prescribed by his advice, but notice the words or phrases (including "the clocks were striking thirteen") that immediately capture our attention and pique our curiosity.

1984

It was a bright cold day in April, and the clocks were striking thirteen. Winston Smith, his chin nuzzled into his breast in an effort to escape the vile wind, slipped quickly through the glass doors of Victory Mansions, though not quickly enough to prevent a swirl of gritty dust from entering along with him.

The hallway smelt of boiled cabbage and old rag mats. At one end of it a coloured poster, too large for indoor display, had been tacked to the wall. It depicted simply an enormous face, more than a metre wide: the face of a man of about forty-five, with a heavy black moustache and *ruggedly handsome features. Winston made for the stairs. It was no use trying the lift. Even at the best of times it was seldom working, and at present the electric current was cut off during daylight hours. It was part of the economy drive in preparation for Hate Week. The flat was seven flights up, and Winston, who was thirty-nine and had a varicose ulcer above his right ankle, went slowly, resting several times on the way. On each landing, opposite the lift-shaft, the poster with the enormous face gazed from the wall. It was one of those pictures which are so contrived that the eyes follow you about when you move. BIG BROTHER IS WATCH-ING YOU, the caption beneath it ran.*

Umberto Eco also has a list of rules, here translated freely by Gio Clairval. As you'll see, they overlap with some of the points already made, but in a most entertaining tongue-in-cheek style:

1   *Avoid alliterations, even if they're manna for morons.*
2   *Don't contribute to the killing of the subjunctive mode, I suggest that the writer use it when necessary.*
3   *Avoid clichés: they're like death warmed over.*
4   *Thou shall express thyself in the simplest of fashions.*
5   *Don't use acronyms & abbreviations etc.*
6   *(Always) remember that parentheses (even when they seem indispensable) interrupt the flow.*
7   *Beware of indigestion... of ellipses.*
8   *Limit the use of inverted commas. Quotes aren't "elegant."*
9   *Never generalize.*
10 *Foreign words aren't bon ton.*
11 *Hold those quotes. Emerson aptly said, "I hate quotes. Tell me only what you know."*
12 *Similes are like catch phrases.*
13 *Don't be repetitious; don't repeat the same thing twice; repeating is superfluous.*
14 *Only twats use swear words.*
15 *Always be somehow specific.*

16 Hyperbole is the most extraordinary of expressive techniques.

17 Don't write one-word sentences. Ever.

18 Beware too-daring metaphors: they are feathers on a serpent's scales.

19 Put, commas, in the appropriate places.

20 Recognize the difference between the semicolon and the colon: even if it's hard.

21 If you can't find the appropriate expression, refrain from using colloquial/dialectal expressions. In Venice, they say "Peso el tacòn del buso." "The patch is worse than the hole."

22 Do you really need rhetorical questions?

23 Be concise; try expressing your thoughts with the least possible number of words, avoiding long sentences—or sentences interrupted by incidental phrases that always confuse the casual reader—in order to avoid contributing to the general pollution of information, which is surely (particularly when it is uselessly ripe with unnecessary explanations, or at least non indispensable specifications) one of the tragedies of our media-dominated time.

24 Don't be emphatic! Be careful with exclamation marks!

25 Spell foreign names correctly, like Beaudelaire, Roosewelt, Niezsche and so on.

26 Name the authors and characters you refer to, without using periphrases. So did the greatest Lombard author of the nineteenth century, the author of "The 5th of May."

27 Begin your text with a captatio benevolentiae, to ingratiate yourself with your reader (but perhaps you're so stupid you don't even know what I'm talking about).

28 Be fastidios with you're speling.

29 No need to tell you how cloying preteritions are [telling by saying you are not going to tell].

30 Do not change paragraph when unneeded.

Not too often.

Anyway.

31 No plurale majestatis, *please. We believe it pompous.*

32 *Do not take the cause for the effect: you would be wrong and thus you would make a mistake.*

33 *Do not write sentences in which the conclusion doesn't follow the premises in a logical way: if everyone did this, premises would stem from conclusions.*

34 *Do not indulge in archaic forms, apax legomena and other unused lexemes, nor in deep rizomatic structures which, however appealing to you as epiphanies of the grammatological differance (sic), inviting to a deconstructive tangent—but, even worse it would be if they appeared to be debatable under the scrutiny of anyone who would read them with ecdotic acridity—would go beyond the recipient's cognitive competencies.*

35 *You should never be wordy. On the other hand, you should not say less than.*

36 *A complete sentence should comprise.*

Mark Twain chimes in with one word to avoid:

Substitute "damn" every time you're inclined to write "very"; your editor will delete it and the writing will be just as it should be.

And F Scott Fitzgerald counseled the writer to pay special attention to verbs:

All fine prose is based on the verbs carrying the sentences... A line like "The hare limped trembling through the frozen grass," is so alive that you race through it, scarcely noticing it, yet it has colored the whole poem with its movement—the limping, trembling and freezing is going on before your eyes.

**MARK TWAIN
(1835–1910)**
Twain's famous works include *The Adventures of Huckleberry Finn*, *The Adventures of Tom Sawyer*, and *Life on the Mississippi*. Twain dreamed in 1858 that his brother would die in a steamboat explosion; this accident occurred a month later, prompting Twain to join the Society for Psychical Research.

FROM ADVICE TO ACTION!

ACTION: When reviewing your first draft, reread Orwell's and Eco's guidelines. If you have broken any of them, be sure it's because doing so creates an effect that you can't create any other way.

Adjectives and adverbs (sparingly)

Despite my chapter title, adjectives and adverbs are not wrong words—but they should be used with caution.

Here's Chekhov again, with more guidance for Gorky:

> Another piece of advice: when you read proof cross out as many adjectives and adverbs as you can. You have so many modifiers that the reader has trouble understanding and gets worn out. It is comprehensible when I write: "The man sat on the grass," because it is clear and does not detain one's attention. On the other hand, it is difficult to figure out and hard on the brain if I write: "The tall, narrow-chested man of medium height and with a red beard sat down on the green grass that had already been trampled down by the pedestrians, sat down silently, looking around timidly and fearfully." The brain can't grasp all that at once, and art must be grasped at once, instantaneously.

"The adjective is the enemy of the noun," said Voltaire. Perhaps in response, Twain said, "The adverb is the enemy of the verb." He added, "When you can catch an adjective, kill it."

Elmore Leonard is one of the modern masters of sparse but punchy description. Here's the second paragraph of his novel *Split Images*:

> The bullet fired from Robbie Daniels's Colt Python did not kill Louverture immediately. He was taken in shock to Good

Samaritan where he lay in intensive care for three days, a lung destroyed, plastic tubes coming out of his nose, his arms, his chest and his penis.

Leonard once explained his ten rules of writing. One was: "If it sounds like writing, I rewrite it." And another: "Try to leave out the part that readers tend to skip."

FROM ADVICE TO ACTION!

ACTION: When reviewing your first draft, test every adjective and adverb. Read the sentence with them and then without them. Which is more powerful?

Also be aware of how many adjectives and adverbs you have used. If there are too many, the reader may feel over-worked. Choose the most powerful ones or those that convey something you can't get over any other way.

26

Developing your style

There's the story and there's how you tell the story. The latter is your style. Some writers forget that the purpose of style is to enhance the experience for the reader, not to call attention to the cleverness of the author.

While style should be a by-product of what you want to say, there may be some approaches that will help you develop yours.

Keep your emotions in check

It is said that sometimes Dickens wept when he gave a reading of the death of Little Nell, but perhaps he wasn't crying when he wrote it. Anton Chekhov suggested that authors keep their emotions in check:

> When you describe the miserable and unfortunate, and want to make the reader feel pity, try to be somewhat colder—that seems to give a kind of background to another's grief, against which it stands out more clearly. Whereas in your story the characters cry and you sigh. Yes, be more cold... The more objective you are, the stronger will be the impression you make.

If you carry some of that objectivity into the writing itself, it may make it stronger, according to F Scott Fitzgerald:

> Reporting the extreme things as if they were the average things will start you on the art of fiction.

Great Expectations

In the section below, young Pip encounters the escaped convict Magwich for the first time. Although it's a terrifying situation, notice how Dickens describes it in a straightforward way:

> *"Hold your noise!" cried a terrible voice, as a man started up from among the graves at the side of the church porch. "Keep still, you little devil, or I'll cut your throat!"*
>
> *A fearful man, all in coarse gray, with a great iron on his leg. A man with no hat, and with broken shoes, and with an old rag tied round his head. A man who had been soaked in water, and smothered in mud, and lamed by stones, and cut by flints, and stung by nettles, and torn by briars; who limped, and shivered, and glared, and growled; and whose teeth chattered in his head as he seized me by the chin.* [The list of descriptions of what had happened to this man makes us imagine him in a bad state, then a worse state, and then a worse state yet. It reads almost like a list of shots in a film, each showing another facet of his condition]
>
> *"Oh! Don't cut my throat, sir," I pleaded in terror. "Pray don't do it, sir."*

Notice that Dickens also keeps to a minimum the description of Pip's reaction ("I pleaded in terror"), leaving it to the reader to imagine what feelings such an encounter would evoke in a young child.

Punctuation and spelling

A few authors have made their mark partly through idiosyncratic use of punctuation and spelling, like e e cummings's refusal to use capital letters, or Joyce's sentences that go on seemingly for ever. Hemingway expressed a different viewpoint:

> My attitude toward punctuation is that it ought to be as conventional as possible. The game of golf would lose a great deal if croquet mallets and billiard cues were allowed on the putting green. You ought to be able to show that you can do it a good deal better than anyone else with the regular tools before you have a license to bring in your own improvements.

Mark Twain was skeptical about hewing to strict rules:

> I never had any large respect for good spelling. That is my feeling yet. Before the spelling-book came with its arbitrary forms, men unconsciously revealed shades of their characters and also added enlightening shades of expression to what they wrote by their spelling, and so it is possible that the spelling-book has been a doubtful benevolence to us.

George Bernard Shaw addressed the question of grammar in a letter to the editor of *The Times* of London:

> There is a busybody on your staff who devotes a lot of time to chasing split infinitives... I call for the immediate dismissal of this pedant. It is of no consequence whether he decides to go quickly or to quickly go or quickly to go. The important thing is that he should go at once.

F Scott Fitzgerald offered his view on one punctuation mark in particular:

> Cut out all those exclamation marks. An exclamation mark is like laughing at your own joke.

If you are uncertain about punctuation and grammar, don't let it stop you from writing. You can either hire an editor or arm yourself with the venerable *Elements of Style*, by Strunk and White— still the best guide and itself a model of simplicity and clarity—and polish your work later.

Dare to find your own

The writer who develops an unusual style may not find the path easy, as Raymond Chandler warned:

> *The most durable thing in writing is style, and style is the most valuable investment a writer can make with his time. It pays off slowly, your agent will sneer at it, your publisher will misunderstand it, and it will take people you have never heard of to convince them by slow degrees that the writer who puts his individual mark on the way he writes will always pay off.*

What writers agree on, though, is that your style has to be a natural development. Jack Kerouac revealed how he happened on his:

JACK KEROUAC (1922-69)

Kerouac is known for his books *On the Road*, *The Subterraneans*, and *Big Sur*. He was one of the original hippies and beat poets. Kerouac always carried a notebook so that he could write at any time.

> *I got the idea for the spontaneous style of On the Road from seeing how good old Neal Cassady wrote his letters to me—all first person, fast, mad, confessional, completely serious, all detailed—with real names in his case, however, being letters. I remembered also Goethe's admonition—well, Goethe's prophecy—that the future literature of the West would be confessional.*

While another writer's style may inspire you, Ayn Rand warned:

> *You cannot borrow another man's soul, and you cannot borrow his style.*

Henry David Thoreau summed it up well:

Who cares what a man's style is, so it is intelligible, as intelligible as his thought. Literally and really, the style is no more than the stylus, the pen he writes with; and it is not worth scraping and polishing, and gilding, unless it will write his thoughts the better for it. It is something for use, and not to look at.

FROM ADVICE TO ACTION!

ACTION: When you review your first draft, consider whether writing your most emotional scenes more dispassionately would make them more powerful. If you've deviated from conventional grammar, spelling or punctuation, is there a good reason for it? And make sure that you haven't succumbed to the lure of the exclamation mark. Finally, don't fret about your style or whether you have one—trust that one will emerge after the first million words or so.

PART V
THE PROCESS

Other than "Where do you get your ideas?" the main questions writers are asked are about the details of their process. Do they write longhand, do they write first thing in the morning or late at night, do they have any rituals? Although all authors have to find their own ways of working, it can be useful to know what is effective for others.

In this section, I consider whether writing needs to be a compulsion, the daily habits of some very successful writers, what they do to overcome writer's block, and more.

27

Is writing a compulsion?

George Orwell thought that writing had to be an obsession, saying:

> All writers are vain, selfish and lazy, and at the very bottom of their motives lies a mystery. Writing a book is a long, exhausting struggle, like a long bout of some painful illness. One would never undertake such a thing if one were not driven by some demon whom one can neither resist nor understand.

Elie Wiesel basically agrees, but without the insults:

> Now with the passing of years I know that the fate of books is not unlike that of human beings: some bring joy, others anguish. Yet one must resist the urge to throw away pen and paper. After all, authentic writers write even if there is little chance for them to be published; they write because they cannot do otherwise, like Kafka's messenger who is privy to a terrible and imperious truth that no one is willing to receive but is nonetheless compelled to go on.

JAMES THURBER (1894–1961)

Thurber's books include *My Life and Hard Times*, and *My World—And Welcome to It*. He wrote extensively for *The New Yorker*, and also 70 fables with satirical morals. Thurber competed in a series of dog shows with his pet poodles.

On a day-to-day basis, the obsession can be less dramatic, as James Thurber described:

> I never quite know when I'm not writing. Sometimes my wife comes up to me at a party and says, Dammit, Thurber, stop writing. She usually catches me in the middle of a paragraph. Or my daughter will look up from the

dinner table and ask, Is he sick? No, my wife says, he's writing something.

Edgar Allen Poe said:

> *Through joy and through sorrow, I wrote. Through hunger and through thirst, I wrote. Through good report and through ill report, I wrote. Through sunshine and through moonshine, I wrote. What I wrote it is unnecessary to say.*

EDGAR ALLAN POE (1809–49)

Poe's most famous works include "The Cask of Amontillado," "The Pit and the Pendulum," and "The Raven." He enlisted in the US army and was discharged to go to the Military Academy at West Point; he left West Point by deliberately getting himself court-martialed.

Age doesn't need to be a signal to stop writing, either. At least for Ray Bradbury, the effect of getting older was the opposite:

> *On my seventieth birthday, when I reflected that so many of my friends were dead or dying, it hit me that it was high time I got more work done. Ever since that time, I have done the active, smart thing by increasing my productivity.*

Although some authors indeed are compelled to write and don't feel right if they miss even one day, others are fine with taking breaks and believe that those are required to refill the well of their imagination. I confess I don't write every day, but depending on writing for your income is a great motivator for learning self-discipline. If you miss too many days, you don't eat. Even if writing isn't a compulsion, eating is.

FROM ADVICE TO ACTION!

ACTION: Are you writing at the pace and in the amount that satisfies you? If not, decide what you could change in order to do so.

28

Places and props

All you really need in order to write is a pen and a piece of paper but, as you'll see, writers have different ideas about the perfect writing environment and the rituals and props that support their writing mood.

William Faulkner's demands were simple:

My own experience has been that the tools I need for my trade are paper, tobacco, food, and a little whiskey.

Haruki Murakami asks for:

a quiet room. Decent desk. Hopefully, music of Telemann. Early in the morning. No work after sunset.

Amy Tan says:

Ideally I would be writing at my desk at my home in Sausalito. If I put headphones on I'm able to write almost anywhere on a computer. I do also write in a journal— which is good for travelling when I can't have my computer. Like in the back of a bus.

Some writers have lots of requirements regarding where and how they work. For instance, Truman Capote said:

I am a completely horizontal author. I can't think unless I'm lying down, either in bed or stretched on a couch and with a cigarette and coffee handy. I've got to be puffing and sipping. As the afternoon wears on, I shift from coffee to mint tea to sherry to martinis. No, I don't use a typewriter. Not in the beginning. I write my first version in longhand (pencil).

Beryl Bainbridge smoked while she wrote and wore white cotton gloves to keep the nicotine stains off her fingers. She described her routines:

> I start off in the kitchen, working with pen and paper on the kitchen table, then I move up to my typewriter on the first floor and later on I go to the word processor which is at the top of the house. The top room is a tip, full of cig ash and bits of paper. I keep the word processor there out of sight, like the telly, because it is so ugly.

Alan Gurganus's habit may disturb the neighbors:

> I say lines out loud a lot. I live alone and my neighbors think I have a very active and busy apartment.

Props

Some authors surround themselves with items that inspire them. Charles Dickens's biographer Michael Slater writes:

> He could not settle to work if he did not have, set out in their regular places on his desk, certain talismanic objects such as his group of duelling bronze frogs, as well as the little china monkey now on view at the Charles Dickens Museum in London.

Marina Warner revealed:

> For my last novel I kept around me:
> 1 bottle bay rum
> 2 oyster shells (fitting together)
> Dried sorrel vine
> Flakes of crystals from the bed of a sulphur spring
> (and 3 others)

The bay rum was for my father, who always used it, so that I could summon him up before me just at a whiff; oysters act as the book's key image, the female sex symbolized as a sea-creature… The sorrel vine and the crystal formed part of the pharmacopoeia that my Sycorax uses in her various experiments in cooking and dyeing and healing, arts which she passes on to her adopted daughter, Ariel.

Kent Haruf has an even busier, and presumably large, desk:

On my desk I keep a sapling chewed by a beaver: I also keep on my desk a bird's nest, a piece of black turf from Northern Ireland, a plastic bag of red sand from the stage at the new Globe Theatre (taken after a production of Shakespeare's Winter Tale), a piece of brick and some paddock dirt from Faulkner's home in Rowan Oaks, an old-fashioned hand warmer in a velvet sack, a blue bandana, a jackknife that once belonged to my maternal grandfather, Roy Shaver, who was a sheep rancher in South Dakota, and an obsidian arrowhead my father found in the North Dakota Badlands, where he was born almost one hundred years ago… The things on my desk and on the walls above it connect me emotionally to memories, ways of living, people and geographical areas that are important to me. It's an emotional attachment to all those things that connects me up with the impulse to write.

Sometimes it's useful to mark the beginning of a project with a ritual or an acquisition, like the one Mary Gordon describes:

On my last trip to Italy I was contemplating a novel in three voices. So I bought three each of three kinds of notebooks: some in a Tuscan candy store, covered in shiny licorice black; some terra-cotta, like the roofs I saw from my window. I bought those in a stationery store near the Pantheon on the same street where I bought a pair of forest-green suede gloves with a raspberry trim. Near Santa Maria in Trastevere I bought three ecclesiastical-looking notebooks covered in black cardboard with a red binding.

FROM ADVICE TO ACTION!

ACTION: Make a list of the minimum demands you have for the setting in which you write, as well as a list of the conditions you'd love to have. Include the characteristics of the location (such as noisy, quiet, with a view, without a view, and so on). Also list any props that might inspire you. Make sure that you have at least the minimum requirements, but also gradually work toward attaining the ideal.

29
How much, for how long?

Newer writers continually worry about whether they are producing enough and wonder how much output is typical. There are about as many answers to that as there are writers. However, it can be encouraging to find that success is not contingent on any particular level of productivity. Reading the variety of approaches may give you some ideas of how to handle your own writing sessions.

It's also good to know that the process is messier than most writers admit when interviewed on talk shows. This has been an issue since before such shows existed. Edgar Allen Poe wrote:

> *Most writers—poets in especial—prefer having it under-stood that they compose by a species of fine frenzy—an ecstatic intuition—and would positively shudder at letting the public take a peek behind the scenes, at the elaborate and vacillating crudities of thought—at the true purposes seized only at the last moment—at the innumerable glimpses of idea that arrived not at the maturity of full view—at the fully-matured fancies discarded in despair as unmanageable—at the cautious selections and rejections—at the painful erasures and interpolations...*

He goes on, but you get the idea.

One word or several thousand?

At one end of the productivity scale we find Oscar Wilde:

> *I was working on the proof of one of my poems all the morning, and took out a comma. In the afternoon I put it back again.*

And at the other end is Anthony Trollope. According to an article in *The New Yorker*:

> Every day for years, Trollope reported in his Autobiography, he woke in darkness and wrote from 5:30 a.m. to 8:30 a.m., with his watch in front of him. He required of himself two hundred and fifty words every quarter of an hour. If he finished one novel before eight-thirty, he took out a fresh piece of paper and started the next. The writing session was followed, for a long stretch of time, by a day job with the postal service. Plus, he said, he always hunted at least twice a week. Under this regimen, he produced forty-nine novels in thirty-five years. Having prospered so well, he urged his method on all writers: "Let their work be to them as is his common work to the common laborer. No gigantic efforts will then be necessary. He need tie no wet towels round his brow, nor sit for thirty hours at his desk without moving,—as men have sat, or said that they have sat."

What was the secret of his productivity? Planning, routine, and ruthless discipline:

> When I have commenced a new book, I have always prepared a diary, divided into weeks, and carried it on for the period which I have allowed myself for the completion of the work. In this I have entered, day by day, the number of pages I have written, so that if at any time I have slipped into idleness for a day or two, the record of that idleness has been there, staring me in the face, and demanding of me increased labour, so that the deficiency might be supplied... There has ever been the record before me, and a week passed with an insufficient number of pages has been a blister to my eye, and a month so disgraced would have been a sorrow to my heart.

Regarding his weekly output, he revealed:

> I have allocated myself so many pages a week. The average number has been about 40. It has been placed as low as 20, and has risen to 112. And as a page is an ambiguous term, my page has been made to contain 250 words; and as words, if not watched, will have a tendency to straggle, I have had every word counted as I went.

Alice Munro follows in his footsteps:

> I am so compulsive that I have a quota of pages. If I know that I am going somewhere on a certain day, I will try to get those extra pages done ahead of time. That's so compulsive, it's awful. But I don't get too far behind; it's as if I could lose it somehow. This is something about aging. People get compulsive about things like this.

In his autobiography, Mark Twain recalls writing *The Innocents Abroad*:

> I was very young in those days, exceedingly young, marvelously young, younger than I am now, younger than I shall ever be again, by hundreds of years. I worked every night from eleven or twelve until broad daylight in the morning, and as I did 200,000 words in the sixty days, the average was more than 3,000 words a day—nothing for Sir Walter Scott, nothing for Louis Stevenson, nothing for plenty of other people, but quite handsome for me.

How long does it take to write a short story? Anton Chekhov had a precise answer:

> To write a story you need five or six days, during which time you must be thinking about it every moment, otherwise you will never be able to frame good sentences. Before it reaches the page, every sentence must spend two days in the brain, lying perfectly still and putting on weight. It goes without

saying, of course, that I am too lazy to mind my own rule, but I do recommend it to you writers, all the more so because I have experienced its beneficent results firsthand and know that the rough drafts of all true artists are a mess of deletions and corrections, marked up from top to bottom in a patchwork of cuts and insertions that are themselves recrossed out and mangled.

How long does it take to write a novel? Amy Tan's answer is:

Years, it seems. For different reasons. It took me three years to write three stories for The Joy Luck Club and then four months to finish the rest of them. It took me a year and a half to write a draft for the next book. It takes me longer and longer. It took me very long to write Saving Fish from Drowning because I got ill and I couldn't even write a sentence for a while. For different reasons I get delayed or paralyzed at some point because of the idea that someone's going to read this and it's going to get published and I wonder: Is this truly the book I want to write? Is this truly a book I want to get published and let go into the world?

It's a question James D. Houston says he gets asked a lot. He adds:

I hardly ever give them the real answer. "It depends," I will say. "A year. Sometimes three or four." The real answer, of course, is that it takes your entire life. I am forty-four, and it took me forty-four years to get this novel finished. You don't mention this to too many people, because it can fill their hearts with sadness, looking at you and thinking, Jesus, forty-four years to come up with this? But it's always the truest answer. You could not have written it any sooner. You write the book when its time has come, and you bring your lifetime to the task, however few or many years you have behind you.

Sometimes circumstances have a major influence on your pace. JK Rowling says that after her mother died:

> I intended to start teaching again and I knew that unless I finished the book [the first Harry Potter] very soon, I might never finish it; I knew that full-time teaching, with all the marking and lesson planning, let alone with a small daughter to care for single-handedly, would leave me with absolutely no spare time at all. And so I set to work in a kind of frenzy, determined to finish the book and at least try to get it published. Whenever Jessica fell asleep in her pushchair I would dash to the nearest café and write like mad.

Some authors are influenced by the demands of their fans. Stephenie Meyer told *Entertainment Weekly*:

> [My fans] count on me to be a fast writer, with a once-a-year release schedule, which, you know, isn't entirely fair. I mean, how long did they give J.K. Rowling? [Laughs] She gets a good couple of years between her books, and [Eragon author] Christopher Paolini gets two or three, too. But I know fans want [the new books], and you wanna give them what they want.

George RR Martin, author of *A Game of Thrones*, has learned how demanding fans can be; ones who are upset that he's not delivering new volumes in his *A Song of Ice and Fire* series fast enough send him hate mail and have set up derogatory websites.

Film and television writers often have to work to strict deadlines if they have been commissioned to write a script. On one sitcom I worked on, one of the stars fell ill at the last minute and we had to come up with a completely new script that didn't feature her. We had a weekend in which to do it. This is the exception, but certainly there are tighter deadlines than for the novelist, and the cost implications are considerable if, for instance, a script isn't ready when the film is due to start production. This means that if you want to write for television or film you need to have a good measure of self-discipline and you can't be a perfectionist.

Writing a feature film typically takes four to six months, although again there are huge variations. Julie Everton, a fellow writing teacher, told me that her friend, noted playwright Phyllis Nagy, says it takes her nine months to write a play: eight months for gestation, the last four weeks for writing.

FROM ADVICE TO ACTION!

ACTION: The important thing is not to try to match anybody else's productivity, but to find out what is sensible for you. Rather than planning to write whenever you can, at whatever pace seems reasonable at the time, set yourself a specific target of a number of words per day or per week or per month, depending on how frequently you have time to write. Experiment to find a level ambitious enough to spur you to action and feel satisfying when you achieve it, but not so challenging that you can't maintain it consistently.

Especially at first, it can be helpful to keep careful track of how many words you write and when you write them. Note the patterns: When you are most productive? What other factors are present during those times? Do more of the things that work best.

If you find yourself getting distracted, use a timer. Set it for 30 minutes to start and during that time do nothing but write: no checking emails or Facebook, no internet searches even if they're relevant, just writing. Once you're used to that, change to 45-minute periods interspersed with 5-minute breaks.

Here we have considered only how long it takes to write your work. How long it takes for it to sell is even less predictable. JK Rowling was delighted when the second agent she approached took her on, but it took the agent a full year to find a publisher and there were many rejections along the way.

Actually, a year is very fast; many successful novelists have toiled for several years, even a decade and more, before finding any kind of acceptance. My screenplay *The Real Howard Spitz* took 13 years from being written to being produced. Along the way it had serious interest from Michael Keaton, director Buck Henry, producer Leonard Goldberg, Robin Williams, and others, but each time the deal failed to materialize or fell through. It was frustrating, despite the fact that I earned money from options along the way. Patience and an irrational optimism are useful for any writer.

30

Confidence

Writers expose themselves repeatedly to rejection: from agents, from publishers, from critics, and from the public. What advice do the classic writers having about coping?

I begin with part of an essay by Mark Twain, in which he relates how he went to seek an opinion of his work—and why he never did it again:

> When I was sixteen or seventeen years old, a splendid idea burst upon me—a brand-new one, which had never occurred to anybody before: I would write some "pieces" and take them down to the editor of the "Republican," and ask him to give me his plain, unvarnished opinion of their value! NOW, as old and threadbare as the idea was, it was fresh and beautiful to me, and it went flaming and crashing through my system like the genuine lightning and thunder of originality. I wrote the pieces. I wrote them with that placid confidence and that happy facility which only want of practice and absence of literary experience can give. There was not one sentence in them that cost half an hour's weighing and shaping and trimming and fixing. Indeed, it is possible that there was no one sentence whose mere wording cost even one-sixth of that time.

However, when Twain got to the building, his confidence vanished:

> At about that crisis the editor, the very man I had come to consult, came down stairs, and halted a moment to pull at his wristbands and settle his coat to its place, and he happened to notice that I was eyeing him wistfully. He asked me

what I wanted. I answered, "NOTHING!" with a boy's own meekness and shame; and, dropping my eyes, crept humbly round till I was fairly in the alley, and then drew a big grateful breath of relief, and picked up my heels and ran!

I was satisfied. I wanted no more. It was my first attempt to get a "plain unvarnished opinion" out of a literary man concerning my compositions, and it has lasted me until now. And in these latter days, whenever I receive a bundle of MS. through the mail, with a request that I will pass judgment upon its merits, I feel like saying to the author, "If you had only taken your piece to some grim and stately newspaper office, where you did not know anybody, you would not have so fine an opinion of your production as it is easy to see you have now."

Our work will be subject to the opinions of others whether we ask for them or not. And when those opinions are negative, it's painful. Anton Chekhov described the ideal to which writers should aspire:

You must once and for all give up being worried about successes and failure. Don't let that concern you. It's your duty to go on working steadily day by day, quite steadily, to be prepared for mistakes, which are inevitable, and for failures.

It's very hard to live up to that. Even a writer at the top of his field, screenwriter William Goldman, admitted:

I don't know how it is for others, but building up confidence is the single hardest battle I face every day of my life.

Chekhov sometimes questioned himself and his writing:

It makes as much sense to write for [critics] as it does to ask someone suffering from a cold to smell flowers. There are times when I get truly discouraged. For whom and to what end do I write? For the public? But I have never actually seen this public and have less faith in its existence than in ghosts: it is uneducated and bad mannered, and even at its best treats us unscrupulously and insincerely. I have no idea whether this public even needs me... Is it money I want? But I have never had money, and because I am not used to having any, I am quite indifferent to it. I simply cannot make myself work for money. Is it praise I want? Praise only irritates me...

Alice Munro attributed her confidence to ignorance:

In writing, I've always had a lot of confidence, mixed with dread that the confidence is entirely misplaced. I think in a way that my confidence came just from being dumb. Because I lived so much out of my mainstream, I didn't realize that women didn't become writers as readily as men, and that neither did people from a lower class. If you know you can write fairly well in a town where you've hardly met any one else who reads, you obviously think this is a rare gift indeed.

Even when the writer can stay motivated long enough to finish a work, it's not long before doubts creep in, as reflected in this quote from Nathaniel Hawthorne:

Some portions of the book are powerfully written; but my writings do not, nor ever will, appeal to the broadest class of sympathies, and therefore will not attain a very wide popularity.

He was talking about *The Scarlet Letter*.
Joyce Carol Oates advised:

One must be stoic, one must develop a sense of humour. And, after all, there is the example of William Faulkner, who considered himself a failed poet; Henry James returning to *prose fiction after the conspicuous failure of his play-writing career; Ring Lardner writing his impeccable American prose because he despaired of writing sentimental popular songs; Hans Christian Andersen perfecting his fairy tales since he was clearly a failure in other genres—poetry, play writing, life.*

That's really the problem. It may be that we are not misunderstood geniuses after all; maybe what we've written actually is bad. Norman Mailer observed:

NORMAN MAILER (1923–2007) Mailer's famous works include *The Executioner's Song, An American Dream*, and *The Naked and the Dead*. He was deeply fascinated by President John F Kennedy, and wrote accounts of various US political conventions between 1960 and 1996.

The sad truth is that a would-be novelist has to start a few books that do give out, or even crash before a sense of the difficulties is acquired. If the same likelihood of failure applied to young race-car drivers, there would not be speedways.

The challenge, then, is to get past the bad stuff and keep writing, on the assumption that sooner or later we'll get better at it, or at least people will think we have. As humorist Robert Benchley said:

It took me fifteen years to discover I had no talent for writing. But I couldn't give it up because by then I was too famous.

To counter your doubts, Hilary Mantel recommends:

the most helpful personal quality a writer can cultivate is self-confidence—arrogance, if you can manage it. You write to impose yourself on the world, and you have to believe in your own ability when the world shows no sign of agreeing with you. A book isn't quickly achieved and the road to publication can be strewn with obstacles. It is especially impor-

tant to be self-confident if you have no contacts and do not know other writers. If you are unpublished, you can still say to yourself, "I am a writer." You should define yourself as such.

FROM ADVICE TO ACTION!

ACTION: A writer's lack of confidence often comes from having an inner critic, who is harsher than any real critic would ever be. Here are three ways to get the inner critic under control when it threatens to undermine your writing:

✐ Challenge it. Write down what it is saying. On paper, statements like "This book is worthless, nobody will want to buy it!" reveal how stark and unrealistic they are. Challenge each one: "Nobody will buy it? Wrong! My mother will buy several copies!" Eventually you'll get down to a more realistic concern: "The book may not sell as many copies as I'd like." That may or may not turn out to be the case, but surely that's no reason to stop writing.

✐ Hear your inner critic's statements in the voice of your favorite cartoon character. When it's Donald Duck saying "You'll never amount to anything as a writer, why not give up now?" it takes the steam out of the statements.

✐ Realize that these thoughts are just that: thoughts, not facts. You have thousands, maybe hundreds of thousands of thoughts every day. They come and they go. Why give such weight to these particular thoughts?

The next time your inner critic attempts to undermine your confidence, use one or more of these three methods... and then get back to work.

31

The critics

s if it weren't enough that most of us struggle with an inner critic, writers also have to cope with outer critics: reviewers.

Chekhov's attitude to critics suggests bitterness. He said:

Critics are like horse-flies which hinder the horses in their plowing of the soil. The muscles of the horse are as taut as fiddle-strings, and suddenly a horse-fly alights on its croup, buzzing and stinging. The horse's skin quivers, it waves its tail. What is the fly buzzing about? It probably doesn't know itself. It simply has a restless nature and wants to make itself felt—"I'm alive, too, you know!" it seems to say. "Look, I know how to buzz, there's nothing I can't buzz about!" I've been reading reviews of my stories for twenty-five years, and can't remember a single useful point in any of them, or the slightest good advice. The only reviewer who ever made an impression on me was Skabichevsky, who prophesied that I would die drunk in the bottom of a ditch.

This was Samuel Johnson's take on the stifling influence of critics:

Criticism, though dignified from the earliest ages by the labours of men eminent for knowledge and sagacity, and, since the revival of polite literature, the favourite study of European scholars, has not yet attained the certainty and stability of science. The rules hitherto received are seldom drawn from any settled principle or self-evident postulate, or adapted to the natural and invariable constitution of things; but will be found, upon examination, the arbitrary edicts of legislators, authorised only by themselves, who, out of vari-

ous means by which the same end may be attained, selected such as happened to occur to their own reflection, and then, by a law which idleness and timidity were too willing to obey, prohibited new experiments of wit, restrained fancy from the indulgence of her innate inclination to hazard and adventure, and condemned all future flights of genius to pursue the path of the Meonian eagle.

By the way, if the Meonian eagle doesn't ring a bell (it didn't for me), Meonia was reputedly the birthplace of Greek epic poet Homer. Johnson seems to be saying that because of the influence of critics, everyone is reduced to following Homer's model of storytelling.

Johnson goes on:

This authority may be more justly opposed, as it is apparently derived from them whom they endeavour to control; for we owe few of the rules of writing to the acuteness of criticks, who have generally no other merit than that, having read the works of great authors with attention, they have observed the arrangement of their matter, or the graces of their expression, and then expected honour and reverence for precepts which they never could have invented; so that practice has introduced rules, rather than rules have directed practice.

To be fair to critics, on another occasion, Johnson said:

It is advantageous to an author that his book should be attacked as well as praised. Fame is a shuttlecock. If it be struck at one end of the room, it will soon fall to the ground. To keep it up, it must be struck at both ends.

Ernest Hemingway described the modern writer's typical experience with critics and confidence:

By the time the book comes out you will have started something else and it is all behind you and you do not want to hear about it. But you do, you read it in covers and you see all the places that now you can do nothing about.

All the critics who would not make their reputations by discovering you are hoping to make them by predicting your approaching impotence, failure and general drying up of natural juices. Not a one will wish you luck or hope that you will keep on writing unless you have political affiliations in which case these will rally around and speak of you and Homer, Balzac, Zola and Link Steffens. You are just as well off without these reviews…

But if the book is good, is about something that you know, and is truly written and reading it over you see that this is so you can let the boys yip and the noise will have that pleasant sound coyotes make on a very cold night when they are out in the snow and you are in your own cabin that you have built or paid for with your work.

Many authors contend that the best way to deal with the critics is to ignore them. Take William Faulkner:

The artist doesn't have time to listen to the critics. The ones who want to be writers read the reviews, the ones who want to write don't have time to read reviews. The critic too is trying to say, "Kilroy was here." His function is not directed toward the artist himself. The artist is a cut above the critic. The critic is writing something that will move everybody but the artist.

Not all authors agree that the impact of negative reviews is without redeeming features. Tennessee Williams said:

I have always been pushed by the negative. The apparent failure of a play sends me back to my typewriter that very night, before the reviews are out. I am more compelled to get back to work than if I had a success.

One consolation is that many times the confident judgments of critics are shown by the passage of time to have been off the mark. Here's a review from the *London Athenaeum*, October 25, 1851. As you read you'll realize the identity of the book being crushed:

This is an ill-compounded mixture of romance and matter-of-fact. The idea of a connected and collected story has obviously visited and abandoned its writer again and again in the course of composition. The style of his tale is in places disfigured by mad (rather than bad) English; and its catastrophe is hastily, weakly, and obscurely managed...

The result is, at all events, a most provoking book,— neither so utterly extravagant as to be entirely comfortable, nor so instructively complete as to take place among documents on the subject of the Great Fish, his capabilities, his home and his capture. Our author must be henceforth numbered in the company of the incorrigibles who occasionally tantalize us with indications of genius, while they constantly summon us to endure monstrosities, carelessnesses, and other such harassing manifestations of bad taste as daring or disordered ingenuity can devise...

We have little more to say in reprobation or in recommendation of this absurd book... Mr. Melville has to thank himself only if his horrors and his heroics are flung aside by the general reader, as so much trash belonging to the worst school of Bedlam literature—since he seems not so much unable to learn as disdainful of learning the craft of an artist.

Nowadays the shafts are just as likely to come from reviewers on online sites, like this amateur critic's assessment of Charlotte Bronte's *Jane Eyre*:

Endless, pointless description. DESCRIPTION, DESCRIPTION, DESCRIPTION!!! The entire book is written in stupid metaphors. *The few places where there is actually any dialogue bore the reader to tears. Honestly, I think that this is dubbed a classic simply because it is older than sand. Gee, maybe if I just go out and slop a few words down on a piece of paper, it'll be a classic in 160 years! It'll be required of every high school sophomore, like this idiotic "story." Excuse me now, I'm off to begin my masterpiece. I'm sure it'll be better than this.*

Should you respond to bad reviews?

TRUMAN CAPOTE (1924–84)

Capote is noted for the novella *Breakfast at Tiffany's* and his true crime novel *In Cold Blood*. For the latter he had the help of his close friend Harper Lee, author of *To Kill a Mockingbird*, who based the character of Dill on Capote.

Truman Capote advised:

Never demean yourself by talking back to a critic, never. Write those letters to the editor in your head, but don't put them on paper.

Chekhov's view was:

Critical articles, even the unjust, abusive kind, are usually met with a silent bow. Such is literary etiquette. Answering back goes against custom, and anyone who indulges in it is justly accused of excessive vanity... The fate of literature (both major and minor) would be a pitiful one if it were at the mercy of personal opinions. Point number one. And number two, there is no police force in existence that can consider itself competent in matters of literature. I agree that we can't do without the muzzle or the stick, because sharpers ooze their way into literature just as anywhere else. But no matter how hard you try, you won't come up with a better police force for literature than criticism and the author's own conscience. People have been at it since the beginning of creation, but they've invented nothing better.

I once had the unfortunate experience of getting nothing but bad reviews for a play of mine produced in Los Angeles. I took out a display ad in *Variety* saying, "The critics are unanimous about *Ricky Rat Waits for the Ratings!*" I didn't go into details, but readers may have assumed that nobody who got all bad reviews would trumpet it. Ticket sales picked up and audiences seemed to enjoy the play more than the critics had.

Unless you can figure out a way to turn negative comments into something useful, saying nothing may be the best strategy, even when the criticism is coming from your peers. Writer and teacher T Alan Broughton said:

> In my syllabus in the introductory course in writing fiction and poetry I warn my students, "When your work is being discussed you should understand that you do not have to defend your writing or yourself before the class; ideally you should present your work, listen to all the responses, and consider at leisure which remarks are useful and which are not. An important part of this process is learning how to be objective about your own work."

Constructive criticism

Stephen Sondheim tells how, at the age of 15, he was able to get Oscar Hammerstein to read a show he'd written to be produced at his school:

> [H]e asked, Do you really want me to treat this as if I didn't know you? Oh yes, I said, to which he replied, In that case, it's the worst thing I've ever read. He saw me blanch and continued, I didn't say it was untalented, but let's look at it. He proceeded to discuss it as if it were a serious piece. He started right from the first stage direction; and I've often said, at the risk of hyperbole, that I probably learned more about writing songs that afternoon than I learned the rest of my life.

Ernest Hemingway told F Scott Fitzgerald:

> *I like to have Gertrude [Stein] bawl me out because it keeps one's opinion of oneself down—way down—She liked the book very much she said—But what I wanted to hear about was what she didn't like and why.*

While I have focused on the impact of negative reviews, a positive review can give a writer's career a great boost, as was the case with Christopher Isherwood's review of Ray Bradbury's *The Martian Chronicles.* Bradbury told the story:

> *The entire scenario set in motion was a fluke. Summertime, 1950, I recognized Isherwood browsing in a Santa Monica bookstore. My book had just come out, so I grabbed a copy off the shelf, signed it and gave it to him. His face fell and my heart sank, but two days later he called and said, "Do you know what you've done?" I asked, "What?" And he simply told me to read his review in the* Times. *His rave turned my life around; the book immediately made the best-seller lists and has been in print ever since.*

Rejecting acceptance

Bradbury pointed out a different challenge when he said:

> *You have to know how to accept rejection and reject acceptance. The early problems of the writer are nothing compared to the later problems. It's not so much accepting rejection, getting rejection slips, but the big problem is rejecting acceptance. In the last seven years I've turned down 15 TV series offers I could have had on my own. I choose to stay free and float easily and keep an eye on myself. A writer must have the firm, hard ability to turn his eye inward upon himself. You write because it's an adventure to watch it*

come out of your hands. *The publicity is pleasant, but it never belongs to you. You're never quite convinced the name on that printed page is you.*

There's also the matter of whether to believe critics when they praise you. On an interview program called *Face to Face*, Evelyn Waugh said:

If someone praises me, I think what an arse and if they abuse me, I think what an arse.

The power of professional critics is giving way to the power of the people. When buying a book on Amazon, for instance, we tend to pay attention to the ratings and reviews of other readers at least as much as to any quotes of professional reviews. Of course, this does mean that you might get, say, 49 negative reviews instead of just one, so all the advice in this chapter still applies. Perhaps the last word on confidence, critics, and failure should go to Samuel Beckett and his famous admonition:

Ever tried? Ever failed? No matter. Try again. Fail again. Fail better.

FROM ADVICE TO ACTION!

ACTION: When you get criticism from others, here are three questions to consider:

✐ Does this person have any business criticizing you in the first place? Do they have expertise or experience that gives them superior knowledge? If not, don't waste any energy worrying about or responding at length to what they've said. A great all-purpose answer is, "Thanks for sharing your opinion." Whenever somebody made a stupid suggestion about a script I'd written, I'd say, "Hmm, that's interesting.

Let me look at that when I do the rewrite." I then totally ignored it and when I handed in the rewrite the person who'd made the comment usually had forgotten all about it. If you need to defuse your emotional reaction as they're making these comments, just imagine them as a fly circling around your head buzzing their little opinions. (If this makes you smile, don't tell them why.)

- Do they mean well but express themselves badly? If so, give them the benefit of the doubt and look past the clumsy expression to whether or not there is any value in what they have said.
- Is there truth to what they're saying, even if their statement isn't totally on target? If so, they've provided you with valuable information.

The next time you find yourself or your writing being reviewed or commented on, ask these three questions. You should find that this turns even a negative criticism into something constructive—or something to be ignored.

32
Writer's block

t's debatable whether there really is a specific condition called writer's block; most of the time the term is used when writers can't think of what to write, or know what they want to write but can't get started, or else get stuck in the middle of a project.

It may be that, as with anxiety attacks, the fear of the block creates the very condition itself. There are a variety of factors that contribute to being blocked. Let's look at them and how to counteract them.

Anxieties and neuroses

At times, a block may be related to other anxieties, as seems to be the case for Lucy Ellmann:

> *Form and structure have never come easily for me; even in pieces three pages long I have trouble knowing what should come when. I blame it on my bad body-image. At the age of twelve I dressed for Halloween as a Blob, sewing myself into a huge laundry bag stuffed with fluff. It was a sign of things to come. I see myself as an amorphous, amoeboid, with no obvious resemblance to the human form. I quake similarly before amorphous piles of my bumble-headed ideas. They need a great deal of coaxing and corseting.*

In the foreword to *Sweet Bird of Youth*, Tennessee Williams described the nature of his block—which didn't stop him from writing some of the most lauded plays in the modern theater:

> *I suddenly remembered a dinner date I once had with a distinguished colleague. During the course of this dinner,*

rather close to the end of it, he broke a long, mournful silence by lifting to me his sympathetic gaze and saying to me, sweetly, "Tennessee, don't you feel that you are blocked as a writer?"

I didn't stop to think of an answer; it came immediately off my tongue without any pause for planning. I said, "Oh, yes, I've always been blocked as a writer but my desire to write has been so strong that it has always broken down the block and gone past it."

… It was literally true. At the age of fourteen I discovered writing as an escape from a world of reality in which I felt acutely uncomfortable. It immediately became my place of retreat, my cave, my refuge. From what? From being called a sissy by the neighbourhood kids, and Miss Nancy by my father, because I would rather read books in my grandfather's large and classical library than play marbles and baseball and other normal kid games, a result of a severe childhood illness and of excessive attachment to the female members of my family, who had coaxed me back into life.

I think no more than a week after I started writing I ran into the first block. It's hard to describe it in a way that will be understandable to anyone who is not a neurotic. I will try. All my life I have been haunted by the obsession that to desire a thing or to love a thing intensely is to place yourself in a vulnerable position, to be a possible, if not a probable, loser of what you most want. Let's leave it like that. That block has always been there and always will be, and my chance of getting, or achieving, anything that I long for will always be gravely reduced by the interminable existence of that block.

Depression

For Hemingway, being blocked related to depression. He described one episode this way:

I've been working hard. Had a spell when I was pretty gloomy, that was why I didn't write first, and didn't sleep for about three weeks. Took to getting up about two or so in the morning and going out to the little house to work until daylight because when you're writing on a book and can't sleep your brain races at night and you write all the stuff in your head and in the morning it is gone and you are pooped. But decided that I wasn't getting enough exercise or something so have been going out and driving myself in the boat for a while in any kind of weather and am o.k. now. It is better to produce half as much, get plenty of exercise and not go crazy than to speed up so your head is hardly normal. Had never had the old melancholia before and am glad to have had it so I know what people go through. It makes me more tolerant of what happened to my father.

Hemingway's father committed suicide in 1928, as Hemingway was to do in 1961.

Depression was a factor for EB White as well, but it delayed rather than stopped him:

The thought of writing hangs over our mind like an ugly cloud, making us apprehensive and depressed, as before a summer storm, so that we begin the day by subsiding after breakfast, or by going away, often to seedy and inconclusive destinations: the nearest zoo, or a branch post office to buy a few stamped envelopes. Our professional life has been a long shameless exercise in avoidance. Our home is designed for the maximum of interruption, our office is the place where we never are… Yet the record is there. Not even lying down and closing the blinds

EB WHITE (1899-1985)
White is known for writing *Charlotte's Web*, *Stuart Little*, and *The Trumpet of the Swan*. His grammar guide, *The Elements of Style*, co-authored with William Strunk, Jr., is widely used in schools and universities in the United States.

stops us from writing; not even our family, and our preoccupation with same, stops us.

If you find yourself seriously depressed, it's important to get help. As someone who has experienced clinical depression myself, I know that it's not a matter of "cheering up" or "getting a hold of yourself," as your well-intentioned family or friends may suggest. It's a medical condition that can be treated.

Part of the process

André Gide advised:

> It would be wise not to worry too much about the sterile periods. They ventilate the subject and instil into it the reality of daily life.

Shelley Jackson suggests that perhaps a block is a normal part of the creative process:

> I sat on an unfinished draft for years because I suspected, correctly, that I didn't know how to finish it. When I finally went back to it, I still didn't know how, but I went ahead and did it anyway. I wish someone had told me that I would never know how to write a novel, only to carry on despite near-total confusion and doubt, and how, once I finished a draft, to figure out what I'd done and make it better.

Roddy Doyle is another novelist with an easy-going approach:

> I don't think I've ever been really blocked. If things are slow or very unsatisfactory, I move on to a different project, and come back to the problem later. I'll happily write crap, knowing it's crap, and edit it properly later. Often, we write six bad sentences before we get to the good seventh one. But we have to write the six first, before we recognize them and realize that the seventh was the true sentence. So, even the bad days are useful.

A temporary block has also become part of Alice Munro's process for each of her books:

> I could be writing one day and think I've done very well; I've done more pages than I usually do. Then I get up the next morning and realize I don't want to work on it anymore. When I have a terrible reluctance to go near it, when I would have to push myself to continue, I generally know that something is badly wrong. Often, in about three quarters of what I do, I reach a point somewhere, fairly early on, when I think I'm going to abandon this story. I get myself through a day or two of bad depression, grouching around. And I think of something else I can write. It's sort of like a love affair: you're getting out of all the disappointment and misery by going out with some new man you really don't like at all, but you haven't noticed that yet. Then, I will suddenly come up with something about the story that I abandoned; I will see how to do it. But that only seems to happen after I've said, No, this isn't going to work, forget it.

Chekhov had similar doubts about the projects he was working on, compared to the ones yet unwritten:

> The plots for five novellas and two novels are languishing in my head. One of the novels was conceived so long ago that several of the characters have already grown old and out of date even before they had a chance to take form on paper. There is an entire army of people in my head begging to get out and just waiting for my command. Everything I have written to this point is rubbish in comparison with what I would want to have written and what I would be thrilled to be writing... Everything I am writing at present bores me and leaves me indifferent, but everything that is still only in my head interests me, moves me, and excites me.

Writers have come up with a variety of practical solutions for these issues.

Consider the bigger questions

Paul Auster feels that a block may be a sign that we need to consider some larger issues:

> Great patience is needed. I have discovered, after many miserable weeks and months of suffering, that when a writer is blocked it generally means that he doesn't know what he is trying to say. You have to go back and examine your motives, your intentions, what you are trying to accomplish. But the essential thing is not to force things merely for the sake of putting words down on the page.

Brainstorm topics

If the difficulty is that you don't have an idea for your next project, you might want to try a method employed by Philip Roth. He told *NPR* how he happened on the subject of his latest novella, *Nemesis*, about a polio epidemic:

> I began [writing] as I sometimes do with a book [by jotting down] on a yellow legal pad all of the historical events that I've lived through that I've not dealt with in fiction. When I came to polio, it was a great revelation to me. I never thought of it before as a subject. And then I remembered how frightening it was and how deadly it was and I thought, "OK, try to write a book about polio..." what I wanted to see is: Could I imagine what it would have been like, had the thing we all feared happened?

Roth used the same method to come up with *The Plot against America*, in which he imagined what would have happened if Charles Lindbergh, rather than Franklin Roosevelt, had won the 1940 presidential election.

Write only what you believe in

Ray Bradbury says:

> The people who have mental blocks are the people who do things they shouldn't be doing. The people who take screenplays they shouldn't write or books they shouldn't write—they're going to wind up with dry spells, because their subconscious says, "I'm going to cut off the water works!"

His solution is very workmanlike: if you write what you love, you never have a dry spell.

Get therapy

Having problems writing a scene halfway through *Carter Beats the Devil* caused Glen David Gold a 17-month gap during which he wondered whether writing fiction wasn't just a symptom of dealing with unresolved childhood traumas. He says:

> So, I got out via therapy, changing my life, skipping ahead to a different scene, and coming back. And then I decided I needed to surprise myself so it wouldn't be just exposition. I was in the library in the stacks and decided I would throw an object into the scene based on the first book I grabbed. Which, no kidding, turned out to be the history of the guillotine. So there was something to break up the exposition, surprise me, and also hang the rest of the scene.

Keep a journal

Dominick Dunne advises:

> I think the best thing any writer can do is keep a journal… During writer's block, your journal is invaluable. Write to yourself about being blocked. Explain to yourself the feelings of frustration you are feeling, or the anger you are having with your talent for letting you down. Describe to yourself the chapter or scene you are writing: who the

characters are and where you are trying to get to in the chapter or scene. Write about it. Believe me, it will start to come, right there in your journal.

Surprise it

HG Wells's advice was:

> If you are in difficulties with a book, try the element of surprise: attack it at an hour when it isn't expecting it.

F Scott Fitzgerald concurred:

> Sometimes you can lick an especially hard problem by facing it always the very first thing in the morning with the very freshest part of your mind. This has so often worked for me that I have an uncanny faith in it.

Play music

Amy Tan says:

> There are many different ways. One is to put on the same music I had on when I was last working on the scene. Music is hypnotic, it aligns all the other senses of the imagination. So that takes me there.

Write one true sentence

Hemingway reassured himself:

> [S]ometimes when I was starting a new story and I could not get it going, I would sit in front of the fire and squeeze the peel of the little orange into the edge of the flame and watch the sputter of blue that they made. I would stand and look out over the roofs of Paris and think, "Do not worry. You have always written before and you will write now. All you have to do is write one true sentence. Write the truest sentence that you know." So finally I would write one true sen-

tence, and then go on from there. It was easy then because there was always one true sentence that I knew or had seen or had heard someone say. If I started to write elaborately, or like someone introducing or presenting something, I found that I could cut that scrollwork or ornament out and throw it away and start with the first true simple declarative sentence I had written.

Stop in the middle

Another tip from Hemingway:

> The best way is always to stop when you are going good and when you know what will happen next. If you do that every day when you are writing a novel you will never be stuck... Always stop while you are going good and don't think about it or worry about it until you start to write the next day. That way your subconscious will work on it all the time. But if you think about it consciously or worry about it you will kill it and your brain will be tired before you start.

Force an association

Ray Bradbury has a method for prompting stories:

> I'll sit at a typewriter and try word association. I'll type the first two words that come into my head, such as "The Veldt" or "The Dwarf." Then I say to my conscious, "All right, you're on your own. I believe in you implicitly. I don't doubt you for a moment. Now, subconscious, tell me everything you have saved up over the years that I don't know about dwarfs. Let me bring on some characters. I'll bring on one to speak for the subject of dwarfs and one to speak against the subject of dwarfs and out of this exchange let's see what kind of life experience we get." My subconscious takes over and says, "Here's my delight," and an hour or two later the story is finished.

Use an image

Peter Carey reveals:

> I used to begin with an image—a strong, symbolic picture—
> and then ask myself, What do you have to do to arrive at this
> point? It's like one of those houses of cards where everything
> underneath has to hold up the top two cards. In the case of
> Illywhacker, I knew that the family was going to end up as
> pets in their own pet shop. The pet shop seemed to me pretty
> much what Australia had become, for all its blustering.

Switch projects

It may be the most drastic solution, but sometimes it makes
sense to scrap what you're writing and write something else.
Lorrie Moore gives an example:

> I often think of an acquaintance of mine who is also a writer
> and whom I ran into once in a bookstore. We exchanged hel-
> los, and when I asked her what she was working on these days
> she said, "Well, I was working on a long comic novel, but then
> in the middle of the summer my husband had a terrible acci-
> dent with an electric saw and lost three of his fingers. It left us
> so sad and shaken that when I returned to writing, my comic
> novel kept getting droopier, darker and sadder and depressing.
> So I scrapped it, and started writing a novel about a man who
> loses three fingers in an accident with a saw, and that," she
> said, "that's turning out to be really funny." A lesson in comedy.

FROM ADVICE TO ACTION!

ACTION: If you find you are experiencing writer's block,
choose any of the above solutions and try it. If it works, great;
if not, carry on with the other solutions one by one until you
find the one that works best for you. If you are experiencing a
serious depression, get professional help.

PART VI
THE WRITING LIFE

Being a writer is more than an occupation. Some consider it a calling, others an art, yet others a craft. Certainly it has an impact on many parts of your life, and in this section we'll look at some of these elements. They include making money, the quest (or avoidance) of fame, the definition and nature of success, and more.

The advice here may help you to clarify why you write and create the lifestyle that best supports your writing.

33

Being alone and handling distractions

s a writer, much of your time will be spent alone—or with imaginary people. For many authors, like Orhan Pamuk, this is a plus:

I'm happy when I'm alone in a room and inventing. More than a commitment to the art or to the craft, which I am devoted to, it is a commitment to being alone in a room. I continue to have this ritual, believing that what I am doing now will one day be published, legitimizing my day-dreams. I need solitary hours at a desk with good paper and a fountain pen like some people need a pill for their health.

Hemingway saw solitude as a good thing, too:

Writers should work alone. They should see each other only after their work is done, and not too often then. Otherwise they become like writers in New York. All angleworms in a bottle, trying to derive knowledge and nourishment from their own contact and from the bottle. Sometimes the bottle is shaped art, sometimes economics, sometimes economic-religion. But once they are in the bottle they stay there. They are lonesome outside of the bottle. They do not want to be lonesome. They are afraid to be alone in their beliefs…

William Saroyan defined the writer as a rebel:

The writer is a spiritual anarchist, as in the depth of his soul every man is. He is discontented with everything and every-body. The writer is everybody's best friend and only true enemy—the good and great enemy. He neither walks with the multitude nor cheers with them. The writer who is a writer is a rebel who never stops.

Some writers are quite happy to work in a bustling environment such as a coffee shop or even a train station or on an airplane, so in this context "alone" means not being distracted by inter-actions with other people, which nowadays can come in the form of emails, instant messages, and other electronic media as well as someone engaging you in conversation. Of course, we are not really alone when writing, it's just that our company is the peo-ple we have created.

This doesn't mean that we have to be hermits the rest of the time. Flannery O'Connor wrote:

There is one myth about writers that I have always felt as par-ticularly pernicious and untruthful—the myth of the "lonely writer"... supposedly, the writer exists in a state of sensitivity which cuts him off, or raises him above, or casts him below the community around him... Probably any of the arts that are not performed in a chorus-line are going to come in for a cer-tain amount of romanticizing, but it seems to me particularly bad to do this to writers and especially fiction writers, because fiction writers engage in the homeliest, and most concrete, and most unromanticizable of all arts... Unless the novelist has gone utterly out of his mind, his aim is still communication, and communication suggests talking inside a community.

FROM ADVICE TO ACTION!

ACTION: If you are not finding enough solitary time to write, what can you do to create more such opportunities? Are you happy working on your own? If not, then writing novels probably isn't for you, but there are other types of writing that are inherently more social, such as journalism, or more collaborative, such as screenplay writing.

Interruptions and distractions

Finding the necessary solitude to write isn't always easy. Ernest Hemingway discovered one way to discourage visitors, as he described in a letter to his editor, Maxwell Perkins:

> *There have been other interruptions of all sorts but I am fairly ruthless about them. Have a big sign on the gate that says in Spanish* Mr H. receives no one without a previous appointment. Save yourself the annoyance of not being received by not coming to the house. *Then if they do come up I have a right to curse them off.*

If other people aren't interrupting us we sometimes find ways to distract ourselves. Amy Tan says:

> *A successful day is when I've not been diverted by distractions like e-mail, when people haven't been interrupting. When I've been fully concentrated in my imagination. When I've been writing with the voice of what the novel should be, not inserting other voices. It's really a discipline—when I sit down at nine o'clock and work all day...*
>
> *Don't take on major projects that are distracting. Don't be persuaded by other people. Don't be a good girl. Don't be a good girl and do blurbs for books. Don't be a good girl and do what other people pressure you to do.*

George Pelecanos confesses:

> *I've weaned myself off the Internet. It's like kicking cigarettes or drugs. Once you do it, you realize that it was a tremendous waste of time. Kids, dogs, and general noise have never been a problem for me. I've never written a book in a quiet place.*

Sometimes it's your own thoughts that distract you, as happens to Shelley Jackson:

I'm constantly assaulted with brilliant ideas that would entail rewriting the entire book. Sometimes I pursue them, but if I didn't eventually buckle down to one approach I'd never finish anything. So I write them down as notes for future use. And then don't use them.

Isaac Bashevis Singer thinks we may be barking up the wrong tree when we resist distractions:

Some writers say they can only write if they go to a far island. They would go to the moon to write not to be disturbed. I think that being disturbed is a part of human life and sometimes it's useful to be disturbed because you interrupt your writing and while you rest, while you are busy with something else, your perspective changes or the horizon widens. All I can say about myself is that I have never really written in peace, as some writers say that they have. But whatever I have had to say I kept on saying no matter what the disturbances were.

ISAAC BASHEVIS SINGER (1902–91)

Singer's works include *Enemies, a Love Story*, *The Golem*, and the Chelm stories. All his material was written first in Yiddish and then translated into English. Many of the men in his family were rabbis, and he began rabbinical training before deciding it was the wrong career for him.

Domestic demands

Family demands often get in the way of writing, a problem many famous male writers have solved by being terrible husbands and fathers.

Women writers have had a harder time, and sometimes there was a price to pay if they insisted on giving time to their writing. Alice Munro has said:

I feel I've done everything backward: this totally driven writer at the time when the kids were little and desperately needed me. And now, when they don't need me at all, I love them so much. I moon around the house and think, There used to be a lot more family dinners.

Emma Tennant offers a solution:

I think it's very hard to write if you have small children... of course many women have children and jobs as well, and I think as far as writing in those cases is concerned it's first thing in the morning that counts. Even if you only get half a page down by the time you have to leave for work or children are awake, there's a sense in which the rest of the day can take care of itself: you don't mind as long as that half page is down. Then, if you're lucky, you'll be able to come back to it in the evening, and correct a bit, or have a thought or two about what the next day's bit will be; again, if you're luckier the next day, you might find that everyone is out and you can do a bit more. People are sometimes taught on creative writing courses that you have to get an awful lot down, and of course this doesn't mean anything at all, and some of the best writers are pleased to get a few hundred words down a day.

Beryl Bainbridge offers another viewpoint:

When I had a house full of children I used to think it would be wonderful to have the place to myself and all the peace I needed to write. Now I realize that it is so much easier to deal with the frustrations of everyday life than to have to face oneself all day long. Sometimes I think of getting a job and then sneaking home in the evenings to write.

EB White found a way to take domestic interruptions in his stride:

I'm able to work fairly well among ordinary distractions. My house has a living room that is the core of everything that goes on—it is a passageway to the cellar, to the kitchen, to the closet where the phone lives. That's a lot of traffic. But it's a bright, cheerful room, and I often use it as a room to write in, despite the carnival that is going on all around me... the members of my household never pay the slightest attention to my being a writing man—they make all the noise and fuss they want to. If I get sick of it, I have places I can go. A writer who waits for ideal conditions under which to work will die without putting a word on paper.

FROM ADVICE TO ACTION!

ACTION: Take an inventory of the extent to which other people are interrupting you or distracting you. To reduce this, you can:

- Ask them to respect the time you need.
- Work in a different place.
- Work at a different time.

Then do an inventory of the ways you distract yourself. To reduce this you can:

- Ration the amount of time you spend online and watching television.
- Work somewhere where there is no internet access.
- Work on a computer that is not internet enabled.
- Work in a space that you have stripped of the distractions that usually hinder you (for instance books and magazines, a telephone, etc.).

34
The day-to-day routine

Probably no two writers have the same routine, but in his autobiography CS Lewis left a charming account of what might be an ideal typical writer's day, as he lived it for a time in a village called Bookham:

I would choose always to breakfast at exactly eight and to be at my desk by nine, there to read or write till one. If a cup of good tea or coffee could be brought me about eleven, so much the better. A step or so out of doors for a pint of beer would not do quite so well; for a man does not want to drink alone and if you meet a friend in the taproom the break is likely to be extended beyond its ten minutes.

At one precisely lunch should be on the table; and by two at the latest I would be on the road. Not, except at rare intervals, with a friend. Walking and talking are two very great pleasures, but it is a mistake to combine them... The return from the walk, and the arrival of tea, should be exactly coincident, and not later than a quarter past four. Tea should be taken in solitude... For eating and reading are two pleasures that combine admirably. Of course not all books are suitable for mealtime reading. It would be a kind of blasphemy to read poetry at table. What one wants is a gossipy, formless book which can be opened anywhere...

At five a man should be at work again, and at it till seven. Then, at the evening meal and after, comes the time for talk, or, failing that, for lighter reading; and unless you are making a night of it with your cronies (and at Bookham I had none) there is no reason why you should ever be in bed later than eleven.

Flaubert had a genteel routine, as described by Frederick Brown's biography of the great writer:

> *Days were as unvaried as the notes of the cuckoo. Flaubert, a man of nocturnal habits, usually awoke at 10 a.m. and announced the event with his bell cord. Only then did people dare speak above a whisper. His valet, Narcisse, straightaway brought him water, filled his pipe, drew the curtains, and delivered the morning mail… Unable to work well on a full stomach, he ate lightly, or what passed for such in the Flaubert household, meaning that his first meal consisted of eggs, vegetables, cheese or fruit, and a cup of cold chocolate. The family then lounged on the terrace, unless foul weather kept them indoors, or climbed a steep path through woods behind their espaliered kitchen garden to a glade dubbed La Mercure after the statue of Mercury that once stood there. Shaded by chestnut trees, near their hillside orchard, they would argue, joke, gossip, and watch vessels sail up and down the river. Another site of open-air refreshment was the eighteenth-century pavilion. After dinner, which generally lasted from seven to nine, dusk often found them there, looking out at moonlight flecking the water and fisherman casting their hoop nets for eel. In June 1852, Flaubert told Louise Colet that he worked from 1 p.m. to 1 a.m.*

Simone de Beauvoir said:

> *I'm always in a hurry to get going, though in general I dislike starting the day. I first have tea and then, at about ten o'clock, I get under way and work until one. Then I see my friends and after that, at five o'clock, I go back to work and continue until nine. I have no difficulty in picking up the thread in the afternoon. When you leave, I'll read the paper or perhaps go shopping. Most often it's a pleasure to work.*

Not every writer has such unchanging routines. John Irving says:

> I don't give myself time off or make myself work; I have no
> work routine… when I'm beginning a book I can't work more
> than two or three hours a day… Then there's the middle of
> a book. I can work eight, nine, twelve hours then, seven days
> a week—if my children let me; they usually don't… An
> eight-hour day at the typewriter is easy; and two hours of
> reading over material in the evening, too. That's routine.
> Then when the time to finish the book comes, it's back to
> those two- and three-hour days. Finishing, like beginning, is
> more careful work.

Domestic requirements are a factor and many writers have a full-
time job as well. In a previous chapter we saw how disciplined
Anthony Trollope was in managing an impressive output despite
his full-time employment. Franz Kafka struggled with the same
challenge. His biographer, Louis Begley, recounts that Kafka
served for 12-hour shifts at first and after a promotion worked
from 8.30 am to 2.30 pm, then had lunch, napped for four hours,
exercised, and had dinner, so it was 11 pm before he started writing. The first hour or more went on writing letters and in his
diary, so his novel writing took place between midnight and one,
two, or three o'clock in the morning. Begley notes:

> [T]his routine left him permanently on the verge of collapse.
> When it was suggested to him that he might organize his
> day better, he said, "The present way is the only possible
> one; if I can't bear it, so much the worse; but I will bear it
> somehow."

Speaking very much like he wrote, Hemingway told the Paris
Review about his schedule:

> When I am working on a book or story I write every morn-
> ing as soon after first light as possible. There is no one to

disturb you and it is cool or cold and you come to your work and warm as you write. You read what you have written and, as you always stop when you know what is going to happen next, you go on from there. You write until you come to a place where you still have your juice and you know what will happen next and you stop and try to live through until the next day when you hit it again. You have started at six in the morning, say, and may go on until noon or be through before that. When you stop you are as empty, and at the same time never empty but filling, as when you have made love to someone you love. Nothing can hurt you, nothing can happen, nothing means anything until the next day when you do it again. It is the wait until the next day that is hard to get through.

When John Grisham first started he had this routine:

The alarm clock would go off at 5, and I'd jump in the shower. My office was 5 minutes away. And I had to be at my desk, at my office, with the first cup of coffee, a legal pad and write the first word at 5:30, five days a week.

After that he would go to his job as a lawyer.

Some writers use extreme methods. John Lanchester wrote in *The New Yorker*:

Perhaps the finest writer ever to use speed systematically... was W. H. Auden. He swallowed Benzedrine every morning for twenty years, from 1938 onward, balancing its effect with the barbiturate Seconal when he wanted to sleep. (He also kept a glass of vodka by the bed, to swig if he woke up during the night.) He took a pragmatic attitude toward amphetamines, regarding them as a "labor-saving device" in the "mental kitchen," with the important proviso that "these mechanisms are very crude, liable to injure the cook, and constantly breaking down." Not recommended.

HG Wells had this genial suggestion:

> *There comes a moment in the day, when you have written your pages in the morning, attended to your correspondence in the afternoon, and have nothing further to do. Then come the hour when you are bored; that's the time for sex.*

FROM ADVICE TO ACTION!

ACTION: Your idea of an ideal routine day in a writer's life may be different from that of CS Lewis and the others described. What would such a day look like for you? Would you work in the morning, afternoon, or evening? What activities would balance your work hours?

Write a list of the factors that would constitute a typical ideal writing day for you. Decide which of these you can implement in the short term and which you will have to work toward over a longer period. It may be that for the time being you can create such a day only once a week, but make the changes you are able to now.

35

Money

S amuel Johnson famously said that no one but a blockhead writes except for money, but of course that's not true. People who are not blockheads write for all kinds of reasons, but if you want to make your living from your writing you face some big challenges.

A handful of authors become fabulously wealthy as a result of their handiwork (hello JK Rowling, John Grisham, Stephen King, and maybe a few dozen others). Authors who achieve "name" status are also able to make money from giving speeches, writing articles, teaching, and other auxiliary activities.

Writers who have huge sudden success can be as surprised by it as the rest of the world. EW.com says of Stephenie Meyer:

> On a lark, she'd gotten up the nerve to contact a handful of literary agents whose names she'd found online, sending each a tease about Twilight. The right one bit, and landed her new client a three-book deal for $750,000. Meyer said, "I'd been hoping for $10,000 to pay off my minivan."

However, most writers never strike it rich. A 1979 survey by the Author's Guild (of America) estimated that the average author's income the previous year was around $10,000 (£6,500). Another survey, conducted in 1993 and reported in the *New York Times*, shockingly concluded that "if anything, the financial situation of authors and playwrights has grown slightly worse in the last 15 years." Although there has not been a recent survey, indications are that writers' circumstances have not improved and, in fact, probably have deteriorated further except in the field of writing for television and film, where strong unions play a major role.

It's also the nature of the game that your income can vary greatly from year to year. Tara K Harper, author of fantasy and science fiction novels, reports on her blog:

My first royalty check for my first novel, was $272, and oh, yes, I was excited. The next check, if I remember correctly, was $358. A year later, the check was around $16k. Some years, I get advances as well as royalties, because I've signed a new contract. In some years, I make equal amounts in royalties as in foreign rights. In some years, foreign rights earn more. Basically, the money goes up and down and can't be counted on till the check clears at the bank.

My experience is similar. I've had six-figure years, and I've had four-figure years. Once in a while a nice residual check shows up when a TV movie or a series episode I wrote is repeated. Even when one of my ancient episodes of *Benson* or *Family Ties* is aired in Malaysia or wherever, a few dollars eventually wend their way to me, and my books bring in varying sums of royalties twice a year. But you can't count on making any particular amount in a given year, and that uncertainty is not something everybody can live with. At the very least, it requires you to live below your means in the good years so that you have some savings to tide you over in the bad ones.

One option is to have another job and write during your spare time. This worked for Anthony Trollope, who was incredibly prolific and successful as a novelist, yet held a full-time job as a postal inspector for many years.

Another classic author, William Makepeace Thackeray, said:

If I had said, "Mama, I want to write a book," what could she have said but "Son, write a book, by all means, but join a profession first…" And, do you know it, it would not have been bad advice. Writing is a perilous craft… luck and not merit plays far too important a part for my liking.

Thackeray made a living from journalism before his success as a novelist.

Writers are often advised to practice their craft for the pleasure of it without concern for whether it provides an income. Ray Bradbury says:

> *Money is not important. The material things are not important. Doing the work beautifully and proudly is important. If you do that, strangely enough, the money will come as a just reward for work beautifully done. A tape recorder, an automobile, they don't really belong to you. What really belongs to you? Yourself, you. That's all you'll ever have. I am ruthless with anyone around me who doesn't think or create always at the top of his form.*

W Somerset Maugham wrote:

W SOMERSET MAUGHAM (1874–1965)
Maugham's best-known work is the novel *Of Human Bondage*, but he was also a successful playwright, at one point having four plays running at the same time in London's West End. He was an ambulance driver in the First World War and a spy in the Second.

> *The moral I draw is that the writer should seek his reward in the pleasure of his work and in the release from the burden of his thoughts, and be indifferent to aught else, care nothing for praise or censure, failure or success, or, one might add, money.*

While I have the greatest respect for Bradbury and Maugham, I have to point out that it's a lot easier to have such lofty ideals once you have become as successful as they have. Rod Serling, playwright, writer for television, and host of the original *Twilight Zone* series, took this practical view:

> *You can become much more independent, much more courageous with a bank account.*

Virginia Woolf agreed, saying that to write fiction, a woman must have money (and a room of her own).

How do you know whether you'll be able to make money writing? Here's Mark Twain's counsel:

> *Write without pay until somebody offers pay; if nobody offers within three years, sawing wood is what you were intended for.*

That may be too harsh; quite a few people take longer than three years to start making significant amounts of money from their writing. Also, sawing wood is not the career opportunity it used to be. But it's true that writers who want to earn a living from their craft have to pay attention to the marketplace as well as to the calling of their muse.

The newspaper and magazine markets are shrinking and some publications are actually paying less than they used to. While they are enjoying greater digital distribution, so far the resulting advertising or subscription revenue has not been enough to guarantee their long-term survival, much less the rates of writers' pay that they previously provided. This has driven more than one freelancer to check out associated fields, such as copywriting, that are more lucrative.

Other than hitting it big with a bestselling novel, writing for film and television is the way to make the most money. However, it's also extremely competitive; getting a staff writing job on a TV show is almost impossible unless you live in Los Angeles (or, to a much lesser extent, New York). You can write your screenplay from anywhere, but the people who buy it will expect you to be available for meetings, so again it's a big help if you already live in the Los Angeles area.

FROM ADVICE TO ACTION!

ACTION: If it's your goal to get your income from writing, here are some questions to consider:

- What kind of writing will you do to earn this money?
- If there are skills you need to develop, how and where can you learn them?
- Are you reading relevant magazines or trade publications to stay informed about what's happening in this field?
- Have you researched what you need to do to break in to this field?

Create a plan that takes the above points into consideration.

36
Fame and success

A handful of authors achieve fame as well as fortune. Usually only the ones who appear on television get to a high level of public recognition. I would guess that most people would pass Danielle Steele or John Grisham on the street without recognizing them, for instance.

Some authors are famous to the people who are fans of their genre. For instance, I have no idea what Tara K Harper looks like, but fans of her *Tales of the Wolves* and people who have attended the fantasy or science fiction conventions at which she has spoken probably would consider her a celebrity.

Becoming famous is not without its dangers. Some people find being a celebrity intoxicating, as Ray Bradbury points out with some unkind words for some of the best-known authors at the time of this quote:

> *Unfortunately, I don't think I keep my ego in check very well. I try to remember that my voice is loud, which is an ego problem. But at least I don't suffer from self-deluding identity problem like, say, Carl Sagan does... he goes around thinking he's Carl Sagan. Just as Norman Mailer thinks he's Norman Mailer and Gore Vidal thinks he's Gore Vidal. I don't think I'm Ray Bradbury. That's a big distinction. It doesn't matter who you are. You mustn't go around saying who you are, or else you get captured by the mask of false identity. It's the work that identifies you.*

Edward Albee adds this warning:

> *One of the things you learn very quickly in our society is that there is not necessarily much relationship between popularity and excellence. Quite often the very best stuff is partici-*

pated in by the fewest people. But you mustn't fall into the trap, either, of assuming that because nobody likes what you have done it is very good. Sometimes people don't like what you've done because it is terrible.

With fame come invitations to address conferences, to chair organizations, to pontificate on radio and television, and to rub shoulders with other celebrities. It sounds kind of cool, but is it really a good thing? Ernest Hemingway thought not:

> Writing, at its best, is a lonely life. Organizations for writers palliate the writer's loneliness but I doubt if they improve his writing. He grows in public stature as he sheds his loneliness and often his work deteriorates.

In a letter, he admitted that this happened to him:

> Am very ashamed not to have written. Was over-run by journalists, photographers and plain and fancy crazies. Was in the middle of writing a book and it is a little like being interrupted in fornication.

Playwright Tony Kushner says:

> in the modern era it isn't enough to write; you must also be a Writer and play your part as the protagonist in a cautionary narrative in which you will fail or triumph, be in or out, hot or cold. The rewards can be fantastic; the punishment dismal; it's a zero-sum game.

A public profile also may lead to demands you may not enjoy and at which you may not excel. Novelist Robertson Davies gives an example:

> The author reads from his work. This is a chancy business, for he may not be a good reader; he may loathe the idea of

public performances; he may simply have no notion of how to make his reading acceptable as a pleasurable experience. Some of the finest writers are bad readers, as anybody who has listened to recordings of the readings of T. S. Eliot or Robert Graves can attest; in dull, strangulated voices, the poets offer their treasures.

Also, events like book signings can turn out to be less exciting than they sound. Many authors have tales of sitting alone at a signing table, praying someone would come up to them. When someone does, often they're just looking for the toilet. One author, and I'm afraid I can't remember who it was, told the story of seeing a young lad hanging around at her signing event. At the end he came up to her and said he didn't have enough money to buy a book, would she buy one for him? She said sure, and held out one of her books. "Oh no," the boy said, "I don't want one of yours."

Lorrie Moore has a suggestion for avoiding the dangers of egotism:

Perhaps one would be wise when young even to avoid thinking of oneself as a writer—for there's something stopped and satisfied, too healthy, in that. Better to think of writing, of what one does as an activity, rather than an identity—to write; I write; we write; to keep the calling a verb rather than a noun; to keep working at the thing, at all hours, in all places, so that your life does not become a pose, a pornography of wishing.

Different writers have different definitions of success, and for some fame is not a factor. May Sarton says:

Fame to me is not writing a bestseller, but knowing that someone, somewhere is reading one of my books... As an example, Journal of a Solitude *has sold 2,000 books a year for 20 years. I receive so many letters from people who tell*

*me my books have changed their lives. I feel loved by so
many people. Let's face it, that's better than money.*

Joseph Heller's take on the matter was:

*As a writer, I feel fairly fulfilled because I wrote only what I
want to write and never have to work with anybody I dislike.
To me, that measures the success: to do what I want to do
and not associate with people I don't want to.*

FROM ADVICE TO ACTION!

Everybody has to come up with their own definition of success,
and fame may or may not be a part of it.

ACTION: Consider these questions:

- What is your definition of success as a writer? Does it
  involve fame? Or just being able to do what you want? Or
  reaching a small but steady stream of readers?
- What would you have to do to achieve that level of
  success?
- What are the steps you can take now to move toward that
  kind of success?

Knowing the exact outcomes you want will help you plan your
progress toward whatever kind of success you desire.

37

Enjoying the life

There's a lot written about the challenges of writing, such as this quote from William Styron:

I get a fine, warm feeling when I'm doing well, but that pleasure is pretty much negated by the pain of getting started each day. Let's face it, writing is hell.

**WILLIAM STYRON
(1925–2006)**
Styron is best known for *Lie Down in Darkness*, *The Confessions of Nat Turner*, and *Sophie's Choice*. He was awarded the Rome Prize for his first novel, but was serving in the Korean War at the time and was unable to attend the ceremony. His experience at his first editing job was so terrible that he deliberately got himself fired.

What about the joy of writing? Some, like William Styron again, tend to define it in terms of how miserable they are when they're not writing:

I've discovered that when I'm not writing I'm prone to developing certain nervous tics, and hypochondria. Writing alleviates those quite a bit.

PG Wodehouse expressed similar thoughts:

I love writing. I never feel really comfortable unless I am either actually writing or have a story going. I could not stop writing.

JB Priestley held that:

Most writers experience only two brief periods of happiness. First when what seems a glorious idea comes flashing into mind and, secondly, when a last page has been written and you have not yet had time to consider how much better it all ought to have been.

Most writers experience a surge of joy at first seeing their book in print, or, like F Scott Fitzgerald, when they get a check:

> Then the postman rang, and that day I quit work and ran along the streets, stopping automobiles to tell friends and acquaintances about it—my novel This Side of Paradise was accepted for publication. That week the postman rang and rang, and I paid off my terrible small debts, bought a suit, and woke up every morning with a world of ineffable toploftiness and promise.

As is much of life, being a professional writer is bittersweet. The sweet is seeing your book in the bookshop; the bitter is noticing that it seems to be the same copy you saw there last month. You have to be careful not to be seen by the employees when you move it higher up on the shelf and turn it so the cover faces out.

The sweet is having your book on the shelves of the numbered top 50 books. The bitter is watching it slowly work its way down the numbers and finally off those shelves entirely as newer books come out.

The sweet is watching someone pick up your book off the shelf and peruse it; the bitter is seeing them put it back instead of buying it.

For a more positive outlook, we go to Leo Rosten:

> It is often claimed that a writer's deepest satisfaction is in being read. I do not think so. His deepest satisfaction lies in the silent alchemy of writing itself. Not to be read is a painful prospect; but it is punishment deferred. The uncontrollable joy lies in the intense and passionate involvement of writing itself, in the stubborn exploration of the self, in that excitement and ecstasy which attend our groping among the shadows and edifices of the soulless world.

Eudora Welty had a similar perspective:

At the time of writing, I don't write for my friends or myself, either; I write for it, for the pleasure of it. I believe that if I stopped to wonder what so-and-so would think, or what I'd feel like if this were read by a stranger, I would be paralyzed. I care what my friends think, very deeply—and it's only after they've read the finished thing that I really can rest, deep down. But in the writing, I have to just keep going straight through with only the thing in mind and what it dictates.

Ultimately, the writers who are happiest are the ones who find joy in the process of writing and don't make their happiness contingent on being published, getting rave reviews, or basking in adoration from the reading public.

FROM ADVICE TO ACTION!

ACTION: Consider whether you have accepted the idea that you're not writing well unless it's painful. If so, it's time to question that belief.

38

What does it take?

So, what does it take to get to the point at which writing becomes the mainstay of your life? Every writer has encountered people who say, "Oh yes, I'd write if I only had the time," as though time were the only requirement for writing something worth reading.

Mark Twain encountered a similar attitude, especially among young people who pestered him for advice on how to make it in the literary business, ideally quickly. He wrote about this in an entertaining article in the November 1870 issue of *The Galaxy* magazine:

> *The young literary aspirant is a very, very curious creature. He knows that if he wished to become a tinner, the master smith would require him to prove the possession of a good character, and would require him to promise to stay in the shop three years—possibly four—and would make him sweep out and bring water and build fires all the first year, and let him learn to black stoves in the intervals; and for these good honest services would pay him two suits of cheap clothes and his board; and next year he would begin to receive instructions in the trade, and a dollar a week would be added to his emoluments; and two dollars would be added the third year, and three the fourth; and then, if he had become a first-rate tinner, he would get about fifteen or twenty, or may be thirty dollars a week, with never a possibility of getting seventy-five while he lived... If he wanted to become a lawyer or a doctor, he would have fifty times worse; for he would get nothing at all during his long apprenticeship, and in addition would have to pay a large sum for tuition, and have the privilege of boarding and clothing himself. The literary aspirant*

knows all this, and yet he has the hardihood to present himself for reception into the literary guild and ask to share its high honors and emoluments, without a single twelvemonth's apprenticeship to show in excuse for his presumption!

Let's assume that you've acquired the rudiments of the craft. What else do you need?

Jack Kerouac offered a sometimes cryptic list for "Belief and Technique for Modern Prose" that includes a number of tips for how to live the writer's life:

Scribbled secret notebooks, and wild typewritten pages, for yr own joy
Submissive to everything, open, listening
Try never get drunk outside yr own house
Be in love with yr life
Something that you feel will find its own form
Be crazy dumbsaint of the mind
Blow as deep as you want to blow
Write what you want bottomless from bottom of the mind
The unspeakable visions of the individual
No time for poetry but exactly what is
Visionary tics shivering in the chest
In tranced fixation dreaming upon object before you
Remove literary, grammatical and syntactical inhibition
Like Proust be an old teahead of time
Telling the true story of the world in interior monolog
The jewel center of interest is the eye within the eye
Write in recollection and amazement for yourself
Work from pithy middle eye out, swimming in language sea
Accept loss forever
Believe in the holy contour of life
Struggle to sketch the flow that already exists intact in mind
Don't think of words when you stop but to see picture better
Keep track of every day the date emblazoned in yr morning

No fear or shame in the dignity of yr experience, language &
knowledge
Write for the world to read and see yr exact pictures of it
Bookmovie is the movie in words, the visual American form
In praise of Character in the Bleak inhuman Loneliness
Composing wild, undisciplined, pure, coming in from under,
crazier the better
You're a Genius all the time
Writer-Director of Earthly movies Sponsored & Angeled in
Heaven

James Michener struck a highly practical note with his advice:

…use every device in the repertory to get to know people in
the publishing business who might be of help later on.
Editors, publicists and agents circulate looking for talent
and are approachable. Go to where they are likely to be.
Introduce yourself, get to know them or, more importantly,
enable them to know you.

Finally, there is William Faulkner's famous statement about what priority writing must have in your life. It has been debated for years and is not for the faint of heart:

Everything goes by the board: honor, pride, decency… to get
the book written. If a writer has to rob his mother, he will not
hesitate; the "Ode to a Grecian Urn" is worth any number
of old ladies.

FROM ADVICE TO ACTION!

ACTION: Decide what you need to do to ramp up your enthusiasm, or live more in the moment, or be more ruthless about taking the time to write, even if it means saying no to other things.

Begin to implement these changes, starting with the small steps.

You will soon experience both the joys and the drawbacks of the writing life. For some it will lead to a lifetime as a professional writer, some will decide to maintain writing as a hobby, and some will abandon it altogether. There's no right outcome, just the one that suits you best.

39

The outlook for the novelist and screenwriter

The media have been calling the novel an endangered species for quite a while. Saul Bellow said:

From the first, too, I had been warned that the novel was at the point of death, that like the walled city or the crossbow, it was a thing of the past.

Now the media would have you believe that the very act of reading books is going out of fashion, and that books, magazines, and newspapers are doomed (at least unless you read them on an iPad, Kindle, or similar device). Haruki Murakami notes:

We have so much competition now. The main problem is time: in the nineteenth century, people—I'm talking about the leisure class—had so much time to spend, so they read big books. They went to the opera and sat for three or four hours. But now everybody is so busy, and there is no real leisure class. It's good to read Moby Dick or Dostoyevsky, but people are too busy for that now. So fiction itself has changed drastically—we have to grab people by the neck and pull them in. Contemporary fiction writers are using the techniques of other fields—jazz, video games, everything. I think video games are closer to fiction than anything else these days.

Reassurance comes from Isaac Bashevis Singer:

[I]f a young man would come to me and I can see that he has talent and he asks me if he should write, I would say go

on and write and don't be afraid of any inventions and any kind of progress. Progress can never kill literature, any more than it can kill religion.

Screenwriters have found that Hollywood is not putting as much money into developing as many projects as it used to. It is focusing on films that cost hundreds of millions to make and that, the movie companies hope, will gross at least a billion dollars. However, more smaller-scale films are being made for companies like HBO and Showtime, and continue to be made by consortia of national broadcasters like the BBC. Some have a cinema release first, others go directly to television.

The fact that broadband has become available to more and more people and at faster and faster speeds means that it's now easy to stream or download movies quickly and easily, via services like Netflix. This makes it possible for independent filmmakers to find audiences all over the world. A film that would not attract a full house at the local multiplex can have an audience of hundreds of thousands spread out across the globe. If filmmakers can find ways to make these people aware of their work, there's a good chance that enough will pay a small fee to watch or download to yield enough income for the filmmaker to keep producing movies.

The ebook phenomenon

With the popularity of smartphones and devices like the iPad and Kindle, the way was cleared for ebooks to take off at a pace that astonished most onlookers. This has also led to a major shift in how writers market their work. No longer dependent on publishers or on printing thousands of copies of their own books before they know whether or not there will be a market for them, writers are utilizing the ebook and print-on-demand technologies. Some have made substantial incomes with ebooks that they priced at 99 cents or $1.99. In some cases these authors have then gone on to achieve lucrative deals with traditional publishers as well.

While the cost of production and distribution of ebooks is negligible, this model works only if the author manages to build a large fan base. Making people aware of your book remains the biggest challenge. Authors who are adept at social media have a head start, but that realm is increasingly crowded, too.

You have an advantage if your work lends itself to exploitation in a variety of media. It's not unusual for there to be a novel and some combination of the game of the novel, a television series or feature film, a supplementary web series, a live stage show, a graphic novel version, a "making of" program, a kids' version, and of course prequels and sequels. These generally are the domain of the bigger media players, but there's nothing to stop a group of freelancers from agreeing on a project to collaborate on, with each responsible for the exploitation of the material in a different way. Whichever one catches on first could boost the success of the others.

There are other formats on the horizon. As of this writing, nobody has cracked the multimedia book format particularly well. One company calls these "Vooks"—a combination of video and books. It works for cookbooks and other how-to books for which a demonstration of some technique adds value, but in the case of fiction the format is less impressive. That's not to say that somebody won't have a breakthrough with it tomorrow—probably it's only a matter of time.

The one constant

People will always want and need to hear stories. The methods and technology will change, perhaps in ways we can't even envision yet. What remains constant is the need for storytellers who are willing to expose their hearts and souls, to serve an apprenticeship to the craft, and to take the risks that accompany all artistic endeavors. If that is you, your future as a writer is secure.

FROM ADVICE TO ACTION!

ACTION: Stay alert to changes in the world of publishing, the media, and information distribution as they happen and consider how you can take advantage of them rather than being daunted by them. Be an early adopter of new technologies and help discover how they can serve the cause of telling stories. Consider:

- How are the current technologies being used to tell stories?
- How could they be used better?
- What changes could be made to traditional ways of storytelling to help fiction continue to thrive?
- Which medium feels the most natural to you, and how can you take maximum advantage of it?

40

The writer's contribution

What does this all add up to? What do writers contribute to the greater good, and what responsibilities come with being a writer?
EB White contended:

A writer should concern himself with whatever absorbs his fancy, stirs his heart, and unlimbers his typewriter. I feel no obligation to deal with politics. I do feel a responsibility to society because of going into print: a writer has the duty to be good, not lousy; true, not false; lively, not dull; accurate, not full of error. He should tend to lift people up, not lower them down. Writers do not merely reflect and interpret life, they inform and shape life.

They also shape their own lives, as Nadine Gordimer says:

We've got to examine the truth. To me, writing, from the very beginning and right until this day, is a voyage of discovery. Of the mystery of life… I still, after all these years, have been following this voyage of discovery, finding out things that I don't know. And when I find them, moving on to other things that are then revealed… The best that is within me, anything worthwhile is in the books. Not in an autobiographical fashion. But I'm talking about the insights, the effort to understand life and transpose it.

Other writers focus on the connections that their work makes with their readers. Isabel Allende says:

I don't write for myself, and I don't think a book is an end in itself. A book is just a bridge, that you cross to touch

ISABEL ALLENDE
(b 1942)

Allende is best known for *The House of the Spirits*, *City of the Beasts*, and *Eva Luna*. While working as a journalist she interviewed Pablo Neruda, who advised her to leave journalism and become a novelist. She translated several novels into Spanish, but lost that job when her employers realized she was changing the endings to give the heroines more strength and intelligence.

somebody and grab someone by the neck and say, "Hey I believe this. You want to hear this story? You want to share this with me, this wonderful experience of storytelling?"

The internet makes the connection with readers easier. Nowadays most authors include their website address and sometimes their email address somewhere within their books. Previously, a determined reader might write a letter to an author care of the publisher and, if the reader was lucky, the publisher would, after a few weeks or months, pass the letter along to the author. Now the whole process is almost instant. Many authors of nonfiction books use the feedback they receive to shape the future editions of their books, while authors of fiction get a good idea of which of their characters are most loved—information that can be very useful to a series author, for instance.

The writer's efforts can have a much larger impact, of course. Kurt Vonnegut noted:

People are willing to take these extraordinary chances to become writers, musicians or painters, and because of them we have a culture. If this ever stops, our culture will die, because most of our culture, in fact has been created by people who got paid nothing for it—people like Edgar Allen Poe, Vincent van Gogh or Mozart. So, yes, it's a very foolish thing to do, notoriously foolish, but it seems human to attempt it anyway.

There you go: a great answer for when your unappreciative spouse, child, or friend asks why you're spending so much time writing. You get to say, "Leave me alone, I'm creating the culture!"

FROM ADVICE TO ACTION!

ACTION: Define the contribution you want to make and then use that as a guideline for your decisions about what you write. If the project takes you toward the contribution you wish to make, it's worth doing; if it doesn't, perhaps it isn't right for you just now.

Afterword

You've now read the advice of many of the best writers of all time, and you've done at least some of the exercises. You've had a look at the website (www.YourCreativeWritingMasterclass.com) and maybe you've read my other writing book, *Your Writing Coach* (also published by Nicholas Brealey Publishing).

You know what's left, don't you?

Yes, it's time to write your book, your screenplay, your play, your stories.

Maybe in a future book you'll be hailed as one of the masters of writing. Or maybe nobody but your mother will have read what you wrote.

The only thing that's certain is that if you don't write it, you'll never know.

Your Masterclass Authors

Here you'll find very brief biographies of the authors quoted in this book (other than the ones already included in sidebars). I've incorporated a couple of quirky facts about each; as you'll see, writers are an idiosyncratic bunch.

EDWARD ALBEE (b 1928). Albee's plays include *Who's Afraid of Virginia Woolf?*, *The Zoo Story*, and *The Goat, or Who is Sylvia?*. He was adopted at the age of two weeks and never felt connected to his family. The first production of an Albee play was in Berlin, though Albee was living in Greenwich Village, New York at the time.

MAYA ANGELOU (b 1928). Angelou's works include *I Know Why the Caged Bird Sings*, *Gather Together in My Name*, and *All God's Children Need Traveling Shoes*, which are three volumes of her six-volume autobiography. At President Clinton's request she recited an original poem for his 1993 inauguration. Along with being a writer, Angelou has worked as a singer, dancer, actor, director, and composer.

MARGARET ATWOOD (b 1939). Atwood's most distinguished novels are *A Handmaid's Tale*, *Life Before Man*, and *The Blind Assassin*, all of which have won awards. Outside her life as a writer she has strong political views about feminism, Canadian identity, and the environment and is a member of the Green Party of Canada.

WH AUDEN (1907–73). Auden is best known for his poems, but he also produced dramatic works such as *Pain on Both Sides* and *The Dance of Death* and numerous essays and reviews. Auden started writing poetry at the age of 13 and during his lifetime published over 400 poems. His topics spanned politics, love, religion, friendship, and nature and were written in variety of styles. He was born in England but moved to America in 1939 and became a US citizen.

PAUL AUSTER (b 1947). Auster's best-known works include *The New York Trilogy*, *The Music of Chance*, and *The Brooklyn Follies*. When he was a child he was struck by lightning. He often uses coincidence as a plot device in an attempt to bring his readers' attention to the bizarre unpredictability of life.

FRANCIS BACON (1561–1626). Bacon was a philosopher and statesman before being knighted in 1603. His most influential work was his revolutionary vision of applying philosophy to scientific methodology and his essay on a Utopian society he called the New Atlantis. Queen Elizabeth I referred to him as the "the young Lord Keeper." However, he lost favor with the Queen when he opposed a bill for a royal subsidy.

BERYL BAINBRIDGE (1932–2010). Bainbridge's best-known works are *Harriet Said*, *Injury Time*, *Sweet William*, *An Awfully Big Adventure*, and *Every Man For Himself*, a historical novel about the sinking of the *Titanic* that won the 1996 Whitbread Award. She also worked as an actress and appeared in a 1961 episode of the soap opera *Coronation Street*. For *Who's Who* and other records she lied about her age, making herself two years younger.

JACQUES BARZUN (b 1907). Barzun's books include *From Dawn to Decadence: 500 Years of Western Cultural Life, 1500 to the Present*, *Teacher in America*, and *The House of Intellect*. He has an abiding interest in classical music and is a preeminent authority on the composer Hector Berlioz. He is a fan of crime and mystery stories and has written introductions for mystery anthologies.

SAMUEL BECKETT (1906–89). Beckett's best-known works are *Waiting for Godot* and *Endgame*. He won the Nobel Prize for Literature in 1969 and was known as one of the main contributors to the "Theatre of the Absurd." As a young man he met James Joyce and helped him with research for *Finnegan's Wake*. In 1945 he had a moment of revelation, that his writing should focus on impoverishment and "subtracting rather than [like Joyce] adding."

SAUL BELLOW (1915–2005). Bellow's novels include *The Adventures of Augie March*, *Herzog*, and *Humboldt's Gift*. His mother wanted him to become a rabbi and he began studying the Bible in Hebrew at age 4. Although he did not like to be considered a Jewish writer, his cultural identity is very present in his writing.

ROBERT BENCHLEY (1889–1945). Benchley's popular humorous essays were published in *The New Yorker* and *Vanity Fair*. He wrote more than 600, which were published in various collections including *The Best of Robert Benchley*. He was a member of the literary group known as the Algonquin Round Table. He also wrote and appeared in a number of short films, one of which won an Academy Award.

JORGE LUIS BORGES (1899–1986): Borges is best known for his collections of short stories with common themes, *Ficciones* and *The Aleph*. Critics credit him with being a pioneer of magical realism, and some believe that it was his progressive blindness that led to the creation of his rich literary symbols.

ELIZABETH BOWEN (1899–1973). Bowen's works include *The Heat of the Day*, *The Last September*, and *The House in Paris*. She kept track of Irish opinions on neutrality for the British Ministry of Information during the Second World War. Bowen stammered, a condition she developed during a period of separation from her father when she was young.

T ALAN BROUGHTON (b 1936) Broughton's books include the novel *A Family Gathering*, the poetry collection *Far from Home*, and the short story collection *Suicidal Tendencies*. His father, Dr. Thomas Robert Shannon Broughton, spent

30 years writing *Magistrates of the Roman Republic*, a massive account of men elected during the Roman Republic.

ROSELLEN BROWN (b 1939). Brown wrote *Before and After*, *Tender Mercies*, and *Civil Wars*. Her first name is a combination of Rosa, her grandmother's name, and Eleanor, in honor of Eleanor Roosevelt. Brown grew up Jewish in non-Jewish neighborhoods, and many of her books address the alienation felt by outsiders.

CHARLES BURNETT (b 1944). Burnett is an African-American writer, director, and producer. His best-known film is *To Sleep with Anger*, starring Danny Glover. While working on it, he supported himself partly with a MacArthur "genius" grant of $250,000.

ITALO CALVINO (1923–1985). Calvino's best-known novels are *Invisible City* and *If on a Winter's Night a Traveller*. Born in Cuba, he grew up in San Remo. Because he refused to enlist in the Fascist military, his parents were held hostage by the Nazis for an extended period.

JULIA CAMERON (b 1948). Cameron is best known for *The Artist's Way*, a book encouraging readers to exercise their creativity with practices including writing freely every morning. She has written several sequels to that book as well as novels, plays, screenplays, and musicals. She married director Martin Scorsese after interviewing him for *Rolling Stone* magazine, though the marriage only lasted two years.

PETER CAREY (b 1943). Carey's novels include *Oscar and Lucinda*, *True History of the Kelly Gang*, and *Illywhacker*. Before becoming known as an author he worked at a series of advertising agencies, eventually establishing his own. He was invited to meet the Queen of England in 1998, but declined the invitation, requesting to reschedule.

RAYMOND CARVER (1939–88). Carver is best known for his collections of short stories, most notably *Will You Please Be Quiet, Please?*, *What We Talk about When We Talk about Love*, and *Elephant*. In the early days of his writing career he worked as a janitor at a hospital, although he spent most of his time there writing. By the end of his career he had turned to heavy drinking and he died of lung cancer.

WILLA CATHER (1873–1947). Cather's best-known novels are *One of Ours*, *The Song of the Lark*, and *Death Comes for the Archbishop*. After a series of bad reviews in the 1930s, she closed herself off from society and refused to publish any of her personal writings. Modern scholars debate whether or not Cather was a lesbian.

MICHAEL CHABON (b 1963). Chabon is known for writing *The Amazing Adventures of Kavalier and Clay*, *The Yiddish Policemen's Union*, and *The*

Mysteries of Pittsburgh. He became famous at the age of 15 for his first novel, which he wrote as his MFA thesis.

ARTHUR CONAN DOYLE (1859–1930). Conan Doyle is famous for writing *The Hound of the Baskervilles*, his other Sherlock Holmes stories, and *The Lost World.* He played cricket for the Marylebone Cricket Club. Sherlock Holmes was based on Sir Arthur's professor, Joseph Bell, a fact that Robert Louis Stevenson spotted when he read the Holmes stories.

JOSEPH CONRAD (1857–1924). Conrad, born Józef Teodor Konrad Korzeniowski, is best known for his novels *Victory*, *The Secret Agent*, and *Heart of Darkness.* His style and antiheroes influenced writers who later formed the modernist movement. Conrad's father was from a noble Polish family, but was exiled for his political activities by the Imperial Russian authorities. Although not able to speak English fluently until his mid-20s, Conrad is regarded as one of the greatest English novelists.

RAY COONEY (b 1932). Cooney, a playwright and actor, wrote *Run for Your Wife*, which ran for nine years in London's West End and remains its longest-running comedy. In France he is known as "the English Feydeau."

ANN CUMMINS. Cummins has written the novel *Yellowcake* and the short story collection *Red Ant House.* She grew up in New Mexico's Navajo Indian Reservation and often writes about the Southwest. She is a professor of creative writing at Northern Arizona University.

ROALD DAHL (1916–90). Dahl is best known for his children's novels *Charlie and the Chocolate Factory*, *Matilda*, and *The BFG.* While Dahl is commonly known as a children's author, he also wrote a large number of short stories for adults. Many of his books contain themes or characters from Norwegian mythology.

DANTE ALIGHIERI (c. 1265–1321). Dante is best known for his epic poem *Divine Comedy*, which includes "Inferno," "Purgatorio," and "Paradiso." By writing high literature in Italian, he moved the language out of the vernacular and into scholarly acceptance. Dante was betrothed from age 12, but was in love with another woman.

ROBERTSON DAVIES (1913–95). Davies is best known for The Deptford Trilogy, The Cornish Trilogy, and The Salterton Trilogy. He was one of the initiators of the Stratford Shakespearean Festival of Canada. He never wrote on a computer, insisting that he didn't want to work quickly, he wanted to work well.

SIMONE DE BEAUVOIR (1908–86). De Beauvoir is best known for her 1949 treatise *The Second Sex*, and for novels including *She Came to Stay* and *The Mandarins.* She had a long relationship with *Jean-Paul Sartre*, but they never had a joint household and she had affairs with many others of both genders.

CHARLES DICKENS (1812–70): Dickens's best-known novels include *David Copperfield*, *A Tale of Two Cities*, and *Great Expectations*. As a child, he helped to support his family by working at Warren's Blacking, where he labeled containers of shoe polish for ten hours a day. He was fascinated by the paranormal and was one of the first members of The Ghost Club.

FYODOR DOSTOYEVSKY (1821–81). Dostoyevsky's most famous works are the novels *The Idiot* and *The Brothers Karamazov* and his epic, *Crime and Punishment*. He grew up in the grounds of a mental hospital and without the consent of his parents would sneak into the hospital to listen to the stories of the patients. The understanding of the human mind he gained from these forbidden visits is reflected in his novels.

RODDY DOYLE (b 1958). Doyle's works include *The Commitments*, *Paddy Clarke Ha Ha Ha*, and *The Woman Who Walked into Doors*. He writes in the working-class Irish vernacular and has been criticized for using offensive language. Doyle is a supporter of Chelsea Football Club.

ALEXANDRE DUMAS (1802–70). Dumas is best known for his novels *The Three Musketeers*, *The Count of Monte Cristo*, and *Twenty Years After*. Dumas was the grandson of a French nobleman and a Haitian slave and was inspired by his mother's stories of his father, a general in Napoleon's army who died when Alexandre was only 4 years old.

DAPHNE DU MAURIER (1907–89). Du Maurier, also known as Lady Browning, is best known for *Rebecca*, *Jamaica Inn*, and "The Birds." Her books were the most often checked-out library books for decades. She was accused of lifting the plot of *Rebecca* from a work by Carolina Nabuco; du Maurier responded by pointing out that the plot was an old one to begin with.

DOMINICK DUNNE (1925–2009): Dunne is best known for *The Two Mrs. Grenvilles*, *A Season in Purgatory*, and *An Inconvenient Woman*. He also worked as a television actor and Hollywood producer. His daughter was murdered after becoming famous for her performance in *Poltergeist*; Dunne wrote for *Vanity Fair* about her murderer's trial.

UMBERTO ECO (b 1932). Eco's novels include *The Name of the Rose*, *Foucault's Pendulum*, and *The Prague Cemetery*. He is also an expert in medievalism and literary theory. In his Milan apartment he has a library of 30,000 books; in the library at his vacation house near Rimini he has 20,000 more.

STANLEY ELKIN (1930–95). Elkin's works include *George Mills*, *Mrs. Ted Bliss*, and *The MacGuffin*. He had multiple sclerosis for decades, but died of a heart attack. Though he is thought of as a Jewish author, he did not consider his religious background to have had much impact on his work.

RALPH ELLISON (1913–94). Ellison wrote *The Invisible Man, Shadow and Act*, and *Going to the Territory*. Ellison was a small child when his father died; he learned years later that his father had named him after Ralph Waldo Emerson in the hopes that he would become a poet. After the tremendous success of *The Invisible Man*, Ellison published collections of essays and short stories, but never completed another novel.

LUCY ELLMANN (b 1956). Ellmann is best known for the novels *Sweet Desserts* and *Varying Degrees of Happiness*, and the screenplay *The Spy Who Caught a Cold*. She emphasizes words by writing them in all capital letters. She is also a book reviewer for the *Guardian*.

JOSH EMMONS (b 1973). Emmons wrote the novels *The Loss of Leon Meed* and *Prescription for a Superior Existence*, and the short story "Arising." He has lectured at four colleges and universities, and now teaches at Iowa's Grinnell College.

PENELOPE FITZGERALD (1916–2000). Fitzgerald is best known for *Offshore*, *The Blue Flower*, and *Innocence*. She began writing historical novels when she had written everything she wanted to say about her own life. The houseboat on the Thames in which she lived sank twice.

GUSTAVE FLAUBERT (1821–80). Flaubert is noted for *Madame Bovary*, *Memoirs of a Madman*, and *Sentimental Education*. *Madame Bovary* is considered possibly the greatest novel of the nineteenth century. Flaubert lived with his mother for much of his life and was open about using the services of both male and female prostitutes.

THOMAS FLEMING (b 1927). Fleming's best-known works include *Now We Are Enemies, A Passionate Girl*, and *Duel: Alexander Hamilton, Aaron Burr and the Future of America*. He makes frequent television appearances to discuss the American Revolution. An Irish-American, Fleming is closely associated with his home town of Jersey City, New Jersey, where he was surrounded by Irish politics from an early age.

EM FORSTER (1879–1970). Forster is best known for *A Room with a View, A Passage to India*, and *Where Angels Fear to Tread*. For two decades, he worked as a broadcaster for BBC radio. His novel *Maurice*, a tale of homosexual love, was written starting in 1913 but not published until a year after Forster's death.

BONNIE FRIEDMAN. Friedman's best-known works are *Writing Past Dark: Envy, Fear, Distraction and Other Dilemmas in the Writer's Life, The Thief of Happiness: The Story of an Extraordinary Psychotherapy*, and "Becoming Visible." She studied at the Bronx High School of Science, even though she had no interest in or aptitude for the hard sciences. Her first published short story appeared in *Playgirl* magazine.

GEORGE GALLO (b 1956). Gallo is a painter, musician, writer, and director. Films he has written include *Wise Guys*, *Midnight Run*, and *Code Name: The Cleaner*. He paints in the style of the Pennsylvania Impressionists.

JANE GARDAM (b 1928). Gardam's best-known works are *God on the Rocks*, *Going into a Dark House*, and *Black Faces, White Faces*. She is currently writing a series of programs about suburbs for BBC radio. She was awarded the OBE in 2009.

ANDRE GIDE (1869–1951). Gide's works include *Les Caves du Vatican*, *Isabelle*, and *Les Nourritures Terrestres*. Gide was an intense advocate of Communism until he spent time in the USSR during the 1930s; thereafter he was equally intensely against it. His books were banned by the Catholic Church in 1952, one year after his death.

GLEN DAVID GOLD (b 1964). Gold's best-known works are *Carter Beats the Devil*, *Sunnyside*, and "The Tears of Squonk." He has also written comic books and one episode of the 1990s cartoon program *Hey Arnold!*. He believes that readers do not question historical writing, and therefore frequently emulates the voice of nonfiction.

WILLIAM GOLDMAN (b 1931). Goldman is best known for his screenplays for *The Princess Bride*, *Butch Cassidy and the Sundance Kid*, and *All the President's Men*. Goldman wrote fake autobiographical details into his novel *The Princess Bride*, which are often mistaken for truth by his readers. His famous quote about the film-making business is "Nobody knows anything."

NADINE GORDIMER (b 1923). Gordimer's novels include *A Guest of Honour*, *The Conservationist*, and *The Pickup*. Most of her novels relate to the culture and politics of South Africa, her home country. She was prominent in the anti-apartheid movement and was one of the first people Nelson Mandela asked to see after he was released from jail.

MARY GORDON (b 1949). Gordon's best-known novels are *The Company of Women* and *The Other Side*, and she also has written three memoirs, including *Circling My Mother*. In 2008 the Governor of New York named her the official New York State Author.

GRAHAM GREENE (1904–91). Greene's most famous novels are *The Quiet American*, *Our Man in Havana*, and *Brighton Rock*. He is also noted for his film noir screenplay *The Third Man*. He attempted suicide on several occasions, supposedly to overcome boredom; he was later diagnosed as having a bipolar disorder. After falling foul of a conman, Greene left Britain to live in the Antibes.

JOHN GRISHAM (b 1955). Grisham's legal thrillers include *The Firm*, which sold more than seven million copies, *The Pelican Brief*, *The Rainmaker*, and *A*

Time to Kill. The latter was his first book and was rejected by 28 publishers before a small publishing house issued an edition of 5,000 copies.

JOHN GUARE (b 1938). Guare's best-known plays are *Six Degrees of Separation* and *The House of Blue Leaves.* He also wrote the screenplay for Louis Malle's film *Atlantic City,* for which he was nominated for an Oscar. He wrote his first play at the age of 11.

ALAN GURGANUS (b 1947). Gurganus is known for writing *The Oldest Living Confederate Widow Tells All, Blessed Assurance,* and *Plays Well with Others.* He originally wanted to be a painter and sometimes illustrates his own works. He served in the Vietnam War and has made statements against the war in Iraq.

TARA K HARPER (b 1961). Harper's well-known works include *Wolfwalker, Shadow Leader,* and *Lightwing.* She plays a variety of instruments, including the dulcimer. She struggled to choose between a career in writing or in space science and compromised by writing science fiction.

KENT HARUF (b 1943). Hauf's prize-winning novels include *The Tie That Binds* and *Plainsong.* All of his novels have the fictional town of Holt, Colorado as their setting. Among the places he worked before becoming a writer are a chicken farm, a presidential library, and Turkey (as a teacher with the Peace Corps).

NATHANIEL HAWTHORNE (1804–64). Hawthorne's best-known works include *Twice-Told Tales, The Scarlet Letter,* and "Young Goodman Brown." Hawthorne was born Hathorne, and added the "w" to his name to distance himself from an ancestor who was a judge in the Salem Witch Trials. Melville's *Moby-Dick* is dedicated to him.

JOSEPH HELLER (1923–99). Heller is famous for writing *Catch-22, Portrait of an Artist, as an Old Man,* and *Something Happened.* "Catch-22" has entered the English language as an idiom because of Heller's book, which did not initially sell well. Heller says that he knew the first and last line of each of his stories before beginning them.

JAMES D HOUSTON (1933–2009). Houston is best known for *Snow Mountain Passage, Continental Drift,* and *Farewell to Manzanar.* He supplemented his income by teaching guitar and playing in a bluegrass band in Santa Cruz, California. Houston began writing while serving in the US Air Force during the Second World War.

WILLIAM DEAN HOWELLS (1837–1920). Howells wrote "Christmas Every Day," *The Rise of Silas Lapham,* and *A Modern Instance.* Before becoming a novelist he worked as an elected clerk in the Ohio State House of Representatives. He was a pioneer of American realistic fiction and thought that all other forms of fiction were a waste of time.

HENRIK IBSEN (1882–1906). Ibsen's major, and in their time controversial, works are *An Enemy of the People*, *Peer Gynt*, *A Doll's House*, *The Wild Duck*, and *Ghosts*. Ibsen began writing plays while training as an apprentice pharmacist after he was forced to leave school at the age of 15. He went on to become one of the most forward-thinking playwrights. He died after suffering a series of strokes.

JOHN IRVING (b 1942). Irving's best-known novels are *The World According to Garp*, *The Cider House Rules*, *Hotel New Hampshire*, and *A Prayer for Owen Meany*. He adapted *The Cider House Rules* for the screen. He has a brief appearance in the film, playing a stationmaster.

SHELLEY JACKSON (b 1960). Jackson is the author of *Patchwork Girl*, *Half Life*, and *The Doll Games*. She pioneered the field of hypertext. Her novella *Skin* was entirely written in one-word tattoos on participants' bodies.

PETER JAMES (b 1948). James has written 25 books, including a series that features Detective Superintendent Roy Grace and is set in Brighton. He is the son of Cornelia James, former glovemaker to Queen Elizabeth II, and he has also worked as a screenwriter and producer.

KEITH JOHNSTONE (b 1933). Johnstone invented Theatresports, a form of improvisational comedy, and documented his approach in two books, *Impro* and *Impro for Storytellers*. He still teaches his approach internationally and tells improvisers "Don't concentrate," "Be obvious," and "Don't be clever" in order to help them release their spontaneity.

SAMUEL JOHNSON (1709–84). Johnson is best known for *A Journey to the Western Islands of Scotland*, *The Idler*, and *A Dictionary of the English Language*. He completed his dictionary single-handedly in nine years, competing for his own satisfaction against the French, whose dictionary was compiled by 40 writers over the course of 40 years. He is buried in Westminster Abbey.

CARL JUNG (1875–1961). Jung's most famous books are *Psychology of the Unconscious*, *Psychological Types*, and *Psychology and Religion*. When he was 38 he began having hallucinations, which he wrote down to analyze and study. Jung's theories are the basis for the Myers-Briggs test.

FRANZ KAFKA (1883–1924). Kafka's books include *The Metamorphosis*, *The Trial*, and *A Country Doctor*. He requested that his friends burn his unpublished writings after his death, but this request was ignored and some of his most-read works were published posthumously.

STEPHEN KING (b 1947). King is best known for *The Shining*, *Carrie*, and *The Stand*. He began writing his seven-volume Dark Tower series when he was 19 and didn't complete it until he was 46. When King was a child he saw a friend being killed by a train, but he does not remember the experience.

MILAN KUNDERA (b 1929). The Czech author's most famous novels are *The Unbearable Lightness of Being* and *The Book of Laughter and Forgetting*. His books were banned by the Communist government of Czechoslovakia until the Velvet Revolution in 1989. Since 1993 he has written his novels in French.

TONY KUSHNER (b 1956). Kushner's most famous works are *Angels in America*, *Caroline, or Change*, and the screenplay for *Munich*. He often continues revising his works after they have been published.

ANNE LAMOTT (b 1954). Lamott 's best-known words are *Operating Instructions*, *Traveling Mercies*, and *Bird by Bird*. She has a large following online, particularly on Facebook. She is a born-again Christian, and she wears a bracelet with her name on one side and "LGB," standing for "love, gratitude, and breath," on the other.

STIEG LARSSON (1954–2004). Larsson wrote *The Girl with the Dragon Tattoo*, *The Girl Who Played with Fire*, and *The Girl Who Kicked the Hornets' Nest*. All three were written for fun in his spare time and published after his death. He changed the spelling of his first name from the original "Stig" to distinguish himself from a contemporary of his by the same name, also a writer.

DH LAWRENCE (1885–1930). Lawrence is best known for his novels *Sons and Lovers*, *Women in Love*, and *Lady Chatterley's Lover*. His works were considered shocking, sometimes pornographic. In 1960, Penguin Books went on trial in England under the Obscene Publications Act for publishing the unexpurgated edition of *Lady Chatterley's Lover*. The prosecutor asked the jury to consider whether it was the kind of book "you would wish your wife or servants to read." The verdict: not guilty.

JOHN LE CARRE (b 1931). Le Carré is the author of *The Spy Who Came in from the Cold*, *Tinker, Tailor, Soldier, Spy*, and *The Constant Gardener*. Before writing his spy novels he worked for MI5 and tracked Soviet sympathizers. When he began writing he was with MI6, which prohibited him from publishing under his own name; his pseudonym translates as "John the Square."

HARPER LEE (b 1926). Lee is best known for her Pulitzer prize-winning novel *To Kill a Mockingbird*, her only novel to be published. Growing up in Monroeville, Alabama, Lee was a tomboy and spent most of her time with her best friend Truman Capote, whom she later assisted with the research for his book *In Cold Blood*. Her novel continues to be a bestseller, but since its publication she has made few public appearances and turned down requests for interviews.

DIANE LEFER. Lefer is best-known for *California Transit*, *The Blessing Next to the Wound* (co-authored with Hector Aristizabal), and "The Tangerine Quandary." She researches her plays and novels by doing the jobs her characters have, including picking potatoes and typing autopsies.

URSULA LE GUIN (b 1929). Le Guin's books include the Earthsea fantasy novels (starting with *The Wizard of Earthsea*), *The Lathe of Heaven*, and *The Left Hand of Darkness*. She was 11 years old when she submitted her first story to the magazine *Astounding Science Fiction* (it was rejected).

ELMORE LEONARD (b 1925). Leonard's novels include *Hombre*, *52 Pick-Up*, *Get Shorty*, *Maximum Bob*, *Out of Sight*, and *Fire in the Hole*. Many have been filmed (with a few exceptions, not doing justice to their source material), and the latter is the basis of the television series *Justified*. Fascinated by the exploits of Bonnie and Clyde and other gangsters when he was a youth, Leonard developed a life-long fascination with guns.

SINCLAIR LEWIS (1885–1951). Lewis is best known for his novel *Babbit*, for which he was the first American to be awarded the Nobel Prize for Literature, as well as *It Can't Happen Here*, *Arrowsmith*, and *Main Street*. He had a love-hate relationship with the movers and shakers of industry, often lampooning them in his fiction but enjoying their approval in real life. Treated for alcoholism as early as 1937, he continued to drink and died of advanced alcoholism at the age of 65.

HP LOVECRAFT (1890–1937). Lovecraft is best known for "The Call of Cthulhu," *The Shadow Out of Time*, and *At the Mountains of Madness*. He is referenced frequently in adventure games, RPGs, and computer games. Although American, he often chose to use English spellings in his writing.

DAVID MAMET (b 1947). Playwright and screenwriter Mamet's works include *Perversity in Chicago*, *American Buffalo*, and the play for which he won the Pulitzer Prize in 1984, *Glengarry Glen Ross*. He was nominated for an Academy Award for the screenplay of *The Verdict*, which starred Paul Newman. He also blogs for *The Huffington Post*.

HILARY MANTEL (b 1952). Mantel is best known for *Wolf Hall*, *Fludd*, and *Beyond Black*. She lived in Botswana for several years with her geologist husband. She was misdiagnosed as psychotic in her 20s and discovered years later that she did not have a mental illness, but endometriosis.

JAY McINERNEY (b 1955). McInerney is best known for his novels *Bright Lights, Big City*, *Story of My Life*, *Brightness Falls*, and *The Last of the Savages*. Dubbed one of the "literary brat pack" of the late twentieth century, he studied under Raymond Carver. The real-life characters of his glamorous world often appear as fictional characters in his novels.

HERMAN MELVILLE (1819–91). Melville's best-known works include *Moby-Dick*, *Billy Budd*, and "Bartleby the Scrivener." He was initially successful, but his popularity dropped off in the 1850s, and his work did not receive much attention for the following 50 years. In 1841, he took a job aboard the whaling ship *Acushnet*, from which he deserted a year later.

STEPHENIE MEYER (b 1973). Meyer was the biggest-selling author of 2008 and 2009 with her Twilight books chronicling the romance of a normal girl and a vampire. Her earnings exceed $50 million. A Mormon, she neither smokes nor drinks and *Twilight* was the first thing she ever wrote.

JAMES MICHENER (1907–97). Michener's best-known books include *Tales of the South Pacific*, *The Fires of Spring*, and *The Drifters*. While serving in the US Navy during the Second World War he was given special assignments because his commanders mistakenly believed him to be the son of an admiral.

HENRY MILLER (1891–1980). Miller's work includes *Tropic of Cancer*, *Tropic of Capricorn*, and *Black Spring*. Many of his novels were banned for obscenity in the United States and had to be smuggled in from France.

DEBORAH MOGGACH (b 1948). Moggach is best known for her novels *The Ex-Wives*, *Tulip Fever*, and *These Foolish Things*. Being something of a tomboy, her childhood hero was William Brown. Her first published writings were articles for newspapers in Pakistan; her first novel was also written there.

RICK MOODY (b 1961). Moody wrote *The Ice Storm*, *The Diviners*, and *Garden State*. He sings with the modern folk group the Wingdale Community Singers, and co-hosts a podcast.

LORRIE MOORE (b 1957). Moore is the author of *Birds of America*, *Who Will Run the Frog Hospital?*, and *A Gate at the Stairs*. In her late teens she won a fiction contest run by *Seventeen* magazine. Her first formally published work was a collection of short stories written for her Master's thesis.

TONI MORRISON (b 1931). Morrison's best-known novels are *The Bluest Eye*, *Song of Solomon*, and *Beloved*. After working as a teacher for a decade, she created a program that facilitates collaborations between top-tier artists and promising students. She won the Pulitzer Prize in 1988 and the Nobel Prize in 1993.

ALICE MUNRO (b 1931). Munro is the author of *The Moons of Jupiter*, *The Love of a Good Woman*, and *Open Secrets*. Despite being a Canadian author, she is most often compared to American Southern writers. She opened a bookstore in Victoria in the 1960s; it is still popular today.

HARUKI MURAKAMI (b 1949). Murakami is best known for *Kafka on the Shore*, *After Dark*, and *Norwegian Wood*. He began running marathons at age 33 and later became a tri-athlete. Before he was an author Murakami ran a jazz coffeehouse with his wife, and many of his books reference music in their titles.

VLADIMIR NABOKOV (1899–1977). Nabokov's works include *Lolita*, *Pale Fire*, and *Speak, Memory*. He had synesthesia, which led him to perceive letters as having color. He was a chess enthusiast and believed that the skills necessary for creating chess problems were the same as those needed for creating literature.

VS NAIPAUL (b 1932). Naipaul's best-known books are *A Bend in the River*, *Magic Seeds*, and *A House for Mr. Biswas*. He was awarded one of the four scholarships available to send Trinidadians to university in Britain. Although he never loved his first wife, he was married to her for 41 years, until she died.

FRIEDRICH NIETZSCHE (1844–1900). Nietzsche's best-known books are *Ecce Homo*, *On the Genealogy of Morality*, and *Untimely Meditations*. Nietzsche gave up his Prussian citizenship at age 24 and was stateless until he died. His poor health compelled him to travel for much of his life in an attempt to find a climate that would suit him.

JOSIP NOVAKOVICH (b 1956). Novakovich's writing includes *April Fool's Day*, *Apricots from Chernobyl*, and *Salvation and Other Disasters*. He studied medicine in Serbia before emigrating to the United States at age 20. In addition to his creative writing he has authored a textbook, *Fiction Writer's Workshop*.

BEN NYBERG has written *One Great Way to Write Short Stories* and *Britain 101*. Nyberg created a systematic approach to short story writing, called the Primer Method, that is included in various university creative-writing curricula.

FLANNERY O'CONNOR (1925–64). O'Connor wrote two novels, *Wise Blood* and *The Violent Bear It Away*, and 32 short stories. Her writing was marked by a fascination with the grotesque. At the age of 6 she was featured in a newsreel, showing off her chicken that could walk backward. She later said, "I was just there to assist the chicken but it was the high point of my life. Everything since has been anticlimax."

ORHAN PAMUK (b 1952). Pamuk's novels include *My Name Is Red*, *The White Castle*, and *Snow*. He received the Nobel Prize in literature in 2006. Between the ages of 22 and 30 he lived with his mother and concentrated on writing and trying to find a publisher for his first novel.

SARA PARETSKY (b 1947). Paretsky's books include *Deadlock*, *Bitter Medicine*, *Burn Marks*, and *Body Work*. All but two of her novels feature VI Warshawski, a female private eye, as protagonist. Advised by her doctor to give up red wine, chocolate, and caffeine, she has found coffee the hardest to sacrifice.

JAMES PATTERSON (b 1947). A former advertising man, Patterson has written 71 novels in 33 years, including thrillers featuring the character Alex Cross, and is the world's bestselling author. In 2005 he founded the James Patterson PageTurner Awards and donated more than $850,000 for people and institutions that spread the excitement of reading and books.

GEORGE PELECANOS (b 1957). Pelecanos is best known for *The Night Gardener*, *A Firing Offense*, and *Shame the Devil*. He wrote many episodes of *The Wire* for HBO. Before publishing his first book, he worked at various food service jobs, including tending bar and washing dishes.

ROBERT PIRSIG (b 1928). Pirsig's best-known works are *Zen and the Art of Motorcycle Maintenance* and *Lila: An Inquiry Into Morals*. He is a diagnosed paranoid schizophrenic, and has repeatedly received shock therapy. 121 publishers rejected *Zen* before William Morrow Publishers bought it.

JB PRIESTLEY (1894–1984). Priestley is best known for *The Good Companions* and the plays *An Inspector Calls* and *When We Are Married*. He made popular broadcasts on BBC radio during the Second World War, which were canceled due to complaints by Churchill's Cabinet.

ANNIE PROULX (b 1935). Proulx's best-known works are *The Shipping News*, *Postcards*, and "Brokeback Mountain." Her first published work appeared in *Seventeen* magazine. She is three times married and three times divorced.

MARCEL PROUST (1871–1922). Proust is best known for his novel *A la recherché du temps perdu* (In Search of Lost Time), originally translated as Remembrance of Things Past. It is revered as a masterpiece, although doubts have often been expressed about how many people complete their reading of it (a modern translated edition runs to six volumes and 4,211 pages). Proust suffered with illness for much of his life and spent most of his final three years in his bedroom, working on his novel and eventually dying of pneumonia and a pulmonary abscess.

ARTHUR QUILLER-COUCH (1863–1944). Quiller-Couch is noted for editing *The Oxford Book of English Verse, 1250–1900* and writing *Adventures in Criticism* and *Hetty Wesley*. He was a Bard of Gorseth Kernow, an organization founded to honor the Celtic history of Cornwall. Sir Arthur wrote the end of *St. Ives*, which Robert Louis Stevenson had not completed.

JEAN RHYS (1890–1979). Rhys wrote *Wide Sargasso Sea*, *Voyage in the Dark*, and *Sleep it Off, Lady*. Rhys began training as an actress at RADA in London but was unable to shed her Caribbean accent and left the program.

LEO ROSTEN (1908–97). Rosten's popular works include *The Joys of Yiddish*, *The Education of H*Y*M*A*N K*A*P*L*A*N*, and *Leo Rosten's Treasury of Jewish Quotations*. He was fluent in Yiddish and English and taught English to immigrants to the United States during the Depression.

JK ROWLING (b 1965). The author of the world-famous Harry Potter series, Rowling was judged by *Forbes* magazine in 2011 to have a net worth of $1 billion. She had overall script approval for the films made from her books and was a producer on the final installment.

SALMAN RUSHDIE (b 1947). Rushdie's works include *Midnight's Children*, *The Satanic Verses*, and *Shalimar the Clown*. He is under fatwa for *The Satanic Verses* and is the main villain in a 1990 Pakistani film, in which he attempts to destroy Pakistan by establishing a casino chain there. He was knighted by the Queen of England in 2007.

JD SALINGER (1919–2010). Salinger's most-noted works are *The Catcher in the Rye*, *Nine Stories*, and *Franny and Zooey*. He was raised Jewish and didn't learn until he was in his teens that his mother was actually an Irish Catholic. After college, Salinger worked in Austria, leaving the country the month before the Nazis annexed it.

WILLIAM SAROYAN (1908–81). Saroyan's best-known work is his Pulitzer Prize-winning play *The Time of Your Life*, and the novel *The Human Comedy*. The latter was also a film (1943), but rather than the film being an adaptation of the novel, it's the other way around. When Saroyan was fired from writing the screenplay of the story, he write it as a novel and published it just before the film was released.

MAY SARTON (1912–95). Sarton wrote *Journal of a Solitude*, *The House by the Sea*, and *Mrs. Stevens Hears the Mermaids Singing*. She was born in Belgium, but is thought of as an American writer. *Mrs. Stevens Hears the Mermaids Singing* was an early work about lesbianism, and initially damaged the reputation of Sarton's previous work.

PAUL SCHRADER (b 1946). Schrader is an American screenwriter and director. He wrote *Taxi Driver* and *Raging Bull*, both directed by Martin Scorsese. Films he directed include *American Gigolo* and *Mishima: A Life in Four Chapters*. Due to his family's religion, he did not see a film until he was 18 years old.

ROD SERLING (1924–75). Serling wrote many influential and award-winning dramas during the "Golden Age" of live television, on anthology series such as the Kraft Television Theater and Playhouse 90. His breakout success was *Requiem for a Heavyweight*, produced in 1956. He became well known to the general public for producing and being the on-camera host of *The Twilight Zone*, which ran for 156 episodes, of which Serling wrote 92. He has a star on the Hollywood Walk of Fame.

WILLIAM SHAKESPEARE (1564–1616). Shakespeare is the best-known and most-performed playwright in the world and produced classics including *Romeo and Juliet*, *Hamlet*, *Macbeth*, and *Othello*, as well as 154 sonnets and other poems. He was an actor and part owner of a theatrical company called the Lord Chamberlain's Men (later the King's Men). He and his wife, Anne Hathaway, had three children. There is speculation about his sexuality, his religion, and even whether he wrote all of the works attributed to him. His gravestone includes a curse on anyone who dares to move his bones.

GEORGE BERNARD SHAW (1856-1950). Shaw's famous plays include *Pygmalion, Heartbreak House,* and *Man and Superman.* He accepted his Nobel Prize, despite reservations, because his wife perceived it to be an honor for Ireland. Before his successful career as a playwright Shaw wrote five novels, none of which was published at the time.

MARY SHELLEY (1797-1851). Shelley's best-known works are *Frankenstein, The Last Man,* and *Falkner.* Her father, William Godwin, deliberately raised her to be a philosopher and cynic. She wrote *Frankenstein* after spending an evening with Lord Byron discussing ghosts; Byron suggested that everyone present that night write his own horror story.

CAROL SHIELDS (1935-2003). Shields wrote *The Stone Diaries, Larry's Party,* and *Unless.* While she is known as a Canadian writer, she was born in the United States and did not become a Canadian citizen until after her marriage in 1957. In addition to her fiction work she wrote a biography of Jane Austen.

GEORGES SIMENON (1903-89). Simenon's books include *Maigret à New York, The Strangers in the House,* and *Le Fils.* He would write up to 80 pages in a day. Maigret, his most famous character, features in 75 of his novels and 28 of his short stories.

STEPHEN SONDHEIM (b 1930). Sondheim's famous musicals include *Into the Woods, Sweeney Todd: The Demon Barber of Fleet Street,* and *A Little Night Music.* Sondheim wrote four musicals under the tutelage of Oscar Hammerstein II, none of which has been produced. He is dissatisfied with his own work on the lyrics of *West Side Story,* believing that they are not consistent with the characters.

SUSAN SONTAG (1933-2004). Sontag's writing includes *In America, The Volcano Lover,* and her play *Alice in Bed.* Before publishing her novels she was known for her essays, mostly on different forms of art. As an activist she called for US military involvement in the war in Bosnia; she lived in Sarajevo during its siege.

SOL STEIN (b 1926). Stein's most famous novel is *The Magician,* which caused controversy among Christians. As well as plays and other novels, Stein is also a writer and editor for the Voice of America, which broadcasts radio programs to more than two million people behind the Iron Curtain. He was also a major influence as a publisher and edited two books that are listed in the top 100 nonfiction books of the twentieth century.

KATHRYN STOCKETT. Stockett's well-received debut novel was *The Help,* about African American maids working in a white household. Stockett was herself raised by an African American domestic worker in Jackson, Mississippi. She got 45 rejection letters for *The Help,* which went on to become a bestseller.

JONATHAN SWIFT (1667–1745). Swift's works include *Gulliver's Travels, A Modest Proposal*, and *Drapier's Letters*. He used various pen names during his lifetime and never published under his own name. He eventually became the Dean of St. Patrick's Cathedral in Dublin.

AMY TAN (b 1952). Tan's best-known novels are *The Joy Luck Club, The Kitchen God's Wife*, and *The Bonesetter's Daughter*. She has three half-siblings living in China, whom she did not meet until she was 35. Her children's book *Sagwa, the Chinese Siamese Cat* has been made into an animated PBS series.

EMMA TENNANT (b 1937). Tennant is known for writing *Pemberley* and *The French Dancer's Bastard*, which are sequels to *Pride and Prejudice* and *Jane Eyre* respectively. Born into the English aristocracy, she has been married four times.

WILLIAM MAKEPEACE THACKERAY (1811–63). Thackeray's best-known works are *Vanity Fair, Catherine*, and *The History of Henry Esmond*. His *The Book of Snobs* spread the modern meaning of the word "snob." He lost much of his inheritance by supporting two newspapers, both of which failed.

HENRY DAVID THOREAU (1817–62). Thoreau's best-known works are *Walden* and his essays "Civil Disobedience" and "Life without Principle." Thoreau wrote extensively about natural history and died from bronchitis contracted while he was counting the rings of tree stumps in a late-night rain storm.

ROSE TREMAIN (b 1943). Tremain wrote *The Road Home, Music and Silence*, and *Sacred Country*. She frequently makes radio broadcasts and writes reviews for the press. Tremain taught creative writing at the University of East Anglia, her alma mater, for eight years.

ANTHONY TROLLOPE (1815–82). Trollope's finest works are *The Warden, Barchester Towers*, and *The Way We Live Now*. His mother was a successful novelist in her time, his father a failed farmer and barrister. Trollope pursued his dream of political office, but described his first and only campaign as "the most wretched fortnight of my manhood." He finish in fourth (last) place. He wrote prolifically for the remainder of his life, also editing *St. Paul's Magazine*.

BRENDA UELAND (1891–1985). Ueland is best known for her book *If You Want to Write: A Book About Art, Independence and Spirit*. She wrote for numerous publications as well as for radio. She was a feminist and was said to have two rules to live by: tell the truth and never do anything you don't want to.

VOLTAIRE (1694–1778). Voltaire is best known for *Candide, Zadig*, and the *Man of Forty Crowns*. Born François-Marie Arouet, he invented the pen name Voltaire from the Latinized spelling of his surname, Arovet, and of the initial letters of *le jeune*, li. His outspoken views on royalty and Christianity earned him a stint in the Bastille and expulsion from Paris. His output was astonishing, including 20,000 letters, and his writing inspired the key figures of the French and American Revolutions.

ALICE WALKER (b 1944). Walker's best-known works are *The Color Purple*, *The Temple of My Familiar*, and *Possessing the Secret of Joy*. She spent her childhood in social isolation due to a disfiguring scar that was later removed. *The Color Purple* was made into a musical and was nominated for 11 Tony Awards.

MARINA WARNER (b 1946). Warner's novels include *The Lost Father* and *Indigo*; her nonfiction books include *From Beast to Blonde: On Fairy Tales and Their Tellers* and *Phantasmagoria*. She is working on a novel inspired by her father's bookshop in Egypt in the 1950s. She has won 14 honorary degrees.

EVELYN WAUGH (1903–66). Waugh's most famous novels are *Decline and Fall*, *A Handful of Dust*, *Brideshead Revisited*, and the Sword of Honour trilogy. *Brideshead* brought him fame and fortune and while in Hollywood to discuss a film version (which failed to appear), he visited Forest Lawn Cemetery. This inspired him to write *The Loved One*, a satirical look at Americans' view of death.

HG WELLS (1866–1946). Wells is most famous for *The Time Machine*, *The Invisible Man*, and *The War of the Worlds*. Wells predicted the Second World War in *The Shape of Things to Come* in 1933, believing that such a war would actually begin in 1940. While deeply spiritual, he did not subscribe to any particular organized religion, believing them all to be true.

NATHANAEL WEST (1903–40). West's most famous novels are *Miss Lonelyhearts*, *The Day of the Locust*, and *The Dream Life of Balso Snell*. It was his experience working as a screenwriter that fed the dark vision of Hollywood portrayed in *The Day of the Locust*. West died in a car accident along with his wife Ellen McKenney, ironically shortly after hearing of the death of his friend F Scott Fitzgerald.

EDITH WHARTON (1862–1937). Wharton's works include *Ethan Frome*, *The Age of Innocence*, and *The House of Mirth*. She was the first woman to win the Pulitzer Prize for literature. She was also a trend-setting interior and garden designer.

ELIE WIESEL (b 1928). Wiesel's books include *Night*, *Dawn*, and *The Gates of the Forest*. When *Night* was first published, it sold very slowly for three years, until it received enough positive critical reviews for Wiesel to begin promoting it in television interviews. He was attacked in 2007 by a Holocaust denier but was not hurt.

OSCAR WILDE (1854–1900). Wilde's works include *The Importance of Being Earnest*, *The Picture of Dorian Gray*, and *An Ideal Husband*. Wilde was a

Master Freemason. The title of *The Importance of Being Earnest* was an inside joke for London homosexuals, who used "I am earnest" as a code phrase to identify themselves to each other.

TENNESSEE WILLIAMS (1911–83). Williams is best known for his plays *A Streetcar Named Desire*, *Cat on a Hot Tin Roof*, and *The Glass Menagerie*. Many of his plays were inspired by his own family life. Before achieving success as a playwright, Williams moved frequently from job to job; his briefest period of employment was at Manhattan's Gotham Book Mart, where he worked for half a day.

PG WODEHOUSE (1881–1975). Wodehouse is best known for his Jeeves and Wooster stories, Blandings Castle stories, and Ukridge stories. In college, he was a school athlete and also performed in plays and musicals. He collaborated with Cole Porter on the lyrics for *Anything Goes*.

VIRGINIA WOOLF (1882–1941). Woolf's most famous works include the novels *Mrs Dalloway*, *To the Lighthouse*, and *Orlando* and her book-length essay, "A Room of One's Own." She was part of the London literary circle that came to be known as the Bloomsbury Group. This included Lytton Strachey, Clive Bell, and Rupert Brooke, among others. She and her husband, Leonard Woolf, founded the Hogarth Press. Virginia Woolf suffered several nervous breakdowns and committed suicide by drowning herself in the River Ouse, her pocket stuffed with stones.

Sources

Below you'll find the sources of the quotes in this book, listed chapter by chapter in order of appearance, as well as publishing information for the books excerpted.

Chapter 1: It starts with (someone else's) words

Martin Amis—*The Paris Review Interviews*, Vol. 3, Picador, 2008.

William Faulkner—*The Paris Review Interviews*, Vol. 4, Picador, 2009.

Vladimir Nabokov—Brian Boyd, *Vladimir Nabokov: The American Years*, Princeton University Press, 1993.

Maya Angelou—*The Paris Review: The Art of Fiction*, No. 119, Fall 1990.

Harper Lee—letter to *O, The Oprah Magazine*, Summer issue, 2006.

Eudora Welty—Eudora Welty & Peggy Whitman Prenshaw, *Conversations With Eudora Welty*, University Press of Mississippi, 1984.

Gabriel García Márquez—*The Paris Review Interviews*, Vol. 4, Picador, 2009.

Ralph Ellison—*The Paris Review Interviews*, Vol. 3, Picador, 2008.

Ray Bradbury—Ray Bradbury, "How to Be Madder than Captain Ahab." Quoted by William Safire and Leonard Safir in *Good Advice on Writing*, Simon & Schuster, 1992.

Salman Rushdie—*The Paris Review Interviews*, Vol. 3, Picador, 2008.

Stephen Sondheim—*The Paris Review Interviews*, Vol. 4, Picador, 2009.

Chapter 2: Memories and fears

Willa Cather—Rene Rapin, *Willa Cather*, Robert M. McBride, 1930.

F Scott Fitzgerald—Matthew Bruccoli (ed.), *F. Scott Fitzgerald: A Life in Letters*, Scribners, 1994.

George Bernard Shaw—*The Bookman*, Vol. 41, Dodd, Mead and Company, 1915.

Eudora Welty—Eudora Welty, *One Writer's Beginnings*, Harvard University Press, 1984.

Josip Novakovich—From "Criss-Crossed With Stories," *Hungry Mind Review*, in Jack Haffron (ed.), *The Best Writing on Writing*, Story Press, 1994.

Haruki Murakami—*The Paris Review Interviews*, Vol. 4, Picador, 2009.

JK Rowling—Biography, www.jkrowling.com.

Charles Dickens—Charles Dickens, *David Copperfield*, Introduction by Hablot K. Browne, Wordsworth Editions, 1962.

Jean Rhys—*The Paris Review Interviews*, Vol. 3, Picador, 2008.

Edna Ferber—John Winkur, *Advice to Writers: A Compendium of Quotes, Anecdotes, and Writerly Wisdom from a Dazzling Array of Literary Lights*, Vintage Books, 2000.

William Styron—William Styron & James LW West, *Conversations with William Styron*, University Press of Mississippi, 1985.

Tennessee Williams—interviewed by Dotson Rader, *The Art of Theater*, No. 81, Fall 1981.

Paul Schrader—interviewed in *Tehelka Magazine*, Vol. 5, Issue 30, August 2, 2008.

Chapter 3: Solitude and dreams

Francis Bacon, Sr.—Robert Chambers & William Chambers, *Chambers's Edinburgh Journal*, Vol. 4, W. Orr, 1845.

Friedrich Nietzsche—*The Gay Science*, trans. W. Kaufmann, Vintage, 1974.

Henry Miller—*Big Sur and the Oranges of Hieronymus Bosch*, New Directions Publishing, 1957.

Franz Kafka—Jon Winokur (ed.), *Advice to Writers*, Pantheon Books, 1999.

Michael Slater—Michael Slater, *Charles Dickens*, Yale University Press, 2009.

HP Lovecraft—Maurice Levy, Lovecraft, *A Study in the Fantastic*, Wayne State University Press, 1988.

Mary Shelley—Introduction to *Frankenstein or The Modern Prometheus*, 1818 text, Oxford World's Classics, 2009.

Stephenie Meyer—*Entertainment Weekly*, interview with Stephanie Meyer by Gregory Kirschling, July 5, 2008, available at EW.com.

Robert Louis Stevenson—Robert Louis Stevenson, *Across the Plains: With Other Memories and Essays*, Cosimo Classics, 2005.

Stephen King—interview with Stan Nicholls, London, September 1998, www.herebedragons.co.uk/nicholls/interviews.htm.

Alan Gurganus—Alan Gurganus, "I Dreamed the Story of a Dream," as told to Naomi Epel, *Writers Dreaming*, Random House, 1993.

Ray Bradbury—Interview with booksense.com, at www.indiebound.com.

Julia Cameron—Julia Cameron, *The Artist's Way: A Course in Discovering and Recovering Your Creative Self*, Pan, 2011.

Chapter 4: Germination

Georges Simenon—*The Paris Review Interviews*, Vol. 3, Picador, 2008.

Jack Kerouac—*The Paris Review Interviews*, Vol. 4, Picador, 2009.

Martin Amis—Clare Boylan (ed.), *The Agony and the Ego*, Penguin, 1993.

William Faulkner—*The Paris Review, The Art of Fiction No. 12*, Spring 1956.

Alice Walker—Susan Sellers (ed.), *Delighting the Heart*, Women's Press, 1989.

Ernest Hemingway—*Paris Review, The Art of Fiction No. 21*, Spring 1958.

Chapter 5: Meeting your characters

Hilary Mantel—Clare Boylan (ed.), *The Agony and the Ego*, Penguin, 1993.

Jane Gardam—Clare Boylan (ed.), *The Agony and the Ego*, Penguin, 1993.

F Scott Fitzgerald—Jon Winokur (ed.), *Advice to Writers*, Pantheon Books, 1999.

Stieg Larsson—"On Stieg Larsson," quoted in *Wall Street Journal*, November 20, 2010.

Mark Twain—Jessica Page Morrell, *Bullies, Bastards & Bitches: How to Write the Bad Guys of Fiction*, Writer's Digest Books, 2008.

Patricia Highsmith—Clare Boylan (ed.), *The Agony and the Ego*, Penguin, 1993.

W Somerset Maugham—Raymond Obstfeld, *Novelist's Essential Guide to Crafting Scenes*, Writer's Digest Books, 2000.

Brenda Ueland—Brenda Ueland, *If You Want to Write: A Book about Art, Independence and Spirit*, Bottom of the Hill Publishing, 2010.

Rose Tremain—Clare Boylan (ed.), *The Agony and the Ego*, Penguin, 1993.

Thomas Fleming—John Darnton (ed.), *Writers on Writing: Collected Essays from the New York Times*, Times Books/Henry Holt, 2001.

Italo Calvino—Italo Calvino, *Invisible Cities*, Harcourt Brace Jovanovich, 1978.

Charles Dickens—Charles Dickens, *Great Expectations*, Longman, 2004.

Robert Louis Stevenson—Robert Louis Stevenson, *Treasure Island*, Penguin Classics, 2003.

Anton Chekhov—Anton Pavlovich Chekhov, Piero Brunello, & Lena Lencek, *How to Write Like Chekhov*, Da Capo Press, 2008.

Chapter 6: What would they do?

Deborah Moggach—Clare Boylan (ed.), *The Agony and the Ego*, Penguin, 1993.

André Gide—Jean Hytier, *André Gide*, F Ungar, 1967.

Ann Cummins—Daniel Alarcon (ed.), *The Secret Miracle*, Henry Holt, 2010.

Rick Moody—Daniel Alarcon (ed.), *The Secret Miracle*, Henry Holt, 2010.

Leo Tolstoy—Leo Tolstoy, *Resurrection*, Penguin Classics, 1966.

Gabriel García Márquez—Gabriel García Márquez, *Love in the Time of Cholera*, Penguin Classics, 2007.

Chapter 7: What they want, what they need, and why it's complicated

Kurt Vonnegut—Kurt Vonnegut & William Rodney Allen, *Conversations With Kurt Vonnegut*, University Press of Mississippi, 1968.

Josh Emmons—Daniel Alarcon (ed.), *The Secret Miracle*, Henry Holt, 2010.

David Mamet—memo to writers of *The Unit*, reproduced at www.movieline.com.

Ayn Rand—*Ayn Rand, The Art of Fiction: A Guide for Writers and Readers*, Plume, 2000.

Herman Melville—Herman Melville, *Moby-Dick*, Wordsworth Editions, 1992.

Charles Dickens—Charles Dickens, *Great Expectations*, Longman, 2004.

Ben Nyberg—Jack Haffron (ed.), *The Best Writing on Writing*, Story Press, 1994.

Daphne du Maurier—Daphne du Maurier, *Rebecca*, Virago Press, 2003.

Anna Massey—article in *The Guardian*, June 28, 2006.

Rosellen Brown—John Darnton (ed.), *Writers on Writing: Collected Essays from the New York Times*, Times Books/Henry Holt, 2001.

Anton Chekhov—letter to Maria Kiselyova, January 14, 1887, Ralph E Matlaw (ed.), *The Stories of Anton Chekhov*, trans. Ivy Litinov, WW Norton, 1979.

Jane Austen—James Edward Austen-Leigh, *A Memoir of Jane Austen*, Oxford University Press, 2002.

Jane Austen—Jane Austen, *Emma*, Wordsworth Editions, 2000.

Paul Schrader—interviewed in *Tehelka Magazine*, Vol. 5, Issue 30, August 2, 2008.

Tony McNabb—presentation to the Four Corners Program, Terrassa, Spain, 2008.

Carl Jung—"Psychology and Religion" in *CW 11: Psychology and Religion: West and East*, 1938.

Chapter 8: What's their status?

Keith Johnstone—*Keith Johnstone, Impro: Improvisation and the Theatre*, Routledge, 1987.

William Shakespeare—William Shakespeare, *Macbeth*, Wordsworth Editions, 1992.

Gustave Flaubert—Gustave Flaubert, *Madame Bovary*, Wordsworth Editions, 1993.

Arthur Miller—Arthur Miller, *Death of a Salesman*, Penguin, 1996.

John Cleese—John Cleese & Connie Booth, *The Complete Fawlty Towers*, Da Capo Press, 2001.

Chapter 9: The character in the mirror

Milan Kundera—*Milan Kundera, The Unbearable Lightness of Being: A Novel*, Harper Perennial Classics, 2009.

Sara Paretsky—Clare Boylan (ed.), *The Agony and The Ego: The Art and Strategy of Fiction Writing Explored*, Penguin, 1993.

Roddy Doyle—Daniel Alarcon (ed.), The Secret Miracle, Henry Holt, 2010.

Stephen King—Daniel Alarcon (ed.), The Secret Miracle, Henry Holt, 2010.

VS Naipaul—*The Paris Review Interviews*, Vol. 4, Picador, 2009.

Haruki Murakami—*The Paris Review Interviews*, Vol. 4, Picador, 2009.

Tennessee Williams—Michiko Kakutani, "The Legacy of Tennessee Williams," *New York Times*, March 6, 1983.

EM Forster—"In Their Own Words: British Novelists," *Among the Ruins: 1919–1939*, BBC Radio.

Eudora Welty—Eudora Welty, *One Writer's Beginnings*, Harvard University Press, 1995.

Carol Shields—John Darnton (ed.), *Writers on Writing: Collected Essays from the New York Times*, Times Books/Henry Holt, 2001.

Bonnie Friedman—Jack Heffron (ed.), *The Best Writing on Writing*, Story Press, 1994.

Ernest Hemingway—Ernest Hemingway, *Selected Letters 1917–1961*, Scribner, 2003.

Chapter 10: Make them talk

Eudora Welty—Eudora Welty & Peggy Whitman, *Conversations With Eudora Welty*, University Press of Mississippi, 1984.

Ernest Hemingway—Ernest Hemingway, *Death in the Afternoon*, Scribner, 1999.

Penelope Fitzgerald—Clare Boylan, *The Agony and The Ego: The Art and Strategy of Fiction Writing Explored*, Penguin, 1993.

Ernest Hemingway—Ernest Hemingway & Larry W Phillips, *Hemingway on Writing*, Simon and Schuster, 1999.

Ernest Hemingway—Ernest Hemingway & William White, *By-line: Ernest Hemingway*, Scribner, 2002.

Annie Proulx—John Darnton (ed.), *Writers on Writing: Collected Essays from the New York Times*, Times Books/Henry Holt, 2001.

DH Lawrence—DH Lawrence, *Women in Love*, Penguin Classics, 2007.

Chapter 11: They're taking over!

William Faulkner—William Faulkner & M Thomas Inge, *Conversations with William Faulkner*, University Press of Mississipi, 1999.

Elie Wiesel—John Darnton (ed.), *Writers on Writing: Collected Essays from the New York Times*, Times Books/Henry Holt, 2001.

Ray Bradbury—*Bookselling This Week*, 1997, and *Book Magazine*, Dec. 1998/Jan. 1999 issue, both available at www.raybradbury.com.

Patricia Highsmith—Patricia Highsmith, *Plotting and Writing Suspense Fiction*, St. Martin's Press, 2001.

Alan Gurganus—Jack Heffron (ed.), *The Best Writing on Writing*, Story Press, 1994.

Alice Walker—Susan Sellers (ed.), *Delighting the Heart: A Notebook by Women Writers*, Women's Press, 1989.

Toni Morrison—Toni Morrison & Carolyn C. Denard, *Toni Morrison: Conversations*, University Press of Mississippi, 2008.

Charles Dickens—Charles Dickens, *David Copperfield* (1850 edition), Project Gutenberg Ebook no. 766, 2009.

Chapter 12: Setting: Where and when?

Peter James—*Books Quarterly*, Issue 39, 2011.

Harper Lee—Harper Lee, *To Kill a Mockingbird*, Popular Library, 1988.

Fyodor Dostoyevsky—Fyodor Dostoyevsky, *Crime and Punishment*, Simon & Brown, 2011.

Sinclair Lewis—Sinclair Lewis, *Babbit*, Signet Classics, 2007.

Gabriel García Márquez—Gabriel García Márquez, *Love in the Time of Cholera*, trans. Edith Grossman, Vintage Books, 2007.

Marcel Proust—Marcel Proust, *Swann's Way*, trans. CK Scott Moncrieff, Henry
    Holt, 1922.

Sol Stein—Sol Stein, *Stein on Writing*, St. Martin's Griffin, 2000.

JB Priestley—JB Priestley, *An Inspector Calls*, Dramatists Play Service, 1998.

Miriam Allen deFord—Brian Aldiss & David Wingrove, *Trillion Year Spree: The
    History of Science Fiction*, Victor Gollancz, 1986.

Chapter 13: POV: Who's telling the story?

Mark Twain—Mark Twain, *The Adventures of Huckleberry Finn*, Tribeca Books,
    2011.

Ernest Hemingway—Ernest Hemingway, *The Green Hills of Africa*, Scribner,
    1998.

JD Salinger—JD Salinger, *Catcher in the Rye*, Back Bay Books, 2001.

Haruki Murakami—Haruki Murakami, *Kafka on the Shore*, Vintage, 2006.

Nathaniel Hawthorne—Nathaniel Hawthorne, "The Haunted Mind,"
    www.ibiblio.org/eldritch/nh/hmind.html.

Jay McInerny—Jay McInerny, *Bright Lights, Big City*, Vintage, 1984.

Nathanael West—Nathanael West, *Miss Lonelyhearts & The Day of the Locust*,
    New Directions, 2009.

Patricia Highsmith—Patricia Highsmith, *Plotting and Writing Suspense Fiction*,
    St. Martin's Press, 2001.

Ursula Le Guin—Ian Jackman (ed.), *The Writer's Mentor*, Random House
    Reference, 2004.

Leo Tolstoy—Leo Tolstoy, *War and Peace*, Vintage, 2008.

John Irving—*Paris Review*, No. 100, Summer/Fall 1986.

Chapter 14: To plan or not to plan?

Edgar Allen Poe—Edgar Allen Poe, "The Philosophy of Composition," *The
    Oxford Book of American Essays*, Cornell University Library, 2009.

PG Wodehouse—"In Their Own Words: British Novelists," *Among the Ruins:
    1919–1939*, BBC Radio.

Shelley Jackson—Daniel Alarcon (ed.), *The Secret Miracle*, Henry Holt, 2010.

George Pelecanos—Daniel Alarcon (ed.), *The Secret Miracle*, Henry Holt,
    2010.

Edward Albee—*Dramatics*, Vol. 65, International Thespian Society, 1993.

Stephen King—Daniel Alarcon (ed.), *The Secret Miracle*, Henry Holt, 2010.

EL Doctorow—*New York Times*, October 29, 1985.

John Guare—John Lahr (ed.), *Playwrights at Work*, Modern Library, 2000.

Paul Auster—Daniel Alarcon (ed.), *The Secret Miracle*, Henry Holt, 2010.

Michael Chabon—Daniel Alarcon (ed.), *The Secret Miracle*, Henry Holt, 2010.

Amy Tan—Daniel Alarcon (ed.), *The Secret Miracle*, Henry Holt, 2010.

Gabriel García Márquez—*The Paris Review: Interviews*, Vol. 2, Picador, 2007.

Chapter 15: Characters become plots (and vice versa)

EM Forster—Sunil Kumar Sarker, *A Companion to E. M. Forster*, Vol. 3, Atlantic, 2007.

Ben Nyberg—Jack Heffron, *The Best Writing on Writing*, Story Press, 1994.

Diane Lefer—Jack Heffron, *The Best Writing on Writing*, Story Press, 1994.

Ray Cooney—*The Times* (London), October 16, 2010.

Kurt Vonnegut—*Lapham's Quarterly*, April 3, 2011.

Chapter 16: Conflict

John Le Carré—John Le Carré, Matthew Joseph Bruccoli, & Judith Baughman, *Conversations with John le Carré*, University Press of Mississippi, 2004.

Ayn Rand—Ayn Rand, *The Art of Fiction: A Guide for Writers and Readers*, Plume, 2000.

Elizabeth Bowen—"Their Own Words: British Novelists," *Among the Ruins, 1919-1939*, BBC Radio.

Raymond Chandler—Raymond Chandler, "Introduction," *Trouble Is My Business*, Vintage, 1988.

Chapter 17: Building the plot

Michael Hauge—*Michael Hauge, Writing Screenplays That Sell*, Collins Reference, 1991.

Emma Tennant—Susan Sellers (ed.), *Delighting the Heart: A Notebook by Women Writers*, Women's Press, 1989.

Orhan Pamuk—*The Paris Review: Interviews*, Vol. 4, Picador, 2009.

Anne Lamott—Anne Lamott, *Bird by Bird: Some Instructions on Writing and Life*, Anchor, 1995.

Robert Pirsig—Robert Pirsig, *Lila*, Bantam Press, 1991.

Hilary Mantel—Clare Boylan (ed.), *The Agony and The Ego: The Art and Strategy of Fiction Writing Explored*, Penguin, 1993.

Chapter 18: Openings, foreshadowing, and Act One

Alexandre Dumas *père*—Jon Winokyr (ed.), *Advice to Writers*, Pantheon Books, 1999.

Anton Chekhov—letter to Alexander Zhirkevich, 1895, in Anton Pavlovich Chekhov, Piero Brunello & Lena Lencek, *How to Write Like Chekhov*, Da Capo Press, 2008.

Philip Roth—Philip Roth & John Searles, *Conversations with Philip Roth*, University Press of Mississippi, 1992.

Gabriel García Márquez—*The Paris Review: Interviews*, Vol. 2, Picador, 2007.

Diane Lefer—Jack Heffron (ed.), *The Best Writing on Writing*, Story Press, 1994.

George Pelecanos—Daniel Alarcon (ed.), *The Secret Miracle*, Henry Holt, 2010.

Sir Arthur Conan Doyle—Sir Arthur Conan Doyle, *The Sign of Four*, Dover Publications, 2003.

Charles Dickens—Charles Dickens, *A Tale of Two Cities*, Prestwick House, 2005.

Ralph Ellison—Ralph Ellison, *Invisible Man*, Vintage, 1995.

Edith Wharton—Edith Wharton, *Ethan Frome*, Penguin Classics, 2005.

Franz Kafka—Franz Kafka, *The Trial*, Schocken, 1999.

Dante Alighieri—Dante Alighieri, *The Divine Comedy, Inferno*, Chartwell Books, 2008.

Mary Wollstonecraft Shelley—Mary Wollstonecraft Shelley, *Frankenstein: or, The Modern Prometheus*, Simon & Brown, 2011.

Joseph Conrad—Joseph Conrad, *Lord Jim*, Oxford University Press, 2008.

Chapter 19: The troublesome middle

Joseph Conrad—Joseph Conrad, "Author's Notes," *Lord Jim*, Oxford University Press, 2008.

Chapter 20: The end and the theme

Charles Dickens—Charles Dickens, *Great Expectations*, original ending based on a proof slip reproduced by Edgar Rosenberg in the WW Norton edition, 1999.

F Scott Fitzgerald—F Scott Fitzgerald, *The Great Gatsby*, Scribner, 1999.

Flannery O'Connor—Flannery O'Connor, *Mysteries and Manners: Occasional Prose*, Farrar, Straus and Giroux, 1969.

Joseph Conrad—Joseph Conrad, "Preface," *The Nigger of the Narcissus: A Tale of the Sea*, Digireads, 2009.

DH Lawrence—DH Lawrence, *Apocalypse and the Writings on Revelation*, Cambridge University Press, 2002.

Chapter 21: Rewriting

Roald Dahl—Donald Murray, "The Maker's Eye: Revising Your Own Manuscripts," in Paul Eschholz, Aldred Rosa, & Virginia Clark (eds.), *Language Awareness: Readings for College Writers*, 8th edn, Bedford/St. Martin's, 2000.

Jacques Barzun—Jacques Barzun, *Simple and Direct: A Rhetoric for Writers*, Harper & Row, 1975.

Jonathan Swift—Jonathan Swift, "On Poetry: A Rhapsody," December 31, 1773.

James Michener—Caryn James, "The Michener Phenomenon," *New York Times*, September 8, 1985.

Joyce Carol Oates—Joyce Carol Oates & Lee Milazzo, *Conversations with Joyce Carol Oates*, University Press of Mississippi, 1989.

Robert Louis Stevenson—letter to Richard Harding Davis, quoted in Richard Duffy, "When They Were Twenty-One," *The Bookman*, January 1914.

Susan Sontag—John Darnton (ed.), *Writers on Writing: Collected Essays from the New York Times*, Times Books/Henry Holt, 2001.

Ernest Hemingway—Ernest Hemingway & William White, *By-line: Ernest Hemingway*, Scribner, 2002.

Joyce Carol Oates—John Darnton (ed.), *Writers on Writing: Collected Essays from the New York Times*, Times Books/Henry Holt, 2001.

EB White—*The Paris Review: Interviews*, Vol. 4, Picador, 2009.

Ernest Hemingway—Ernest Hemingway, *Selected Letters 1917–1961*, Scribner, 2003.

Mark Twain—letter to Sir Walter Bessant, 22 February 1898, www.twain-quotes.com.

Samuel Johnson—Jon Winokur (ed.), *Advice to Writers*, Pantheon Books, 1999.

Sir Arthur Quiller-Couch—Rudolph Flesch, *The Art of Readable Writing*, Macmillan General Reference, 1994.

Roddy Doyle—Daniel Alarcon (ed.), *The Secret Miracle*, Henry Holt, 2010.

Finding Your Style

Diane Lefer—Jack Heffron (ed.), *The Best Writing on Writing*, Story Press, 1994.

EB White—William Strunk & Elwyn Brooks White, *The Elements of Style*, Penguin, 2008.

Chapter 22: Clarity, simplicity

Robert Louis Stevenson—Robert Louis Stevenson, *The Art of Writing*, Kessinger, 2004.

Mark Twain—Kate Kinsella (ed.), *Prentice Hall Literature: Timeless Voices, Timeless Themes*, Vol. 1, Pearson Education, 2002.

Willa Cather—Willa Cather, *Willa Cather on Writing*, University of Nebraska Press, 1988.

Franz Kafka—Franz Kafka, *Metamorphosis*, Classix Press, 2009.

Raymond Carver—Raymond Carver, *What We Talk About When We Talk About Love: Stories*, Vintage, 1989.

Graham Greene—Graham Greene, *The Comedians*, Penguin Classics, 2005.

Evelyn Waugh—Evelyn Waugh, *Brideshead Revisited*, Back Bay Books, 2008.

George Gallo—George Gallo, "Midnight Run," *Scenario*, Vol. 5, No. 3, 2000.

Charles Burnett—Charles Burnett, "To Sleep with Anger," *Scenario*, Vol. 2, No. 1, 1996.

Chapter 23: Conciseness

Anton Chekhov—letter to Maxim Gorky, December 3, 1898, Ralph E Matlaw (ed.), *The Stories of Anton Chekhov*, trans. Ivy Litvinov, WW Norton, 1979.

Mark Twain—letter to Henry Rogers, April 26-28, 1897, *Harper's Magazine*, Vol. 135, 1917.

Ernest Hemingway—Ernest Hemingway, *Death in the Afternoon*, General Books, 2010.

EL Doctorow—John Darnton (ed.), *Writers on Writing: Collected Essays from the New York Times*, Times Books/Henry Holt, 2001.

Stanley Elkin—Tom LeClair & Larry McLaffery (eds), *Anything Can Happen: Interviews with Contemporary American Novelists*, University of Illinois Press, 1983.

Anton Chekhov—Anton Chekhov, *The Cook's Wedding and Other Stories*, BiblioBazaar, 2007.

EL Doctorow—John Darnton (ed.), *Writers on Writing: Collected Essays from the New York Times*, Times Books/Henry Holt, 2001.

James Patterson—*Success Magazine*, February 2011.

Chapter 24: It's in the details

CS Lewis—CS Lewis, Lyle W Dorsett & Marjorie Lamp Mead, *C. S. Lewis' Letters to Children*, Simon & Schuster, 1996.

Mark Twain—Stephen Blake Mettee, *The Portable Writer's Conference: Your Guide to Getting Published*, Quill Driver Books, 2007.

Anton Chekhov—Larner Underwood, *The Quotable Writer*, Lyons Press, 2004.

Gabriel García Márquez—T*he Paris Review: Interviews*, Vol. 2, Picador, 2007.

Anton Chekhov—letter to AP Chekhov, May 10, 1886, Anton Pavlovich Chekhov, Piero Brunello, & Lena Lencek, *How to Write Like Chekhov*, Da Capo Press, 2008.

Jane Austen—Jane Austen, *Northanger Abbey*, Pearson Education/Longman, 2004.

Flannery O'Connor—Flannery O'Connor, "The Nature and Aim of Fiction," *Mysteries and Manners: Occasional Prose*, Farrar, Straus and Giroux, 1969.

Margaret Atwood—Margaret Atwood, *The Blind Assassin*, Anchor, 2001.

Vladimir Nabokov—Vladimir Nabokov, *Lolita*, Vintage, 1989.

William Shakespeare—William Shakespeare, *Romeo and Juliet*, Wordsworth Editions, 2000.

William Shakespeare—William Shakespeare, *As You Like It*, Wordsworth Editions, 2000.

Jorge Luis Borges—*Paris Review*, July 1969.

EL Doctorow—cited numerous times but origin unclear.

Chapter 25: The right word and some wrong ones

Mark Twain—Mark Twain, "William Dean Howells," in Mark Twain & Charles Neider, *The Complete Essays of Mark Twain*, Da Capo Press, 2000.

Mark Twain—Joseph Twadell Shipley, *Origins of English Words*, Johns Hopkins University Press, 2001.

George Orwell—George Orwell, *Politics and the English Language and Other Essays*, Lulu Press, 2010.

George Orwell—George Orwell, 1984, *Plume*, 2003.

Umberto Eco—trans. Gio Clairval on gioclairval.blogspot.com, February 23, 2010.

Mark Twain—Mark Twain, *The Autobiography of Mark Twain*, Charles Neider (ed.), Harper Perennial Modern Classics, 2000.

F Scott Fitzgerald—letter to Frances Scott Fitzgerald, 1938, Larry W Phillips (ed.), *F. Scott Fitzgerald on Writing*, Scribners, 1985.

Anton Chekhov—Sept. 3, 1899, Ralph E Matlaw (ed.), *The Stories of Anton Chekhov*, trans. Ivy Litinov, WW Norton, 1979.

Voltaire—Ben Yagoda, *When You Catch an Adjective, Kill It*, Broadway Books, 2007.

Mark Twain—Ben Yagoda, *When You Catch an Adjective, Kill It*, Broadway Books, 2007.

Elmore Leonard—Elmore Leonard, *Split Images*, Avon Books, 1995.

Elmore Leonard—Elmore Leonard, "Writers on Writing; Easy on the Adverts, Exclamation Points, and Especially Hooptedoodle," *New York Times*, July 16, 2001.

Chapter 26: Developing your style

Anton Chekhov—letter to Lydia Avilova, March 19, 1892 & April 29, 1892, Ralph E Matlaw (ed.), *The Stories of Anton Chekhov*, trans. Ivy Litinov, WW Norton, 1979.

F Scott Fitzgerald—F Scott Fitzgerald, *The Crack-up*, New Directions, 2009.

Charles Dickens—Charles Dickens, *Great Expectations*, Longman, 2004.

Ernest Hemingway—letter to Horace Liveright, Ernest Hemingway & Carlos Baker, *Ernest Hemingway Selected Letters 1917–1961*, Scribner, 2003.

Mark Twain—Mark Twain & Charles Neider, *The Autobiography of Mark Twain*, Harper Perennial Modern Classics, 2000.

George Bernard Shaw—Sir Ernest Gowers, *The Complete Plain Words*, David R. Godine, 2002.

F Scott Fitzgerald—Fred Metcalf (ed.), *The Penguin Dictionary of Modern Humorous Quotations*, Penguin, 2001.

Raymond Chandler—Raymond Chandler, *Raymond Chandler Speaking*, University of California Press, 1997.

Jack Kerouac—*The Paris Review: Interviews*, Vol. 4, Picador, 2009.

Ayn Rand—Ayn Rand, *The Art of Fiction: A Guide for Writers and Readers*, Plume, 2000.

Henry David Thoreau—Henry David Thoreau, *The Selected Essays of Henry David Thoreau*, Wilder Publications, 2008.

Chapter 27: Is writing a compulsion?

George Orwell—George Orwell, *Why I Write*, Penguin (Great Ideas Series), 2004.

Elie Wiesel—John Darnton (ed.), *Writers on Writing: Collected Essays from the New York Times*, Times Books/Henry Holt, 2002.

James Thurber—James Thurber & Thomas French, *Conversations With James Thurber*, University Press of Mississippi, 1989.

Edgar Allen Poe—*The Devorian*, Dover College, 1883.

Ray Bradbury—interview in *Playboy*, 1996, available at www.raybradbury.com.

Chapter 28: Places and props

William Faulkner—*The Paris Review: Interviews*, Vol. 2, Picador, 2007.

Haruki Murakami—Daniel Alarcon (ed.), *The Secret Miracle*, Henry Holt, 2010.

Amy Tan—Daniel Alarcon (ed.), *The Secret Miracle*, Henry Holt, 2010.

Truman Capote—*Paris Review*, No. 16, 1957.

Beryl Bainbridge—Clare Boylan (ed.), *The Agony and The Ego: The Art and Strategy of Fiction Writing Explored*, Penguin, 1993.

Alan Gurganus—Jack Heffron (ed.), *The Best Writing on Writing*, Story Press, 1994.

Michael Slater—Michael Slater, *Charles Dickens*, Yale University Press, 2009.

Marina Warner—Clare Boylan (ed.), *The Agony and The Ego: The Art and Strategy of Fiction Writing Explored*, Penguin, 1993.

Kent Haruf—John Darnton (ed.), *Writers on Writing: Collected Essays from the New York Times*, Times Books/Henry Holt, 2001.

Mary Gordon—John Darnton (ed.), *Writers on Writing: Collected Essays from the New York Times*, Times Books/Henry Holt, 2001.

Chapter 29: How much, for how long?

Edgar Allen Poe—Edgar Allen Poe, "The Philosophy of Composition," in *The Oxford Book of American Essays*, Cornell University Library, 2009.

Oscar Wilde—Oscar Wilde & Alvin Redman, *The Wit and Humor of Oscar Wilde*, Courier Dover, 1959.

Anthony Trollope—Anthony Trollope, *An Autobiography*, Oxford University Press, 2009.

Alice Munro—*The Paris Review: Interviews*, Vol. 2, Picador, 2007.

Mark Twain—Mark Twain & Charles Neider, *The Autobiography of Mark Twain*, Harper Perennial Modern Classics, 2000.

Anton Chekhov—Anton Pavlovich Chekhov, Piero Brunello, & Lena Lencek, *How to Write Like Chekhov*, Da Capo Press, 2008.

Amy Tan—Daniel Alarcon (ed.), *The Secret Miracle*, Henry Holt, 2010.

James D. Houston—Carl Edgarian & Tom Jenks, *The Writer's Life*, Vintage Books, 1997.

JK Rowling—Biography, www.jkrowling.com.

Stephenie Meyer—*Entertainment Weekly*, interview with Stephanie Meyer by Gregory Kirschling, July 5, 2008, available at EW.com.

Chapter 3O: Confidence

Mark Twain—*The Galaxy*, Vol. 10, 1870.

Anton Chekhov—Anton Chekhov, *Letters of Anton Chekhov to his Family and Friends with Biographical Sketch*, Kessinger Publishing, 2005.

William Goldman—William Goldman, *Five Screenplays with Essays*, Applause Theatre Book Publishers, 1994.

Anton Chekhov—Anton Chekhov, Piero Brunello, & Lena Lencek, *How to Write Like Chekhov*, Da Capo Press, 2008.

Alice Munro—*The Paris Review: Interviews*, Vol. 2, Picador, 2007.

Nathaniel Hawthorne—Nathaniel Hawthorne & Joel Myerson, *Selected Letters of Nathaniel Hawthorne*, Ohio State University Press, 2002.

Joyce Carol Oates—Joyce Carol Oates, *The Faith of a Writer*, HarperCollins, 2004.

Norman Mailer—Norman Mailer, *The Spooky Art: Thoughts on Writing*, Random House, 2004.

Robert Benchley—Fred Metcalf (ed.), *The Penguin Dictionary of Modern Humorous Quotations*, Penguin, 2001.

Hilary Mantel—Clare Boylan (ed.), *The Agony and The Ego: The Art and Strategy of Fiction Writing Explored*, Penguin, 1993.

Chapter 31: The critics

Anton Chekhov—Maksim Gorky, Aleksandr Ivanovich Kuprin, & Alekseevich Bunin, *Reminiscences of Anton Chekhov*, BW Huebsch, 1921.

Samuel Johnson—Samuel Johnson & Sir John Hawkins, *The Works of Samuel Johnson, LL.D*, Printed for J. Buckland, 1787.

Samuel Johnson—Samuel Johnson & George Birkbeck Norman, *Wit and Wisdom of Samuel Johnson*, Hill, Clarendon Press, 1888.

Ernest Hemingway—Ernest Hemingway & Larry W Phillips, *Ernest Hemingway on Writing*, Simon and Schuster, 1999.

William Faulkner—*The Paris Review: Interviews*, Vol. 2, Picador, 2007.

Tennessee Williams—*Vetoes: Webster's Quotations, Facts and Phrases*, ICON Group International, 2008.

Truman Capote—Truman Capote & M Thomas Inge, *Truman Capote: Conversations*, University Press of Mississippi, 1987.

Anton Chekhov—Anton Pavlovich Chekhov, Simon Karlinsky, & Michael Henry Helm, *Anton Chekhov's Life and Thought: Selected Letters and Commentary*, Northwestern University Press, 1997.

T Alan Broughton—Jack Heffron (ed.), *The Best Writing on Writing*, Vol. 2, Story Press, 1995.

Stephen Sondheim—*The Paris Review: Interviews*, Vol. 4, Picador, 2009.

Ernest Hemingway—Ernest Hemingway, *Selected Letters 1917–1961*, Scribner, 2003.

Ray Bradbury—Jon Winokur, *Advice to Writers*, Pantheon Books, 1999.

Evelyn Waugh—television interview with John Freeman, *Face to Face*, original air date June 26, 1960.

Samuel Beckett—Asja Szafraniec, *Beckett, Derrida, and the Event of Literature*, Stanford University Press, 2007.

Chapter 32: Writer's block

Lucy Ellmann—Clare Boylan (ed.), *The Agony and The Ego: The Art and Strategy of Fiction Writing Explored*, Penguin, 1993.

Tennessee Williams—Tennessee Williams & Lanford Wilson, "Foreword," *Sweet Bird of Youth*, New Directions, 2008.

Ernest Hemingway—Ernest Hemingway, *Selected Letters 1917–1961*, Scribner, 2003.

EB White—EB White, *The Second Tree from the Corner*, Harper Perennnial, 1978.

André Gide—Jon Winokur (ed.), *Advice to Writers*, Pantheon Books, 1999.

Shelley Jackson—Daniel Alarcon (ed.), *The Secret Miracle*, Henry Holt, 2010.

Roddy Doyle—Daniel Alarcon (ed.), *The Secret Miracle*, Henry Holt, 2010.

Alice Munro—*The Paris Review: Interviews*, Vol. 2, Picador, 2007.

Anton Chekhov—Anton Pavlovich Chekhov, Piero Brunello, & Lena Lencek, *How to Write Like Chekhov*, Da Capo Press, 2008.

Paul Auster—Daniel Alarcon (ed.), *The Secret Miracle*, Henry Holt, 2010.

Philip Roth—Philip Roth, "On Writing, Aging and 'Nemesis,'" *NPR*, October 14, 2010 (transcription on www.npr.org).

Ray Bradbury—*San Mateo Times*, January 28, 1997.

Glen David Gold—Daniel Alarcon (ed.), *The Secret Miracle*, Henry Holt, 2010.

Dominick Dunne—Jon Winokur (ed.), *Advice to Writers*, Pantheon Books, 1999.

HG Wells—Peter Kemp (ed.), *The Oxford Book of Literary Quotations*, Oxford University Press, 1997.

F Scott Fitzgerald—F Scott Fitzgerald, *The Letters of F. Scott Fitzgerald*, Scribner, 1963.

Amy Tan—Daniel Alarcon (ed.), *The Secret Miracle*, Henry Holt, 2010.

Ernest Hemingway—Ernest Hemingway & Sean A Hemingway, *A Moveable Feast: The Restored Edition*, Simon and Schuster, 2009.

Ernest Hemingway—Ernest Hemingway & William White, *By-line: Ernest Hemingway*, Scribner, 2002.

Ray Bradbury—Bill Strickland, *On Being a Writer*, F & W Publications, 1992.

Peter Carey—*The Paris Review: Interviews*, Vol. 2, Picador, 2007.

Lorrie Moore—Clare Boylan (ed.), *The Agony and The Ego: The Art and Strategy of Fiction Writing Explored*, Penguin, 1993.

Chapter 33: Being alone and handling distractions

Orhan Pamuk—*The Paris Review: Interviews*, Vol. 4, Picador, 2009.

Ernest Hemingway—Ernest Hemingway, *Green Hills of Africa*, Arrow, 2008.

William Saroyan—William Saroyan & Aram Saroyan, *The William Saroyan Reader*, Barricade Books, 1994.

Flannery O'Connor—Flannery O'Connor, *Mysteries and Manners: Occasional Prose*, Farrar, Straus and Giroux, 1969.

Ernest Hemingway—Ernest Hemingway, *Selected Letters 1917–1961*, Scribner, 2003.

Amy Tan—Daniel Alarcon (ed.), *The Secret Miracle*, Henry Holt, 2010.

George Pelecanos—Daniel Alarcon (ed.), *The Secret Miracle*, Henry Holt, 2010.

Shelley Jackson—Daniel Alarcon (ed.), *The Secret Miracle*, Henry Holt, 2010.

Isaac Bashevis Singer—*The Paris Review: Interviews*, Vol. 2, Picador, 2007.

Alice Munro—*The Paris Review: Interviews*, Vol. 2, Picador, 2007.

Emma Tennant—Susan Sellers (ed.), *Delighting the Heart: A Notebook by Women Writers*, Women's Press, 1989.

Beryl Bainbridge—Clare Boylan (ed.), *The Agony and The Ego: The Art and Strategy of Fiction Writing Explored*, Penguin, 1993.

EB White—*The Paris Review: Interviews*, Vol. 4, Picador, 2009.

Chapter 34: The day-to-day routine

CS Lewis—CS Lewis, *Surprised by Joy: The Shape of My Early Life*, Houghton Mifflin Harcourt, 1995.

Gustave Flaubert—Frederick Brown, *Flaubert: A Biography*, Harvard University Press, 2007.

Simone de Beauvoir—*Paris Review*, Spring/Summer, 1965.

John Irving—*Paris Review*, Summer/Fall, 1986.

Franz Kafka—Louis Begley, *The Tremendous World I Have Inside My Head: Franz Kafka: A Biographical Essay*, Atlas, 2008.

Ernest Hemingway—*Paris Review*, No. 18, 1958.

John Grisham—*San Francisco Chronicle*, February 5, 2008.

John Lanchester—John Lanchester, "High Style," *New Yorker*, January 6, 2003.

HG Wells—Norman Ian MacKenzie & Jeanne MacKenzie, *H. G. Wells: A Biography*, Simon and Schuster, 1973.

Chapter 35: Money

Samuel Johnson—James Boswell, *The Life of Samuel Johnson*, David Womersley (ed.), Penguin Classics, 2008.

Tara K Harper—www.tarakharper.com.

William Makepeace Thackeray—Margaret Forster & William Makepeace Thackeray, *Memoirs of a Victorian Gentleman*, Morrow, 1979.

Ray Bradbury—Bill Strickland, *On Being a Writer*, F & W Publications, 1992.

W Somerset Maugham—W Somerset Maugham, *The Moon and Sixpence*, Arc
    Manor, 2006.
Rod Serling—Bill Strickland, *On Being a Writer*, F & W Publications, 1992.
Virginia Woolf—Virginia Woolf, *A Room of One's Own*, Amereon, 1996.
Mark Twain—*The Galaxy*, November 1870.

Chapter 36: Fame and success

Ray Bradbury—interview in *Playboy*, 1996, available at www.raybradbury.com.
Edward Albee—*Dramatics Magazine*, Vol. 65, International Thespian Society,
    1993.
Ernest Hemingway—from his recorded speech accepting the Nobel Prize for
    Literature, cited in Bryan Patrick Harnetiaux & Ernest Hemingway, *The
    Snows of Kilimanjaro: A Full-Length Play*, Dramatic Publishing, 1995.
Ernest Hemingway—Ernest Hemingway, *Selected Letters 1917–1961*, Scribner,
    2003.
Tony Kushner—Tony Kushner & Robert Vorlicky, *Tony Kushner in
    Conversation*, University of Michigan Press, 1998.
Robertson Davies—Clare Boylan (ed.), *The Agony and The Ego: The Art and
    Strategy of Fiction Writing Explored*, Penguin, 1993.
Lorrie Moore—*Messenger Magazine*, No. 35, Fall-Winter 1997.
May Sarton—May Sarton & Earl G Ingersoll, *Conversations with May Sarton*,
    University Press of Mississippi, 1991.
Joseph Heller—Bill Strickland, *On Being a Writer*, F & W Publications, 1992.

Chapter 37: Enjoying the life

William Styron—*The Paris Review: Interviews*, Vol. 4, Picador, 2009.
PG Wodehouse—*The Paris Review: Interviews*, Vol. 3, Picador, 2008.
JB Priestley—John Boynton Priestley, *The Moments, and Other Pieces*,
    Heinemann, 1966.
F Scott Fitzgerald—F Scott Fitzgerald, "Early Success," *American Cavalcade*,
    October 1937.
Leo Rosten—Leo Rosten, The Return of Hyman Kaplan, Gollancz, 1959.
Eudora Welty—*The Paris Review: Interviews*, Vol. 2, Picador, 2007.

Chapter 38: What does it take?

Mark Twain—*The Galaxy*, November 1870.
Jack Kerouac—Jack Kerouac & Regina Weinrich, *You're a Genius All the Time:
    Belief and Technique for Modern Prose*, Chronicle Books, 2009.
James Michener—Jack Heffron (ed.), *The Best Writing on Writing*, Story Press,
    1994.
William Faulkner—Donald M Kartiganer, *Faulkner and Psychology*, University
    Press of Mississippi, 1994.

Chapter 39: The outlook for the novelist and screenwriter

Saul Bellow—John Darnton (ed.), *Writers on Writing: Collected Essays from the New York Times*, Times Books/Henry Holt, 2001.

Haruki Murakami—*The Paris Review: Interviews*, Vol. 4, Picador, 2009.

Isaac Bashevis Singer—*The Paris Review: Interviews*, Vol. 2, Picador, 2007.

Chapter 40: The writer's contribution

EB White—*Writers at Work*, 8th series, Penguin, 1988.

Nadine Gordimer—interview on

VQROnline.org/webexclusive/2007/03/12/gordimer-interview.

Isabel Allende—Ian Jackman, *The Writer's Mentor*, Random House Reference, 2004.

Kurt Vonnegut—Bill Strickland, *On Being a Writer*, Writer's Digest Books, 1989.

Also from Nicholas Brealey Publishing

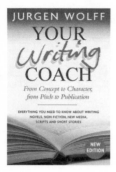

YOUR WRITING COACH
FROM CONCEPT TO CHARACTER,
FROM PITCH TO PUBLICATION

THE No.1 BESTSELLER ON WRITING,
NOW IN A NEW AND EXPANDED EDITION

"Full of encouraging examples and practical tips,
many of them more far-reaching than they seem at
first glance."
—*Financial Times*

Have you always wanted to write a book, short story or screenplay but never quite known where to start? Do you think you won't be able to come up with a plot, or create vivid characters, or find the time? Whatever is stopping you from becoming a writer, *Your Writing Coach* has the answers. It will guide you even after you've finished your writing project by showing you how to get an agent and how to market what you've written.

With exercises, quotes, examples and methods drawn from a variety of disciplines, *Your Writing Coach* reveals:

- How to grab and hold the reader's attention
- How to create plots and craft characters
- How to decide whether to self-publish
- How to market yourself and your work using new media

"With compassion, wit and the wisdom gleaned from a long and successful writing career, Jurgen Wolff guides you, step by step, on the inner and outer journey to writing success."
Robert Cochran, co-creator and executive producer, *24*

UK £10.99 / US $19.95
Paperback Original 978 1 85788 577 4